# TAX GUIDE FOR RESIDENTIAL REAL ESTATE

## THE COMPLETE TAX HANDBOOK FOR HOMEOWNERS AND INVESTORS

**CONTED MEDIA CORPORATION**

# TAX GUIDE
# FOR
# RESIDENTIAL
# REAL ESTATE

## THE COMPLETE TAX
## HANDBOOK FOR
## HOMEOWNERS AND INVESTORS

# MICHAEL P. SAMPSON

**CONTED MEDIA CORPORATION**
**614 G STREET, SW**
**WASHINGTON, DC 20024**

CONTED MEDIA CORPORATION
614 G Street, SW
Washington, DC   20024

# DEDICATION AND ACKNOWLEDGEMENTS

One of the rewards of being a college professor is the insight gained from the questions asked by your students. During the past twenty years, I have had the pleasure of talking with the many real estate professionals attending my lectures and seminars, and the hundreds of CPAs enrolled in my University tax courses. By paying attention to their questions and comments, I have been able to learn a great deal about what is going on in the real world without the anxiety of experiencing it myself. I have vicariously become aware of the realities of the real estate markets and the tribulations of dealing with tax administration. This book is largely a distillation of these perspectives. In appreciation, the book is dedicated to these students, both past and present.

I also want to acknowledge the teachers and writers who have shown me the creative side of real estate, and how the tax law can add to the fun. Among many others, I am deeply indebted to (in alphabetical order): Sandy Botkin, Bob Bruss, Fred Crane, Pete Fortunato, Ken Harney, Benny Kass, Jack Miller, Jimmy Napier, and Neal Peirce.

Many individuals contributed their talents and suggestions as the book progressed. Without their encouragement and tolerance, it would have been impossible to overcome the frustrations of trying to explain any relevance of the tax law to real estate. I offer my thanks to them all, and especially to my friends Dan McGinley for dealing with the endless details of production, to Fernande Pruden for her computer expertise, and to my cat, Elektra, for her devotion and her supervision of my all-night writing sessions. Additionally, I cannot forget the help of the staff of Prentice-Hall Information Services in preparing the book's first edition.

Finally, I express my sincere gratitude to the United States Congress and the Internal Revenue Service for making all this necessary.

Washington, DC
December, 1992

# CONTENTS

# CONTENTS

# CONTENTS

## PART TWO
## TAX BREAKS FOR HOME OWNERSHIP

**Chapter 4**

## TAX BREAKS WHILE YOU OWN
## YOUR HOME

# CONTENTS

## Chapter 5

## TAX BREAKS WHEN YOU SELL YOUR HOME          103

# CONTENTS

CONTENTS

# CONTENTS

## Chapter 8

# CONTENTS

# CONTENTS

## PART FOUR

## CREATIVE FINANCING AND TAX-DEFERRED TRANSACTIONS

## Chapter 10

### TAX CONSEQUENCES OF SELLER FINANCING     212

# CONTENTS

# CONTENTS

# CONTENTS

# CONTENTS

# INTRODUCTION

The purpose of this book is to give you a "red-flag" tax background for residential real estate ownership with as little pain as possible. The book is specifically designed for real estate professionals, small-unit rental property investors, and anyone concerned with personal financial planning. It is also intended to provide tax guidance for homeowners.

Some real estate tax books seem forbidding for the layperson. This may be partly because the books attempt to address tax implications of every conceivable real estate activity. This problem is compounded by the incomprehensible language used by tax specialists to communicate with each other. Sometimes the jargon seems to be deliberately designed to confuse the uninitiated.

Residential real estate is a popular investment. It doesn't matter whether the property is a personal residence, a vacation home, or a rental investment. For all, you get real estate's unique economic benefits. As a bonus, you get special tax breaks. There is a catch, however. To make the breaks work, you must understand the tax dynamics. Studying the details of federal tax law might not be your favorite pastime. You might be quickly discouraged by the law's sheer volume, complexity, and frequent changes.

An easy excuse is to dismiss the whole subject as being one only for tax experts. The problem is that tax experts don't make your investment decisions. Thus, you should have a "red-flag" awareness of tax implications. A "red-flag" awareness makes it possible for you to spot potential tax problems, and more important, to spot potential tax opportunities. You are then in a position to explore the tax details more fully with a tax expert.

This book addresses only the tax nuts and bolts for *residential* property: principal residences, vacation homes, and rental property. Tax matters relating solely to commercial property are excluded. Many points, however, apply for both. You may be surprised that some important tax topics are omitted. This was done deliberately -- because either the topic has little relevance for residential real estate (for example, the rehabilitation tax credits), or the topic doesn't affect many homeowners and rental property investors (for example, capitalization of construction interest and taxes). Further, this book addresses only the Federal income tax. Other Federal taxes, such as the estate and gift taxes, as well as taxes levied at the state and local levels, are not discussed.

Every attempt is made to minimize "legalese" and tax jargon. Sometimes, however, specialized terminology is necessary to understand the law. In these situations, we pinpoint and explain the specialized terms.

The Tax Reform Act of 1986 (1986 TRA) revolutionized the tax law. This massive legislation changed most investment strategy rules we followed in the past. Happily, tax benefits for home ownership emerged almost unchanged. Also, small-unit residential rental property continues to provide tax relief. Tax benefits for large-scale residential "tax shelter" syndicates, however, are largely eliminated, so that they are much less important in the overall real estate investment picture. Accordingly, we do not discuss such syndicates in this book. However, many of the rules discussed for small investors also apply for large-scale syndicates.

Part One of the book introduces you to the wonderful world of taxation and the penalties for not abiding by the rules. We discuss economic implications of tax incentive mechanisms, and guide you through the tax and legal steps for successful acquisition and disposition of real estate.

Part Two is a course for maximizing the tax benefits of home ownership. If politicians are willing to protect these tax breaks against all political odds, you should use them effectively. A home is more than a place to live. It is also one of the best tax shelters. People get significant tax savings while they own their homes, and big tax breaks when they sell them. Part Two is a road map for pocketing these extra tax dollars.

Part Three guides you through the maze of tax benefits for those who own rental property. Along with the tax breaks, however, there are tax pitfalls. New traps were added by the 1986 TRA. Many are surprised to learn that expenditures they thought were deductible, aren't; and that they have income they didn't know about. There is also a discussion of the revised Alternative Minimum Tax (AMT) in Chapter 9. After tax reform, the AMT is a reality to be confronted by many rental property investors.

Part Four explores tax implications of creative financing and opportunities for tax deferral. Seller financing is often the pivotal factor to make a transaction work when interest rates are high or the institutional financial market is tight. Such transactions are riddled with tax traps to ensnare unsuspecting taxpayers. The traps are not limited to sales of investment property. In some respects, seller-financed home sales are even more dangerous. For instance, you may not realize that notes a seller takes from a buyer are ticking time bombs waiting to explode into unexpected tax liabilities. We also discuss two other creative solutions for a tight money market: shared equity financing, and lease-options. Both are recent developments in the residential real estate market.

Real estate exchanges are not common in many parts of the country. Chapter 11 discusses the enormous economic and tax benefits of this fascinating technique. Finally, we examine the tax treatment of involuntary conversions of property by condemnation or destruction. This subject is important because of urban expansion. Increasingly, cities, counties, and states are taking private property to provide public services. There are tax benefits when you understand the tax rules. Not understanding the law results in bigger tax bills.

The appendices provide essential background information for those not familiar with the structural mechanics of the tax law. Appendix A describes the mechanics of the individual income tax calculation. If you are not familiar with this calculation, you should read this appendix before proceeding further. Appendix B discusses the rules for capital gains and losses, and related matters. The 1986 TRA largely eliminated the distinction between capital gains and other types of income. However, the capital asset rules continue to be important in some situations.

### A Note About Footnotes

The technical footnotes are provided for the convenience of tax advisors. They refer to the Internal Revenue Code, Income Tax Regulations, rulings, and court decisions, and quickly pinpoint the source of the information discussed in the text. The footnotes provide a starting point and will save you expensive research time. Where possible, the facts of illustrative examples are taken directly from the actual court cases, rulings and Regulations cited.

# GENERAL CONCEPTS

## CHAPTER 1

*Financial Analysis of
Residential Property
Ownership*

## CHAPTER 2

*Basic Concepts for Building
a Tax Plan*

## CHAPTER 3

*Acquiring and Disposing of
Real Estate*

*part*

# Chapter

# ONE

## FINANCIAL ANALYSIS OF RESIDENTIAL

## PROPERTY OWNERSHIP

Why own residential property? If your investment criteria require stable income and appreciation in value, residential rental property is a natural candidate. Money market funds, bonds, and other fixed income investments offer you income security, but no appreciation potential. Stocks offer both income and potential appreciation, but you must bear the risks of the stock market and the decisions of corporate managers. Works of art, oriental rugs, and other "collectibles" sometimes appreciate, but don't provide current income.

Residential real estate, on the other hand, has a long track record for both appreciation and income. Basic investment goals, therefore, should encourage you to break down the doors to buy residential property. Why might you hesitate?

Maybe you fear the unknown. Compared to many alternatives, real estate requires a large initial financial commitment. Often, the down payment and closing costs consume all your available investment funds. Maybe you are afraid to put all your eggs into one basket. Maybe you are afraid of mortgages that tie up your assets and income for many years in the future. Maybe you are not sure where you will get the cash to carry these debts. Maybe you worry about vacancies and management problems. Maybe you fear government intervention such as rent control. Is it any wonder you are apprehensive?

Do other types of investments have similar perils? Let's look at corporate stock, one of the most popular investment vehicles. When you invest in stock, the problems described above are not so obvious because you are one step removed from the day-to-day business operations of the corporation. Still, the problems are there. What about your fear of rental property losses because of vacancies? Is this unwelcome possibility any different from loss of corporate income because of declining sales? In many situations, both result from the same economic circumstances. What about management problems? The inefficiency and misdeeds of some corporate managers are widely publicized. To make matters worse, as a small shareholder you have no effective control over who the managers are, or how they operate. If things go wrong, your only practical solution is to sell the stock -- often at a loss. However, you have complete control over management of your investment real estate. If professional managers are ineffective, you can replace them.

The fact remains, however, that real estate usually requires a substantial up-front financial commitment. It is therefore imperative that you examine and understand all relevant tax and financial consequences. Frequently, prior planning prevents problems that might arise later. This point cannot be over-emphasized:

### *ADVANCE PLANNING SAVES YOU MONEY!*

How do you overcome this fear of the unknown? Remember that before you can learn to swim, you must jump into the water. The same is true for real estate ownership.

Perhaps you should jump into real estate by buying a home. From earliest childhood, we take home ownership for granted as an important part of the American dream. Therefore, you might be more comfortable to commit a large part of your resources to buying a home than to make the same financial investment for rental property. After owning a home, you will become accustomed to owning real estate. You will learn that the burden of paying a mortgage is no greater than that of paying rent. Your imagined catastrophes don't happen. After you become comfortable with owning a home, the transition to owning rental property becomes easier.

Your emotional reactions to the "creature comforts," although important when you buy a home, must not be the sole motivating factor when you buy rental real estate. You must also analyze the investment aspects. You need more than a vague notion that residential property has a good track record for appreciation in value.

Home ownership requires the same up-front commitment and debt burdens as rental property ownership. Still, prospective home buyers seldom analyze the purchase from a financial standpoint. Consider the following situation. You visit a stockbroker for investment advice. She suggests that you invest $60,000 in her favorite stock, and explains that you can finance one-half the purchase price on margin (by borrowing). How much financial and tax information would you require before you invest a substantial portion of your life savings? At the very least, you should require financial statements and a history of the company. You also should examine your cash position to figure out whether you can afford to borrow to buy the stock.

On the other hand, how would you approach a $60,000 home purchase? You might make the decision on an emotional basis without adequately understanding the financial and tax implications. Why should your approach be different for the two investments? Both require substantial outlays of cash. Both require heavy future debt payments.

The tools for analyzing financial and tax dynamics of home ownership and rental property ownership are similar. A few simple yardsticks can give you a quick measure of the relative financial merits of real estate as compared to alternative investments. The remainder of this chapter explores these techniques. First, we look at the financial aspects of real estate ownership. Then we integrate the impact of the tax law into the analysis. Finally, recognizing that corporate stock is one of the most common investment alternatives, we pull these ideas together to compare investments in securities to alternative investments in a home or in rental property.

## YARDSTICKS FOR FINANCIAL ANALYSIS
## OF REAL ESTATE OWNERSHIP

o  "Cash in is good, cash out is bad."

o  "Sell things for more than you pay for them."

o  "When you buy, use somebody else's money."

These three easy-to-remember sentences are the foundation for four useful financial analysis yardsticks: cash flow, cash-on-cash return, appreciation in value, and overall return. Let's look at each of these in detail.

### Cash Flow

Ideally, your investments produce positive cash flow (the cash-in is more than the cash-out). If negative cash flow (more cash-out) is inevitable, you should minimize it. Rental property gives you more flexibility for regulating cash flow than most investment alternatives. For example, once you invest, you have no control over the interest on savings deposits, money market funds, or bonds. Dividends on stock depend upon earnings and decisions of the corporation's directors. Cash income from rental real estate, however, is largely within your control.

In addition, the tax law makes Uncle Sam a partner who shares in cash expenditures both for homeowners and for rental property investors. You may think that a home's cash flow is always *out*, not *in*. Homeowner tax deductions, however, give you tax savings not available for other investments. Thus, though you don't collect rent from your home investment, you might have positive cash flow from tax savings.

As a homeowner, you get a big fringe benefit along with your investment. You get a free place to live. If you don't own a home, you probably pay rent for a place to live. Thus, when you compare home ownership to investment alternatives, you must offset your rent against the other investment's income to measure your true cash return. As illustrated by the rent vs. buy analysis below, home ownership tax savings can give you a better after-tax cash flow than that of securities investments.

### Cash-on-Cash Return

This yardstick compares an investment's after-tax positive cash flow to the amount of cash you have invested (equity). It doesn't take into account the investment's appreciation in value.

## Appreciation in Value

Real estate's long term track record for appreciation in value is well known. In the past, it has consistently outperformed most other types of investment. This trend should continue because of the economic law of supply and demand. Almost every human need is directly or indirectly related to real estate, and "they aren't making any more of it."

Appreciation is relevant only if it is stable and if you can use it effectively to accomplish your economic objectives. J. P. Morgan, when asked to give special insight into the workings of the stock market, said, "It will fluctuate." This reality severely restricts the usefulness of increases in stock prices. A large "paper" gain in a particular stock today can easily disappear tomorrow. Often, fluctuations have nothing to do with the specific stock, or with economic conditions in general. By comparison, although there are temporary fluctuations, experience shows that, over the long term, residential property appreciation is not likely to disappear.

If the appreciation is stable, how do you use it to get you effectively from economic point "A" to a desired economic point "B" without tax erosion? Here again, real estate out-performs stock. There are two ways you can use an investment's appreciation:

o Pledge it as collateral for a loan to finance your other economic objectives (using other people's money), or

o Sell it and use the proceeds to finance other economic objectives.

**Leverage**. Using other people's money has long been a benchmark for investment strategy. The financial advantages of leverage are that:

o A property's appreciation belongs to the owner regardless of who finances it, or how much is financed, and

o Tax benefits generally apply equally for property financed by borrowed dollars and that financed by owner dollars.

Leverage is even more important during periods of inflation. The dollars you pay back in the future will be worth less than the value of the real estate you purchase today with those borrowed dollars. Additionally, inflation is usually accompanied by higher interest rates and less institutional money to finance investments. Real estate, however, can cope effectively with these developments because you can use creative financing techniques not available for other investments (see Chapters 10 and 11).

Corporate stock is not very useful as collateral for loans because of price volatility. The easiest route is to borrow on margin. However, this type of leverage has severe limitations. First, the amount you can borrow is regulated by the Federal government, and rarely exceeds 50% of the investment's cost. Stockbrokers extol the financial benefits of margin borrowing by asserting that "you can buy twice as much stock with your available investment dollars." Even if you have never invested in real estate, wouldn't you balk at the "opportunity" to make a 50% down payment for a home or rental property? Second, if the market value of the stock declines, you face the unpleasant prospect of a *margin call*. This means that you must put up additional cash to maintain the required loan/equity ratio. Otherwise, you must sell the stock at a loss or borrow money elsewhere to pay your stockbroker. Finally, you are restricted about how you use the money. Usually, you can only use it to buy more stock.

Another alternative is to pledge the stock as collateral for a loan from a financial institution. Again, because of price volatility, banks are not particularly impressed with securities as collateral. Although you are allowed to use the loan proceeds for any purpose, financial institutions are usually unwilling to lend more than a small percentage of the market value. Thus, you can't use the investment's appreciation to the fullest extent.

The story is different for real estate. It is becoming easier to borrow by pledging the equity in your property as collateral. Second mortgages and home equity lines of credit are commonplace. Because residential real estate values are stable, financial institutions are willing to lend a higher percentage of the market value than they will for securities. Further, you can use the borrowed funds for any purpose you desire. And, if the value of the property should decline, you won't have a margin call.

**Sale or Other Disposition**. If you plan carefully, you can take advantage of your real estate's appreciation without creating taxable income. Tax deferral techniques let you use your equity without cutting Uncle Sam in on the profit (see Chapters 10, 11, and 12). This is usually not possible for alternative investments.

**Overall Return**

This is the total of the cash-on-cash return and appreciation compared to the amount of cash you have invested. Because of the volatility of appreciation of securities, this measure is not very useful for such investments. However, it is a more solid measure of the economic potential of real estate.

## THE ROLE OF TAXES IN FINANCIAL DECISION MAKING

We've all learned that the world's only certainties are death and taxes. And there is an old saying that "if you can't beat it, capitalize on it." To date, nobody has devised a way to avoid death. However, an entire industry is available to help you avoid and capitalize on taxes.

For most of its history, the income tax law has been used by the Federal government as a tool to engineer economic and social behavior. This is because it is much easier politically to give special benefits to an activity indirectly through the tax law than it is to subsidize the activity directly. The tax subsidy approach has three serious drawbacks. First, it is an inefficient way to allocate resources. Second, by necessity, tax incentives create "loopholes" not equally available for all taxpayers. This results in a general perception that the tax system is inequitable and unfair. Third, the law becomes very complex when incentives are injected into the system. The complexities are beyond the comprehension of many taxpayers, and this aggravates the perception of unfairness.

In a tax system that relies on voluntary compliance, a widespread perception of unfairness is a death knell for the system. If you feel that you carry a disproportionate burden of supporting the government, you might question why you should comply, particularly when many wealthy individuals and corporations pay little or nothing because of tax loopholes. Tax cheating ceases to be a social disgrace, and becomes a desirable activity to "even things up." Meanwhile, the Treasury suffers.

As tax loopholes and complexities proliferate, taxpayers demand reform. As a result, we have had major tax legislation on the average of every 18 months during the past 34 years. In addition, there have been many tax bills for specialized matters. Many of these have been called "tax reform." However, this tax reform has generally been restricted to narrowing existing loopholes, and attempting to increase compliance by using expanded penalties and reporting requirements. There has not been any significant change to the underlying philosophy that the tax system is an appropriate tool for economic manipulation.

## Impact of the Tax Reform Act of 1986

The monumental Tax Reform Act of 1986 (1986 TRA) reversed this trend. Rather than tinkering with the existing system, the 1986 TRA fundamentally reversed the direction of tax policy. It attempted to remove tax considerations as motivating factors for making economic decisions. It's primary purpose was to reestablish fairness. Lawmakers felt that this was necessary to restore faith in the tax system and the legislative process. With renewed faith, they anticipated that tax compliance would improve and Federal revenues would increase. In the quest to restore fairness, the goal of simplification was sacrificed.

The key to the 1986 TRA was low tax rates. A much broader tax base pays for the low rates. This is accomplished by eliminating many special tax deductions and credits. An especially important target of the law was "tax shelters," or investments designed primarily to save taxes for investors despite the lack of the investment's economic viability.

Although the goal was to eliminate tax incentives, political expediency required the retention of some incentives. As the law developed, it became obvious that some tax benefits are "sacred cows" and that others are merely "holy cows." Holy cows can be eliminated without fatal political consequences. Killing sacred cows means political disaster. Despite the political perils, three of the long-standing sacred cows emerged from tax reform slightly wounded. The sanctity of the home mortgage interest, charitable contributions, and tax-exempt municipal bond interest was invaded, but these benefits retain most of their prior tax vigor. Congress retained other benefits in modified form. Thus, the tax system is still a factor for making economic decisions. But its influence is reduced, and you must redirect your tax planning strategy.

Real estate has always been a major beneficiary of tax subsidies. The ongoing tax commitment can be traced in major tax bills through the 1981 tax law. Since then, tax trends for real estate have been mixed. Tax changes in 1982 and 1984 were biased in favor other types of investment.

Although the 1986 TRA's overhaul almost eliminates tax benefits for large tax shelter syndicates, it preserves substantially all tax benefits for homeowners, and many benefits for small-unit residential rental property investors. Despite what happens to tax benefits for rental property in future legislation, it seems clear that the tax law will continue to favor home ownership. Even in the most heated debates about closing tax "loopholes," politicians continue to protect homeowners.

### Understanding Tax Rates - Old and New

Income tax rates determine the extent of Uncle Sam's participation in an investment. Although this isn't the most exciting aspect of the tax law, you must understand how the rate system works before you can crank tax consequences into a financial analysis.

**Tax Rates Before the 1986 TRA.** Tax rates under the old law (before 1987) were steeply progressive. This means that the law applied increasingly higher tax rates to increasingly higher segments (brackets) of income. There were many tax brackets that ranged from 11% to 50%. Thus, in the highest bracket, you saved fifty cents in taxes for every deductible dollar you spent. Put another way, Uncle Sam picked up one-half of the expenditure.

**Tax Rates After the 1986 TRA.** Probably the most revolutionary aspect of the 1986 TRA was that it abandoned the basic philosophy of a progressive tax rate system, and adopted a modified *flat* rate system with much lower rates. In its purest form, a *flat tax* means that all taxpayers pay tax at the same rate regardless of how much income they have. Still, for practical reasons, the new rate system provides a few lower rate brackets.

**Impact of State Income Taxes.** In addition to the Federal income tax, you must crank state income taxes into your analysis. The structures of state income taxes vary, but most of them "piggy-back" on the Federal income tax. This means that you begin your state tax calculation with your Federal adjusted gross income (see Appendix A). You then make adjustments for certain specified items. Generally, these adjustments do not involve tax deductions related to home ownership or residential real estate investment.

Therefore, for purposes of financial analysis, you can combine your highest applicable Federal and state tax rates to figure out the overall income tax impact. We develop these ideas below.

### How Tax Rates Apply for Financial Analysis

There are two distinct meanings for the terms "tax bracket" or "tax rate." Sometimes we use the "marginal" tax rate (bracket), and at other times we use the "effective" tax rate (bracket). The two concepts have different economic implications.

**Marginal Tax Rate.** We use the marginal tax rate for tax planning. The marginal rate is the combined Federal and state percentage rates applied to the top dollar of taxable income. When you decrease or increase your taxable income, the marginal rate determines Uncle Sam's (and the state's) percentage of participation as a tax partner. For purposes of the following examples and discussions, we refer to the combined Federal and state marginal rates as "Uncle Sam."

> **Example:** Bailey has taxable income of $60,000. Her marginal tax rate is 40% (that is, the rate applied to the sixty-thousandth dollar). If she spends one additional deductible dollar, she reduces her taxable income by one dollar. This saves her 40 cents of taxes. Thus, the extra dollar of expenditure only costs her 60 cents. Uncle Sam is a 40% partner in financing the expenditure.

Sometimes your tax partnership is even better. Suppose that you can deduct an extra dollar without actually spending any money. The deduction for depreciation can do this. If your real estate is increasing in value, an extra dollar of depreciation costs you nothing. In the above example, deducting an extra depreciation dollar saves 40 cents of tax. Since you have no economic outlay, this is like having Uncle Sam give you a check for 40 cents as a gift. In this respect Uncle Sam is better than a real-life partner. How many partners are willing to give you cash without demanding something in return? This illustrates the importance of depreciation for real estate investments. If all other things are equal, you should maximize depreciation deductions (see Chapter 8). Note, however, that in some situations, the tax law limits this *shelter* benefit by imposing the passive loss rules (see Chapter 7).

Your tax partnership works both ways. Uncle Sam is willing to participate in expenditures, but he also wants his share of the partnership's income.

**Example:** Suppose in the above example that instead of spending one dollar, Bailey raises the rent by one dollar, thus increasing her taxable income by that amount. She must pay Uncle Sam his share of 40 cents on the additional dollar of income, so that her share of the tax partnership additional income is only 60 cents.

**Effective Tax Rate.** You determine your effective tax rate by dividing your total taxable income into your total tax liability. This number isn't very useful for tax planning. It merely tells you what overall percentage of your taxable income you pay to the government. If anything, this information is depressing. In tax planning, our primary focus is on the dollars added and subtracted from the top of your taxable income rather than the overall percentage of your income you pay to the government.

**What to Expect With Tax Rates.** Both the Congress and state legislatures constantly tinker with tax rates. Political considerations motivate most of this tinkering. For example, when Congress wants to give a "tax cut," the usual approach is to lower the rates rather than expand the tax base by curtailing deductions and other tax benefits. This approach, although simplistic, is easy for the voters to understand (at least they think they understand). As a result of this tinkering, you must regularly reassess the financial status of your investments as the rates change.

## HOME OWNERSHIP - YOUR CASTLE AND YOUR FINANCIAL SHELTER

Now let's pull all this together. To illustrate how financial analysis works, we use the financial yardsticks (with tax consequences cranked in) to compare a stock investment with a home purchase. The illustrations show the interplay between actual and tax cash flows to determine your bottom-line economic result.

### Rent vs. Buy Analysis

Assume you are married and recently inherited $15,000. Your adjusted gross income (see Appendix A) is $40,000, and you presently live in an apartment, paying $400 per month rent. A stockbroker advises you that the stock market is the way to go for your inheritance. However, you want to investigate the possibility of using it to buy your first home.

First, the stock investment. Assume that the margin rules allow you to borrow an amount equal to the cash you invest at an interest rate of 11%. Thus, your $15,000 cash buys stock worth $30,000, which yields 9 1/2%. The stockbroker says that it is reasonable to expect the stock's value to increase 5% during the current year. Your combined Federal and state marginal tax rate is 35%.

Here is how the investment analysis yardsticks work for the stock investment. Remember that a home gives you a free place to live, so you must reduce the stock's cash return by the rent.

*Cash Flow:*

| | |
|---|---:|
| Income from stock @ 9 1/2% | $ 2,850 |
| Less: Interest on margin loan | 1,650 |
| Net cash income | $ 1,200 |
| Less: Tax thereon @35% | 420 |
| Net after-tax income | $ 780 |
| Less: Nondeductible rent | 4,800 |
| Net cash outflow | $(4,020) |

*Cash-on-Cash Return on Investment:*

| | |
|---|---:|
| Cash return (tax savings) | $ 780 |
| Equity investment in stock | $15,000 |
| Cash-on-cash return | 5.2% |

*Appreciation in Value:*

| | |
|---|---:|
| $30,000 investment @ 5% | $ 1,500 |

*Overall Return on Investment:*

| | |
|---|---:|
| Cash return + appreciation | $ 2,280 |
| Investment in securities | $15,000 |
| Overall return | 15.2% |

Now let's look at the home purchase. The $15,000 cash enables you to purchase a $75,000 home with a 30 year amortizing mortgage of $60,000 at 9.25%. The first year's interest is $5,534, and real estate taxes are $1,500. If the stockbroker is willing to predict that the stock will appreciate 5% in the current year, we'll make the same assumption for the home. Here is how the yardsticks measure a home's investment potential:

---

*Cash Flow:*

| | |
|---|---:|
| Deductible interest | $ 5,534 |
| Deductible real estate taxes | 1,500 |
| Total deductible expenses | $ 7,034 |
| Less:  Tax savings @35% | 2,462 |
| Net cash outflow | $(4,572) |

*Cash-on Cash Return on Investment:*

| | |
|---|---:|
| Cash return (tax savings) | $ 2,462 |
| Equity invested | $15,000 |
| Cash-on-cash return | 16.4% |

*Appreciation in Value:*

| | |
|---|---:|
| $75,000 investment @ 5% | $ 3,750 |

*Overall Return on Investment:*

| | |
|---|---:|
| Cash return + appreciation | $ 6,212 |
| Equity invested in home | $15,000 |
| Overall return | 41.4% |

*Summary of Rent vs. Buy Analysis:*

| | Stock | Home |
|---|:---:|:---:|
| Cash outflow | ($4,020) | ($4,572) |
| Cash-on-cash return | 5.2% | 16.4% |
| Appreciation | $1,500 | $3,750 |
| Overall return | 15.2% | 41.4% |

---

Let's analyze the numbers. It is true that the cash outflow is greater for the home than for the stock. However, when you compare the homeowner cash flow (tax savings) to that of the stock, the cash return for the home is over three times that for the stock. This isn't bad for an investment you didn't think had any positive cash flow at all! Remember, this happy result is because of your tax partnership with Uncle Sam. Because of greater leverage, the appreciation and overall return for the home are almost three times that for the stock.

In this analysis we don't take into account the amount of the mortgage payments you apply to reduce the loan principal. This is because principal payments merely convert your cash equity into real estate equity. In this respect, an amortizing mortgage is like a forced savings account. In the example, you have put $389 into real estate equity "savings" during the first year. In each year after that, the amount applied to principal increases as the amount of interest paid (and the resulting tax deduction) decreases. This means that positive cash flow decreases during each year you own your home. Although we don't consider principal payments for investment analysis, it is important that you make sure you have sufficient cash to cover them.

## RENTAL PROPERTY AS AN INVESTMENT

The financial advantages of real estate are magnified for rental property. Tax breaks for homeowners are also available for rental property. However, rental property enjoys many additional tax deductions. In addition to interest and real estate taxes, you can deduct all expenses of maintaining the property (repairs, insurance, management fees, utilities, etc.). And, of course, there is the best of all tax deductions -- depreciation, the "Gift from Uncle Sam."

Real estate's superior leverage potential is particularly important for rental property because purchase-money financing increases the basis for depreciation (see Chapter 3). Hence, depreciation deductions don't require the corresponding cash outlay necessary for other deductions. You get a double-barreled benefit. There is no outlay of cash, and if the property maintains or increases its value, there is no economic loss.

### Comparative Investment Analysis

We can adapt the homeowner rent vs. buy analysis to

compare an investment in stock to an investment in residential rental property. We use the same criteria: cash flow, cash-on-cash return, appreciation in value, and overall return.

To illustrate, assume you are married and have accumulated $20,000 in a savings account. You are considering a stock investment yielding 10% with annual projected appreciation of 5%. You can borrow an additional $20,000 on margin at 12% interest, so that your total investment in stock is $40,000. Your combined Federal and state marginal tax rate is 35%

---

### Cash Flow:

| | |
|---|---:|
| Income from stock | $ 4,000 |
| Less: Interest on margin | 2,400 |
| Net taxable income | $ 1,600 |
| Less: Tax thereon @35% | 560 |
| Cash flow | $ 1,040 |

### Cash-on-cash Return on Investment:

| | |
|---|---:|
| Cash return (tax savings) | $ 1,040 |
| Amount invested | $20,000 |
| Cash-on-cash return | 5.2% |

### Appreciation in Value:

| | |
|---|---:|
| $40,000 investment @ 5% | $ 2,000 |

### Overall Return on Investment:

| | |
|---|---:|
| Cash flow + appreciation | $ 3,040 |
| Amount invested | $20,000 |
| Overall return | 20.3% |

---

Assume you can get a 30-year bank loan at 9 1/2% for an investment house. The required down payment (including closing costs) is 20%. Thus, you can borrow $80,000 to purchase a $100,000 investment property. The first year interest payment is $7,378, real estate taxes are $1,600, and estimated repairs and other costs are $800. Of the purchase price, $18,000 is allocable to land

and $82,000 to the building. Depreciation for the first year is $2,858. You can get $850 per month rent ($10,200 annually) and you expect that the property will appreciate 5% in the first year. We assume that you qualify for the special $25,000 deduction for passive losses (see Chapter 7).

---

*Cash Flow:*

| | | |
|---|---|---:|
| Rental income | | $10,200 |
| | | |
| Less: | Interest | $ 7,378 |
| | Real estate taxes | 1,600 |
| | Other cash expenses | 800 |
| Total cash deductions | | $ 9,778 |
| | | |
| Cash flow | | $ 422 |
| Less: Depreciation | | (2,858) |
| Tax Loss | | $(2,436) |
| | | |
| Tax savings @ 35% | | $ 853 |
| Add: Rental income (above) | | 10,200 |
| Total positive cash flow | | $11,053 |
| Less: Cash expenses (above) | | 9,778 |
| Net cash flow | | $ 1,275 |

*Cash-on-cash Return on Investment:*

| | |
|---|---:|
| Cash return (tax savings) | $ 1,275 |
| Amount invested | $20,000 |
| Cash-on-cash return | 6.4% |

*Appreciation in Value:*

| | |
|---|---:|
| $100,000 investment @ 5% | $ 5,000 |

*Overall Return on Investment:*

| | |
|---|---:|
| Cash flow + appreciation | $ 6,275 |
| Amount invested | $20,000 |
| Overall return | 31.4% |

### Summary of Stock vs. Rental Property Analysis

|                     | Stock    | Rental   |
|---------------------|----------|----------|
| Cash flow           | $1,040   | $1,275   |
| Cash-on-cash return | 5.2%     | 6.4%     |
| Appreciation        | $2,000   | $5,000   |
| Overall return      | 20.3%    | 31.4%    |

As in the case of the rent vs. buy analysis, greater leverage for real estate results in greater appreciation, which, in turn, is reflected in the overall return. Thus, like home ownership, rental property shows its economic superiority over a stock investment. Here, the addition to your equity "savings account" (principal payments) is $519. This example also shows how an investment with before-tax positive cash flow produces a tax loss because of the depreciation deduction. This results in further positive cash flow because of tax savings (the "gift from Uncle Sam").

## WINNERS AND LOSERS AFTER THE 1986 TRA

It is clear that many real estate syndicates structured as we know them have ceased to be viable investments. Passive investors' positive cash flow generated from tax savings ceased. To make up for the loss of tax cash flow, rents needed to be increased. This was not easy in some rental markets. For instance, some segments of the commercial market, such as office buildings, were unable to force higher rents on tenants. This resulted in widespread loan defaults and foreclosures. The effect on the banking industry is painfully apparent. It was somewhat easier to increase rents for residential projects, but here too, there is only so much the market will bear.

Single family houses (and other small-unit residential property) have become more attractive for small investors. The exception permitting deductions of up to $25,000 of passive rental losses (see Chapter 7) is specifically designed to accommodate residential property investors. In the overall real estate investment picture, rental houses stand out as one of the few remaining old-style tax shelters (albeit a small shelter). Moreover, the increased rent level for large residential projects should spill over into the single family rental market. The combination of these factors, plus the tax benefits, indicates that residential real estate should continue to be a sound financial investment.

# Chapter

# TWO

## BASIC CONCEPTS FOR BUILDING

## A TAX PLAN

You would never begin construction of a building without a blueprint. It explains four essential elements for successful completion of the job. First, it describes how the structure is designed. Second, it shows how the design accomplishes the building's function. Third, it adapts the building to the peculiarities of its site. Finally, it specifies the materials to be used.

You should also have a blueprint before buying real estate. Whether the potential investment is your home or a rental property, you should understand the design, the function, the site, and the building materials for your tax plan. In this chapter we discuss the first three of these elements. The specific tax rules applicable in various situations are the building materials for the tax plan. We discuss these rules in subsequent chapters.

### HOW TO DESIGN A TAX PLAN

The starting point for designing a tax plan is to determine how the tax rates apply to you. As discussed in Chapter 1, the rates are the "zoning" regulation for the plan, and indicate how much Uncle Sam participates as a financing partner.

## Tax Consequences of Spending Money

Money is the mortar that holds an investment together. However, money is not always easy to come by, so it is important to plan your expenditures to get the biggest tax bang for the buck. Also, when possible, use somebody else's money.

Spending money can have three different tax consequences. First, and best, you get an immediate tax benefit from a deduction or credit. Second, and not quite as good, you capitalize the expenditure and deduct it in future years. For example, you must capitalize building costs, and then deduct them in subsequent years as depreciation. Third, and worst, you get no tax benefit, either now or in the future. This is what happens to your personal expenses such as food, clothing, and repairs for personal-use property.

## Shaping the Design — Tax Planning
## Targets For Investment

The overall shape, or design of your tax plan depends upon your tax objectives. The actual appearance of the plan depends upon the building materials, or tax rules you use to achieve your overall objectives. Like all building materials, detailed tax rules are numerous and complex.

Fortunately, the tax rules fit into one of four overall tax planning categories or targets. You can use these targets in various combinations to shape your tax plan. The targets have technical tax labels which are sometimes used interchangeably. For instance the term *deduction* is sometimes used to describe a tax *credit*. This is unfortunate, because the various targets have different economic consequences. Thus, before embarking on any tax plan, you must understand the mechanics of each tax target, and grasp its economic implications.

**Exclusions from Income**. The general tax rule is that "gross income is all income from whatever source derived." This broad definition implies that gross income includes any increase in economic wealth. However, Congress has decided that some increases should not be subject to the income tax, and are thus *excluded*. Excluded income never enters into the tax calculation.

Many types of income are excluded, each with its own exclusion rationale. For example, the law excludes the value of property you inherit or property you receive as a gift. The reason is that such property is subject to the estate and gift taxes. Some exclusions are designed to promote social welfare and economic well-being. Examples are social security benefits, employer medical insurance plans, group life insurance plans, etc.

The economic benefit of excluded income depends upon your marginal tax rate. The higher your marginal rate, the bigger the benefit.

**Example:** Karadbil's employer pays part of the premiums for her medical insurance. Although the employer's premium payments are additional economic compensation, they are excluded from her income. Thus, in the 35% marginal tax bracket, she gets 100 cents of benefit from each dollar her employer contributes, but she avoids paying 35 cents of tax.

The most important residential property exclusion is the over-55 exclusion for gain from the sale of a principal residence (see Chapter 5).

**Deductions from Income.** Deductions reduce your gross income to determine your taxable income. As illustrated in Chapter 1, the economic benefit of a deduction depends on your marginal tax rate. The higher the rate, the more the benefit. There are more deductions available for real estate than for any other type of investment.

**Credits Against the Tax Liability.** A tax credit is a dollar-for-dollar offset against your tax liability. Unlike exclusions and deductions, your marginal tax rate is immaterial for determining a tax credit's economic benefit. A dollar of tax credit gives you a full dollar of tax benefit. It is equivalent to a dollar of tax payment.

The tax credit is the most potent mechanism to encourage investment. Credits have the same economic impact for all taxpayers, regardless of their marginal tax rates. The most important tax credits for real estate are those for rehabilitating old commercial or historic buildings, and for constructing low-income housing.

**Deferral of Tax on Gains.** The normal tax rule is that gains from sales or exchanges of property are taxed in the year of the transaction. In some situations, however, you may defer, or postpone taxation until a later time.

Real estate offers more opportunities for tax deferral than any investment alternative. The home-sale rollover allows you to postpone tax on gain from the sale of your principal residence (see Chapter 5). You may defer gain from your investment or business real estate by using a like-kind real estate exchange (see Chapter 11). The installment method of reporting allows you to defer tax on personal, investment, or business property when you finance the sale by carrying back a note (see Chapter 10).

Tax deferral is like a loan from the government for the amount of tax postponed. This casts Uncle Sam into a new role for real estate investors. Chapter 1 discusses his role as a partner for financing expenditures. Tax deferral makes him a financing partner for acquiring property. In effect, he is your banker. His astonishing loan terms, however, are not available from any real-life lender.

First, Uncle Sam's loans are interest-free. He allows you to postpone your tax, but does not require you to pay interest during the deferral period. This amounts to an interest-free "loan" for the amount of tax otherwise payable. Most banks (but not Uncle Sam) require you to pay interest.

Second, you may take out the loan at any time, in any amount, and you don't have to apply for it. You don't need Uncle Sam's prior permission for tax deferral. You simply arrange your transaction to qualify according to the tax law. It doesn't matter when the transaction occurs, or how much tax is postponed. Most banks (but not Uncle Sam) require prior application and approval for a loan.

Third, you may repay the loan whenever you want to repay it, and Uncle Sam has no right to call it. The deferred tax is payable when you dispose of the property you received the tax-deferred transaction in a subsequent taxable transaction. The timing of the disposition is entirely up to you, and Uncle Sam sits quietly on the sidelines in the meantime. Most banks (but not Uncle Sam) require a loan repayment schedule, or require that the loan is payable on demand.

Finally, you may never have to repay the loan at all. You can avoid repayment simply by dying! This is because the basis of the property your beneficiary inherits from you is stepped-up to its market value when you die (see Chapter 3). Thus, there is no gain because the beneficiary's basis equals the property's market value. Nobody ever has to pay your postponed tax. Most banks (but not

Uncle Sam) require that somebody eventually repays a loan. This opportunity for complete (legal) tax avoidance is the tax law manifestation of the philosophy that many people use to govern their lives: "Always put off until tomorrow what you should do today, because if you put it off long enough, you probably won't have to do it." For your real estate investments, this is sound advice, indeed.

> Example: McGinley, a married taxpayer, has taxable income of $80,000. His combined Federal and state marginal tax rate is 35%. He sells his home for a $50,000 gain, which increases his taxable income to $130,000. The tax on the additional $50,000 is $17,500. McGinley uses the home-sale rollover to postpone the $17,500 tax. If he can obtain 80% financing for a new home, the tax saving, used as an additional down payment, enables him to buy a new home worth $87,500 more than he otherwise could ($17,500 tax savings plus $70,000 additional mortgage).

### Three Sentence Course in Tax Planning

When you design your tax plan, you must consider not only technical tax rules, but also the overall purpose and policy of the tax system. The Internal Revenue Code is an enormously complex document with a bewildering array of rules. Each provision is designed to accomplish a specific economic or social objective. If you apply a tax rule according to the legislative intent, you won't have any problem. However, if you try to be clever and manipulate the rule to accomplish an objective not intended, you can be in trouble.

To frustrate such abuses, the courts have developed overriding judicial principles to rearrange your clever tax schemes to reflect their economic reality. Thus, you must review your transactions, however artfully arranged, in the light of these principles. This is particularly important in creative financing situations, as discussed in Chapters 10 and 11. These are the three overriding judicial principles:

**Substance over Form.** The economic substance of a transaction controls its tax consequences. If its technical form differs from its economic substance, the form is disregarded, and the transaction is taxed according to its economic reality.[1] This is sometimes called the "duckness" test. If it looks like a duck, quacks like a duck, and waddles like a duck, by George, it's a duck, even if you call it a cow!

**Step-Transaction**. If you divide a transaction into a series of separate steps, each of which gets more favorable tax treatment than the overall transaction considered as a whole, the steps are ignored, and the transaction is taxed as if the steps don't exist.[2]

**Business Purpose**. The tax law ignores a transaction or action if it has no substantial economic or business purpose other than saving taxes.[3]

In addition to overriding judicial principles, you must remember that the burden of proof rests with you, not the government. This means that the Internal Revenue Service (IRS) may reject your version of a transaction, and the ball is then in your court to prove that your interpretation of the law should prevail. Sometimes it is difficult to sustain this burden. It is dangerous to be uncooperative with the IRS, or to stretch the literal letter of the law too far. Your psychological gratification in winning a tax battle over a particular issue is easily offset by your economic pain when you lose the war.

These ideas can be summarized in an easy-to-remember three sentence course in tax planning:

o **Bulls Make Money, Bears Make Money, Pigs Get Slaughtered**. This well-known rule of the stock market also applies for tax planning. Most court decisions, IRS rulings, and legislative changes adverse to taxpayers are monuments to tax "pigs" trying to get unwarranted tax benefits.

o **If It Seems Too Good To Be True, It Is**. Many artful technical tax planning schemes designed to get unwarranted tax benefits are easily overturned by applying the overriding judicial principles.

o **In the Long Run, the IRS Has All the Marbles**. Your burden of proof gives the government a powerful negotiating position in tax disputes.

## UNDERSTANDING THE FUNCTION OF YOUR TAX PLAN

When you build a structure you should understand why you are building it, and how it will serve its function. The same is true when you build a tax plan. Unlike a bricks-and-mortar building, however, the ultimate tax function of a real estate investment is not always entirely clear at the outset.

The way you use the property determines your tax consequences while you own it and when you dispose of it. Although you may have many economic reasons for owning a property, there are only four tax functions or motivations.

**Personal Use.** Most residential property owners use it as a principal residence. This function permits a few tax deductions during ownership (see Chapter 4) and permits deferral or exclusion of gain from its sale (see Chapters 5 and 6). You also might own residential property as a vacation or second home. Although you get deductions during ownership similar to those for a principal residence, you cannot defer or exclude gain from sale.

**Investment.** You own investment property primarily for appreciation over time, and/or for current cash return from rents and tax benefits. You get many more tax benefits during ownership for investment property than for personal-use property (see Chapter 8). However, the passive loss limitation rules might curtail some of these benefits (see Chapter 7). You may also defer gain in a qualifying exchange (see Chapter 11).

**Trade or Business.** This is property you use in your business activities. Examples: a building where a real estate office is located, a factory building for a manufacturing business, business automobiles, equipment, furniture, etc. You get the same tax benefits for business property that you get for investment property, including tax deferral in a qualifying exchange. However, the passive loss limitation rules do not apply to tax benefits for business property like they do for investment property (see Chapter 7).

**"Dealer" Property.** The tax law defines *dealer* property as "property held by the taxpayer primarily for sale to customers in the ordinary course of his business."[4] Essentially, this definition describes inventory. Such property gets very few tax deductions during ownership, and is denied capital gain treatment when sold. You cannot defer gain from its sale or exchange. Example: Lots resulting from a subdivision. See Appendix B for a discussion of dealer property.

Sometimes you might emit mixed signals about why you own a particular piece of real estate. Your actions may cloud your real motivation. In these situations, the IRS will choose the motivation most suited to its purpose, i.e., maximizing your tax bill. Remember that you have the burden of proving that your motivation is different from what your actions imply.

The IRS frequently disputes whether you own property as an investment or as a personal vacation home. The vacation home limitation, establishes legislative guidelines to settle the dispute (see Chapter 7). Another classic dispute is whether you own property (such as a horse farm) as a bona-fide business, or you are trying to masquerade your hobby as a business to get extra tax benefits. Again, there are legislative guidelines (the hobby loss limitation - see Chapter 4). Perhaps the most troublesome disputes concern the classification of property as an investment, or as dealer property. In the past, the IRS target was to deny long-term capital gain treatment for sales of such property. Now that ordinary income rates do not differ substantially from long-term capital gain rates, this traditional arena of battle is much less important. However, the dealer vs. investor distinction still has other important tax implications (see Appendix B).

Sometimes you might use property for more than one purpose at the same time. For instance, you may live in part of a house (personal use) and rent the remainder to tenants (investment use). Or you may use part of your home as a business office. The tax law treats each part of multi-use property separately, and accords the appropriate tax benefits (and detriments) to each part.

In all these situations, it is important for you to identify the specific tax function for your property in advance, and treat the property accordingly while you own it and when you dispose of it. In all events, avoid sending out mixed signals. All of your actions, and all documentation relating to the property, should point to the tax motivation you want to establish. In subsequent chapters, we discuss how you do this in specific situations.

## ADAPTING TO THE BUILDING SITE
## FOR YOUR TAX PLAN

The building site for a tax plan is the environment created by the tax law. Like any other environment, the tax environment has many nitty-gritty rules governing the behavior of the inhabitants, and those who disobey the rules are punished. In this chapter, we describe the general ground rules, or nuts and bolts, of the tax environment for all taxpayers regardless of their business or investment activities. First, we identify who they are, and the planning opportunities for shifting income from one taxpayer to another. Then we look at tax accounting methods, reporting requirements, penalties, and statutes of limitations.

### The Inhabitants of the Environment --
### Types of Income Tax Payers

The starting point for tax planning is to identify who (or what) is taxed. Sometimes, income can be shifted from one taxpayer to another to achieve overall tax savings. The income tax law defines four distinct taxable entities: individuals, estates, certain trusts, and corporations.

First, a word about partnerships, often used for real estate investments. Partnerships are not taxpaying entities, but they have many tax ramifications. Even when a partnership does not distribute its earnings to the partners, its income is included in the partners' individual tax returns according to their partnership agreement. The partnership must report its income and the share of that income taxable to each partner. It also must make many tax elections such as accounting methods, depreciation and inventory methods, etc. Because losses pass through to the partners, the partnership is the vehicle most frequently used for real estate investment syndicates.

The restrictions on using passive losses to offset income from other sources (compensation, interest, etc.) have curtailed syndicates whose primary purpose is to provide tax shelter to the partners. Thus, the tax role of partnerships for real estate investment has rapidly declined for achieving this goal. However, for most small-unit residential investors, the law continues to permit a limited amount of passive losses to offset other income (see Chapter 7). In these situations, a partnership still might be useful. An alternative may be a shared-equity financing agreement (see Chapter 11).

**Individuals.** Individual taxpayers are living, breathing, human beings. Age is irrelevant. When you take your first breath, you become a potential individual taxpayer. With your last dying gasp you cease to be an individual taxpayer, and are reclassified as an estate (see below). Your children are potential taxpayers and give you opportunities for splitting income within your family unit to achieve overall tax savings. These possibilities are discussed below.

If you operate your business as a proprietor, you report its income (or loss) on your individual income tax return (IRS Form 1040, Schedule C). The same is true for reporting income or loss from rental property you own as an individual or as a joint owner with someone else (IRS Form 1040, Schedule E). The reporting procedure is different if you own your business or investments in a corporation. Here, you report the operating results on a corporation income tax return (IRS Form 1120). The corporation's income appears in your individual tax return only when you are paid a dividend.

**Estates.** An estate is the legal entity that administers the property of a deceased individual between the date of death and the time the property is distributed to the beneficiaries. During this period, the estate reports and pays tax on the income from its assets. Don't confuse the status of an estate as an income taxpayer with the Federal estate tax. The estate tax is a separate tax levied on the value of the estate's assets at the time of a decedent's death.

**Trusts.** A trust is a legal entity established by a contract between the person transferring property to the trust (grantor) and the person who administers it (trustee). The contract describes how the trustee is to administer the assets, and how he will distribute the income to the beneficiaries. You may establish trusts during your lifetime (*inter-vivos* or *living* trusts), or by a provision in your will (testamentary trusts).

Trusts are very flexible legal devices. You can design them to accomplish many tax and non-tax objectives. Trusts are created to care for minors or other dependent relatives, to avoid probate, or to shift the taxability of income to other taxpayers. You may retain many administrative powers, and may retain the power to alter, amend, or completely revoke the trust.

A trust has tax consequences only if you give up the power to alter, amend or revoke it. If you retain any of these powers, the trust is called a revocable trust, and it is treated for all Federal tax purposes (income, estate, and gift) as if it didn't exist. Its income is included in your individual tax return, and its assets are included in your taxable estate for the Federal estate tax. Although revocable trusts have no tax consequences, they provide many non-tax advantages as ownership vehicles for real estate (see Chapter 3).

When you give up all powers to alter, amend or revoke the trust, it is called an irrevocable trust. Income tax consequences depend upon how the trustee is directed to dispose of the trust's annual income. Regardless of whether the trust is inter-vivos or testamentary, it is classified for income tax purposes into one of two categories.

o **Simple Trusts** -- The trustee distributes the trust's entire income annually to the beneficiaries. A simple trust is not a taxpaying entity. The trust merely acts as a conduit, and income is reported in the tax returns of the beneficiaries.[5]

o **Complex Trusts** -- The trustee has the power to accumulate the trust's income and add it to the principal. Sometimes the trustee is directed to accumulate all income, but more often, he has discretion either to distribute income to the beneficiaries or to accumulate it. If he accumulates the income, the trust becomes a taxpaying entity, and pays tax on the income retained. When income is eventually distributed to the beneficiaries, the tax previously paid by the trust is credited against the beneficiaries' tax according to a complex set of rules.[6]

**Corporations.** A corporation is an artificial entity created by a charter from a state government. Generally, corporations are taxpayers that are separate and distinct from their owners, the shareholders. A corporation's income subject to the following progressive rates:

| Taxable Income: | |
|---|---|
| Not over $50,000 | 15% |
| Over $50,000 but not over $75,000 | 25% |
| Over $75,000 | 34% |

The benefit of the lower rates phases out between taxable income of $100,000 and $335,000, by a 5% surtax. When income exceeds $335,000, the effect of the phase-out is that all taxable income (beginning with the first dollar) is taxed at 34%.[7]

When income is distributed to the shareholders as a dividend, it is included in their income and is taxed again. If only a few shareholders own a corporation, they might be tempted to accumulate the income in the corporation to avoid the second tax. To discourage such attempts, the law imposes penalty taxes on unreasonably accumulated income.

A special election (Subchapter S) allows a corporation's income to bypass the corporate tax and be taxed directly to the shareholders, even though the income is not distributed to them.[8] When the income is eventually distributed, there is no additional tax. The election also permits shareholders to deduct limited amounts of corporate losses from other income. Often, Subchapter S is described as an election permitting a corporation to be taxed like a partnership. This is not entirely true. For many tax purposes, an electing corporation continues to be treated as a corporation, not a partnership. The election is complex, and you can have severe adverse tax consequences if you inadvertently fail to comply with its requirements. You should use Subchapter S cautiously, and if you make the election, you should have continuous expert tax advice.

### Income Splitting

Income splitting is the technique for diverting your high tax bracket income to a lower bracket related taxpayer. Low tax bracket family members such as small children and elderly parents are likely candidates. If you can shift your to a lower income taxpayer, you essentially "pour" it into a lower marginal tax bracket.

You can't shift your earned income, or income from your personal services, to another taxpayer.[9] Therefore your fees, salaries, wages, commissions, etc. are always taxed to you. You can transfer income from property, however, if you transfer the property that produces the income. Thus, you may shift rents, dividends, interest, etc., to another taxpayer.

There are restrictions on the benefit of income splitting with your children under age 14. Their unearned income in excess of $600 is taxable at your marginal tax rate.[10] However, the child can offset $600 of unearned income with his standard deduction (see Appendix A). Thus, if you transfer property producing income of $1,200 to your child, $600 is not taxed (standard deduction), and $600 is taxed at the lowest individual rate. This treatment applies regardless of how the child acquires the income-producing property.

It doesn't matter whether the property came from the parents, grandparents, other parties related or unrelated, or from the child's own savings. The $600 base amounts are adjusted annually.

The restriction doesn't apply for unearned income of your children over age 14, or for other related taxpayers. Thus, if you transfer property to an unmarried child over 14, $600 of the property's income is not taxed because of his standard deduction, and the remainder is taxed at his normal tax rates rather than yours.

As an alternative to an outright gift, you can shift the property's income by using an irrevocable trust. The terms of the trust can delay the beneficiary's possession of the property until any later date. The terms also might delay payment of the income to the beneficiary by directing the trustee to accumulate it. In this case the trust itself becomes a taxpayer because it is a complex trust (see above), and is taxed at the rates applicable to trusts.

### The Impact of Tax Accounting Methods

Earlier in this chapter, we focused on the economic impact of tax planning objectives or targets. In addition, you must determine the timing of these elements to structure the overall design of your tax plan. In what tax year is income taxed? When are expenses deducted? Generally, answers to these questions depend upon your taxable year, and the overall tax accounting method you select.

Every taxpayer must select a taxable year for reporting income.[11] This can either be a calendar year (January 1 - December 31), or a fiscal year. A fiscal year is any twelve month period ending on the last day of any month other than December. The selection of a taxable year depends upon your natural business cycle. Generally, the year-end you select should coincide with the slowest time for your business. For example, the calendar year is not appropriate for a New England ski resort, where operations are at their peak on December 31. On the other hand, a calendar year is appropriate for a retail store where business is heaviest during the Christmas season, and where inventories are at the lowest level on December 31.

The two basic overall tax accounting methods are the cash method and the accrual method.[12] You must select one of these methods for each of your business or investment activities. If you have more than one business or investment activity, you may select different methods for each activity. Similarly, you may select one tax accounting method for your business or investment activities, and another for your personal income and deductions.

> **Example:** Foley operates a real estate brokerage office as a proprietor. In addition, she has twelve rental houses. She selects the accrual method for reporting her brokerage income, and the cash method for the investments. In addition, she reports her personal interest income and personal deductions by using the cash method.

**Cash Method.** The cash method is used by most individual taxpayers. It cannot be used by corporations. Under the cash method, you include income in the year when you actually or constructively receive it. You deduct expenses in the year when you pay them.

You constructively receive income when it becomes available to you without restrictions, even though you don't take actual possession of the cash.

> **Example:** Interest is credited quarterly on Einhorn's savings account. On December 31, 19X1, the interest for the fourth quarter is credited to the account, and Einhorn has an unrestricted right to withdraw it. However, Einhorn is busy preparing for a New Year's Eve party, so he doesn't withdraw it until January 14, 19X2. Since he has an unrestricted right to receive the cash in 19X1, the interest is included in his 19X1 income, even though he takes possession of the cash in 19X2.

> **Example:** Williamson is a practicing CPA. During December, 19X1, he bills his clients $80,000 for services rendered. He receives payment of $50,000 of this amount. Deciding that he would rather not pay tax on the $50,000 in 19X1, he stores the payment checks in his safe until January 20, 19X2, when he deposits them in the bank. Since he has an unrestricted right to receive the cash in 19X1, the income is included in that year even though he does not cash the checks until 19X2.

Generally, you deduct expenses in the year you pay them. However, you must capitalize some cash expenditures and deduct them in the future tax years to which they relate. Examples are capital improvements, prepaid expenses such as fire insurance, prepaid interest, and inventories.

The cash method of reporting gives you considerable leeway for tax planning called *income shifting*. You can manipulate the timing of cash receipts and disbursements. Subject to the constructive receipt rule, you can defer or accelerate income by delaying or speeding up the receipt of cash. Similarly, you can often accelerate or delay deductions by timing your cash payments.

Income shifting traditionally has been used to accomplish two tax planning objectives. The first objective is to neutralize the effect of the progressive tax rates. For instance, if you are in a high marginal bracket this year, the goal is to accelerate deductions to reduce your marginal bracket, or to delay income until the following year when your marginal bracket might be lower. The reduction and compression of the individual tax rate brackets has largely nullified this strategy. However, you still have limited leeway to pursue this objective.

The second objective is to postpone the payment of tax to a future year, and use the postponed tax money in the meantime. This opportunity for an "interest-free" loan from the government is still available, and is a useful tax planning strategy.

You have considerable discretion for timing many personal deductions. For instance, you can make next year's charitable contributions this year, or pay this year's state income taxes now rather than waiting for the due date next year. You should usually accelerate deductions even though you must borrow to make the payments if the cost of borrowing is less than your marginal tax rate. However, you must spend the money before the end of the tax year.

**Accrual Method.** The accrual method of tax accounting is similar to the *generally accepted accounting principles* for financial reporting. It attempts to match income and expenses in the year they are incurred regardless of when payments are made or received.

The year for reporting income and expenses is controlled by your legal right to receive income and your legal obligation to pay for expenses. Income is taxed when *all events* have transpired to give you the right to receive payment. Expenses are deductible when your liability to pay is fixed, provided that the services have been performed or goods have been delivered.

> **Example:** Oglethorp, a CPA, performs services for clients and bills them in December, 19X1. He receives payment in 19X2. Under the cash method, the income is reported in 19X2, when he receives the cash. However, under the accrual method, since the services were performed and billed, *all*

*events* have transpired to give him the legal right to receive the income in 19X1. Thus, he includes it in 19X1 income.

**Example:** Assume Oglethorp has a charge account with his local office supplies store. In December, 19X1, he gets a delivery that is billed to his account. He pays the account in 19X2. Under the cash method, the deduction is in 19X2, the year of payment. However, under the accrual method, since *all events* have transpired to fix his legal liability, and since the goods have been delivered, the deduction is in 19X1.

## Recordkeeping Requirements

You are not permitted any tax deduction or other tax benefit unless you have adequate records. The records must prove two things. First, they must show how much you paid. You can use a cancelled check or a receipt marked "paid." Second, the records must show exactly what you paid for. You prove this with a receipt or invoice describing the item purchased or service rendered. Many taxpayers assume that a cancelled check alone is adequate documentation. This is not always the case. Although the check proves how much you paid, it doesn't necessarily prove what was purchased. You should keep descriptive receipts or invoices in addition to the check.

For some deductions, the law has more extensive documentation requirements that go beyond proof of the amount and purpose of the expenditure. This is the case for travel and entertainment expenses, automobile expenses, and deductions related to home computers. If you don't have records containing the information required by the law, your deductions are disallowed.

## Tax Compliance

Tax compliance simply means that you must obey the law. If you don't, you are punished. Although this seems like a straightforward and acceptable idea, it has disturbing practical implications. There are two ways a government can skin a fiscal cat. It can tax its skin off or it can administer its skin off by making compliance more difficult. The first alternative is politically unpopular, since it usually means raising taxes. The second is more acceptable. Who can argue with forcing people to obey the law? However, the policing process is inconvenient, and sometimes even painful.

In the quest for increased tax revenue, the trend since 1982 has been to tighten tax compliance rather than raising taxes. This has involved two elements. First, you have much greater reporting obligations. You have been enlisted by the government as a self-contained IRS agent to divulge all kinds of information about yourself and others. Second, penalties for noncompliance have increased dramatically. The impact of long-standing penalties has been increased, and creative new penalties have been devised.

**Reporting Requirements.** You have always been required to file tax returns to report the details of your income. Until recently, however, there were relatively few situations where you were required to report your financial dealings with others. Aside from wages and tax withholding, and dividends and interest paid, the government relied on voluntary reporting of other transactions. This has changed. The 1982 tax act created many new reporting requirements. Among other things, securities brokers are now required to report the proceeds of sales of securities, commodities, futures contracts, and precious metals. State and local governments are required to report the amount of state income tax refunds. The new requirements can be troublesome and expensive.

Someone also must report real estate transactions, including sales of single-family homes. Details of transactions must be reported to the IRS by the first person on the following list involved in the transaction:[13]

o The person (attorney or title company) responsible for closing the transaction,

o The mortgage lender,

o The seller's real estate broker,

o The buyer's real estate broker,

If you fail to file a required information return you are subject to a penalty of $50.00. The maximum amount of such penalties is $250,000.[14]

**Interest and Penalties.** You must pay interest if you underpay your tax, and in some situations, the government must pay you interest on your overpayments. The interest rate you pay is the Treasury rate on three-month bills plus three percentage points (adjusted quarterly). The rate the government pays you is the three-month Treasury bill rate plus two percentage points.[15]

The law imposes both criminal and civil penalties for non-compliance. Criminal penalties punish you with fines or imprisonment for specific crimes defined in the law. Hopefully, you won't have to worry about criminal penalties. There are numerous civil penalties, but most taxpayers encounter only a few of them.

**Failure to File**. The penalty is 5% per month of the tax due (as shown on the return) up to a maximum of 25%. The penalty begins on the due date of the return, including extensions. Before the penalty is computed, however, the amount of tax required to be shown is reduced by amounts withheld from wages and payments of estimated tax.[16].

**Failure to Pay**. Generally, the penalty is one-half of one percent per month (up to a maximum of 25%) of the tax shown on the return. In any month where both the failure to file *and* the failure to pay penalties are applicable, the failure to file penalty is reduced by the failure to pay penalty. For both penalties, a part of a month counts as a full month.[17]

**Negligence and Fraud Penalties**. The negligence penalty is imposed if you understate your tax because of negligence. Negligence is defined as intentional disregard of rules and Regulations without intent to defraud. Although this includes many possible transgressions, there are two situations where you are in danger of being penalized. First, when you fail to include items subject to information reporting (see discussion above). Second, when you don't keep the required records to support tax deductions. The penalty is 20% of the amount of the understatement of tax due to negligence.[18]

The fraud penalty is imposed if the IRS determines that you understated your tax liability because of fraud with the intent to evade tax. The amount of the penalty is 75% of the amount of the underpayment because of fraud.[19] Fraud results from a taxpayer's deliberate action to deceive, misrepresent or conceal facts, etc. The government has the burden of proving fraud.

**Substantial Understatement of Tax Penalty**. The penalty is 20% of an underpayment of tax attributable to an understatement (tax required to be paid less tax shown) if the understatement exceeds the *greater* of 10% of the tax required to be shown $5000 ($10000 for corporations). You may avoid the penalty by either fully disclosing all the facts on the tax return, or by proving that there is *substantial authority* for your position.[20]

### Statutes of Limitations

A statute of limitations is a time limit for you to assert your legal rights. As time passes it becomes increasingly difficult to prove events because evidence may be lost or destroyed, and witnesses die or otherwise become unavailable. The purpose of the time limitation is to prevent parties from pursuing "stale" claims. Once the period of limitation expires, you cannot pursue your claim. Statutes of limitations exist for all types of civil and criminal actions at both the Federal and state levels. For tax purposes, both you and the government are subject to limitation periods.

**Assessment by the Government.** Generally, the IRS may impose (assess) additional tax on you within three years after you file your tax return. If you file early, the three-year period begins to run on the due date of the return (usually April 15 of the following year).[21]

In two situations, the government's period for imposing tax is extended. First, If you omit gross income in excess of 25% of the income you show on your return, the limitation period for the government is extended to six years. Second, if you don't file a return, or if the return is fraudulent, there is no statute of limitation.

**Refunds for Taxpayers.** If you overpay your tax, you can file a claim for refund. You must file the claim within three years from the date you filed the return, or within two years after you pay the tax, whichever is later. If you file early, you are deemed to have filed on the due date (usually April 15 of the following year).[22]

Special statutes of limitations apply for some types of transactions. For example the limitations periods are extended for the home-sale rollover (see Chapter 5), and for involuntary conversions (see Chapter 12).

## FOOTNOTES

1. *U.S. v. Phellis*, 257 US 156 (1921).

2. *Warner Co. v. Comm'r*, 26 BTA 1225 (1932) Acq.

3. *Gregory v. Helvering*, 293 US 465 (1935).

4. Internal Revenue Code (IRC) §1221(1).

5. IRC §§651 and 652.

6. IRC §§661 through 663.

7. IRC §11(b)(1)(C).

8. IRC §1361 through 1379.

9. *Lucas v. Earl*, 281 US 111 (1930).

10. IRC §1(g).

11. IRC §441(b).

12. IRC §446; Reg. §1.446-1.

13. IRC §6045(e).

14. IRC §6721.

15. IRC §6621.

16. IRC §6651(a)(1).

17. IRC §6651(a)(2).

18. IRC §6662(a),(b)(1), and (c).

19. IRC §6663.

20. IRC §§6662(a),(b)(2), and (d).

21. Generally see IRC §6501.

22. IRC §6511.

Chapter

# THREE

## ACQUIRING AND DISPOSING
## OF REAL ESTATE

This chapter explores important considerations for acquiring and disposing of real estate. The way you acquire property has important tax and non-tax consequences. The deed and other recorded documents lock you into the way the property is titled. Along with the property, you also acquire something the tax law calls "basis." This is the starting point for tax planning. You may be in trouble if you don't give proper (or any) attention to these matters in advance. This is unfortunate, because you can avoid many future problems with careful planning at the outset. Prior planning is particularly important when you buy a home.

When you dispose of property in a sale or exchange, the first step is to calculate the amount of the gain or loss. Then you determine whether the transaction is taxed in the current year, and, if so, how it is taxed. This chapter discusses tne mechanics for calculating gain or loss. Tax deferral is discussed in Chapters 10 through 12.

### LEGAL FUNDAMENTALS FOR
### ACQUIRING REAL ESTATE

The way you take title to property may have important implications when you deal with the property later. For instance, titling is important when you dispose of the property, or if you have a divorce. Title is always a crucial consideration if you transfer the property in an estate plan. Your purchase contract should clearly state how the property is to be titled. Make sure your settlement agent is careful to insure that all acquisition documents are titled correctly before they are recorded.

Most jurisdictions charge recording fees or transfer taxes to re-record a document, even if it is merely to change the title for the same owner. These fees can be expensive, sometimes amounting to as much as two or three percent of the property's value. Prior planning can avoid these additional costs.

Homes and residential rental property are usually titled in some form of individual ownership. The property can be owned by a single individual, or it can be concurrently owned by two or more individuals. You also can title property in the name of an artificial entity such as a corporation, partnership, or trust. Although corporations and partnerships are seldom used for home ownership, revocable trusts have significant non-tax legal advantages. Partnerships and revocable trusts are useful vehicles for owning rental property. Corporations are rarely used to own small-unit residential property, whether held for personal use or for investment.

## Concurrent Property Ownership by Individuals

If you are a concurrent owner of property you are called a co-tenant, and you have an undivided interest in the entire property rather than an individual interest in a specific part of it. As a co-tenant, you (along with the other co-tenants), can transform your undivided interest into ownership of a specific part of the property in a legal proceeding called *partition*. The four principal types of individual concurrent ownership have different legal characteristics. The most important characteristic is survivorship, which means that if you die, your interest in the property passes to the other co-owners rather than to your heirs.

**Tenancy in Common.** Each co-tenant has an undivided interest in the property, with a right to its possession and enjoyment. The interests need not be equal or acquired at the same time or in the same document. A tenancy in common does not have survivorship. This means that when you die, your interest passes to your heirs as specified in your will. If you have no will, your interest passes to your heirs under the state's law of intestate succession (the procedure for distributing property owned by people who die without a will).

> **Example:** Larry, Curley, and Moe acquire a rental house as tenants in common. Moe has a one-half undivided interest and Larry and Curley each have a one-quarter interest. Curley conveys half of his interest to Shemp, making Curley and Shemp one-eighth co-tenants. Moe dies, and his heirs (taken as a whole) become a one-half co-tenant with the surviving tenants.

Unrelated rental property investors usually take title as tenants in common. In a sense, it is a "poor man's" partnership. For tax purposes, however, it is not as flexible as a partnership and you should not use it as a substitute if you intend to have a partnership.

Income from property held as a tenancy in common is apportioned and taxed to the co-tenants according to their percentages of ownership. For expenses, the courts have held that as a co-tenant, you may deduct only the portion of the expenses attributable to your percentage ownership, even if you pay more than your proportionate share.[1] This is because you are personally liable only on your share of the expenses. Any expenses you pay in excess of your proportionate share are treated as advances to the other co-tenants, for which you may seek reimbursement. Income and deductions related to the tenancy in common are reported on each co-tenant's individual income tax return.

Gain or loss from sale of property is determined by allocating the amount realized among the co-tenants in the ratio of their proportionate interests. Each co-tenant's basis is determined under the normal basis rules for purchase, inheritance, gift, etc., discussed below.

**Joint Tenancy.** A joint tenancy has the right of survivorship. When you die, your ownership interest automatically passes equally to the surviving co-tenants. Your heirs (unless they are also co-tenants) have no legal claim to your share.

> **Example:** Huey, Dewey and Louie own a rental house as equal joint tenants. Upon Huey's death, his one-third interest automatically passes equally to Dewey and Louie. The two survivors then each own a one-half interest.

A joint tenancy is a volatile form of ownership, and its stringent requirements sometimes are inappropriate for real estate investment. If any requirement is violated, the joint tenancy becomes a tenancy in common, and the survivorship feature ceases to exist. The law calls this *severance*.

To create a joint tenancy, the interests of all co-tenants must vest at the same time, all co-tenants must acquire their interests by the same deed, all co-tenants must have equal interests, and all co-tenants must have the same right of possession and enjoyment. Thus, if you convey property you own individually to yourself and others as joint tenants, a joint tenancy is not created because you acquired your interest before the others acquire theirs. If any co-tenant conveys his interest, the joint tenancy is destroyed because the new owner and existing co-owners acquired their interests at different times and in different deeds. The joint owners cannot have unequal interests. For instance, one of two co-tenants cannot have a one-third interest and the other a two-thirds interest.

Because jointly owned property passes outside the will and probate estate of a deceased joint tenant, it is sometimes called a "poor man's will." However, you can have many tax and non-tax complications by using joint tenancies as a substitute for a will, so you must be wary. A revocable trust (discussed below) is a safer way to avoid probate.

Many states have *anti-survivorship* statutes stipulating that survivorship does not exist unless your deed specifically states that you intend that survivorship shall exist, and/or that you do not intend a tenancy in common. Without such "magic words" a deed creates a tenancy in common. This could wreak havoc if you used the joint tenancy as a substitute for a will. If the title is not correctly drafted, instead of passing to the other joint tenants, your interest passes to your heirs under the state's laws of intestate succession.

Each joint tenant includes his proportionate share of a property's income in his individual income tax return. Unlike a tenant in common, however, if a joint tenant pays more than his share of the expenses, he may deduct the entire amount. This is because he is assumed to be jointly and severally liable for all expenses related to the property.[2] Gains and losses from dispositions of jointly owned property are treated similarly to those for property of tenancies in common.

**Tenancy by the Entireties**. This is a special form of joint ownership for married people that, like a joint tenancy, has the survivorship feature. Thus, upon the death of one spouse, the surviving spouse automatically becomes the sole owner. If a couple is divorced, the tenancy by the entireties is converted into a tenancy in common. Each former spouse can get a separate equal share of the property in a partition proceeding.

Many states have altered the common-law nature of the tenancy by the entireties. In some states, *anti-survivorship* statutes and other requirements of joint tenancies also apply for tenancies by the entireties. Other states take the opposite approach and create presumptions that property titled in the names of both or either of the spouses creates a tenancy by the entireties with the right of survivorship. You should therefore understand what you are getting yourself into before automatically titling your property, particularly your home, in this manner.

Tenancy by the entireties is the most common ownership form for married people. For purposes of the home-sale rollover and over-55 exclusion, the method of titling marital property is a neutral factor (see Chapter 6). There is considerable room for flexibility.

**Community Property**. Nine states have a system for marital property ownership known as *community property*. Generally, property acquired during marriage by the efforts of either spouse belongs one-half to each spouse. It does not matter whose efforts generated the funds to acquire the property. Property owned separately by a spouse before marriage, and property acquired by gift or inheritance usually are not community property.

The states differ about what happens when a spouse dies. In some states, one-half of the property passes to the surviving spouse, and the other half goes to the deceased spouse's heirs. In other states, the deceased spouse's share passes automatically to the surviving spouse in a manner similar to a tenancy by the entireties. In some states you can elect to take title as joint tenants or tenants in common. Since the laws of the community property states differ in many respects, you must examine the consequences in each state. The nine community property states are Arizona, California, Nevada, New Mexico, Idaho, Louisiana, Texas, Washington, and Wisconsin.

### Using a Revocable Trust for Ownership of Real Estate

If you create a trust and retain the power to alter, amend or revoke it, the trust is called a revocable trust. Revocable trusts are also called *living trusts*. Sometimes a revocable trust created for the specific purpose of owning real estate is called a *land trust*. Some states have special laws governing land trusts, and in some states, such as Illinois, they have been used for many years.

For all Federal tax purposes, a revocable trust is treated as if it didn't exist (see Chapter 2). Its income and deductions are reported in the income tax return of the grantor. No gift tax is payable when the trust is created, and the trust property is included in the grantor's taxable estate. Some states impose tax on revocable trusts, so you should examine state law before using them.

Although revocable trusts have no tax consequences, under state law they are legal entities separate from their creators (grantors). You can make yourself the trustee, and can retain complete power to administer the trust's property as if you owned the property in your name. Using a revocable trust as an alter-ego allows you to avoid state property law complexities.

The most important function of revocable trusts is to avoid the cumbersome and expensive court administration of your estate, called *probate*. If you transfer your property through a will, it is subject to probate. If the property is owned by a trust, however, the trust survives your death, even though the trust was merely your alter-ego during your lifetime. Thus, a revocable trust can serve as a substitute for your will. You can spell out how the trustee administers and transfers the trust's property after your death. These can be the same directions that you would give to your executor in a will. Revocable trusts are especially useful to avoid the problem of *ancillary administration* of real estate located outside your state. Most states require that real estate located within their boundaries be administered under their probate laws, and sometimes, the administrator must be a resident of the state. In many situations, your executor will fail to qualify to administer your out-of-state real estate. This results in expense and coordination difficulties. Because property owned by a revocable trust avoids all probate, these problems don't arise.

### Condominiums

Condominium ownership is a combination of individual and concurrent ownership of property. As a condominium owner, you have separate ownership of a specific unit and, for the property's common elements, you are a tenant in common with the owners of other units. The unit can be an apartment, townhouse, or detached house. Common elements include the land where the unit is built, hallways, recreational facilities, parking areas, spaces between the units, etc. A transfer of a condominium unit also transfers the undivided interest in the common elements. The details of condominium ownership are governed by special condominium laws that have been enacted by all states.

### Cooperatives

A cooperative is an indirect form of property ownership. An entity, usually a corporation, purchases or constructs the property. By virtue of your ownership of the corporation's stock, you have the right to occupy a specific unit. You do not own the real estate separately. The tax law has a special provision allowing you to take the tax deductions for your allocated share of the cooperative corporation's mortgage interest and real estate taxes (see Chapter 4).

## TAX BASIS - HOW YOU GET IT, AND WHY IT MATTERS

Your property's tax basis is the starting point for tax planning. You acquire this tax characteristic when you acquire the property. The amount of basis depends upon how you acquire the property. Different rules apply for purchases, gifts, inheritances, and other special tax-oriented acquisitions. Basis is increased by acquisition costs, and basis can change while you own the property. Some expenditures after you acquire the property increase the basis, and some tax deductions, such as depreciation, reduce it. The original basis, adjusted for these factors, is called the *adjusted basis*. Basis is important in two tax contexts: (1) calculating your gain or loss from the property's disposition, and (2) determining your depreciation deduction for investment property. All property has a tax basis, and the basis cannot be less than zero.

### Purchased Property

The basis of purchased property is its cost.[3] This includes not only the cash you give, but also any amount of the purchase price financed by someone else. Thus, the amount of all mortgages increases the property's basis, whether they are assumptions of existing debt or purchase-money debt.[4] It doesn't matter whether the financing is from an outside institutional source or from a note carried back by the seller. The basis is not increased, however, by refinancing the original loan for a larger amount, or by obtaining a second mortgage while you own the property. Basis is also increased by the amount of the seller's delinquent real estate taxes you pay or assume.[5]

Inclusion of debt in basis gives real estate one of its greatest tax benefits. Real estate has a greater potential for leverage than other investments. Since the basis for depreciation is increased by using other people's money, you are able to obtain valuable tax deductions without spending your own money. As discussed in Chapter 2, these deductions mean cash in your pocket. The amount of cash depends upon your marginal tax rate.

### Property Received as a Gift

Generally, the donee's basis for gift property is the same as the basis of the donor. This rule merely shifts a pre-gift gain from the donor to the donee.[6]

> **Example:** Weaver gives property with a basis to him of $80,000 to his daughter. The market value of the property is $100,000, so that if he had sold it his gain would have been $20,000. The daughter's basis is $80,000, the same as Weaver's basis. Thus, if she sells the property for $100,000, the $20,000 gain is hers.

If the value of the property exceeds the donor's basis at the time of the gift, the basis may be increased by a portion of any gift tax paid. For gifts after 1976, the amount added is the gift tax attributable to the increase in the property's value during the donor's ownership. In no event, however, can the donee's basis exceed the value of the property at the time of the gift.[7]

> **Example:** Assume in the above example that Weaver pays gift tax of $6,000 on the gift. $20,000 ($100,000 less $80,000) or 20% of the property's value is due to appreciation during Weaver's ownership. Therefore, $1,200 of the gift tax ($6,000 x 20%) is added to the daughter's basis, which is $81,200.

A different rule applies if the property's value at the time of the gift is *less* than the donor's basis. The donee's basis for gain or loss is held in limbo until the donee disposes of the property. If the donee disposes of the property at a price greater than the donor's basis, gain is calculated by using the donor's basis. However, if the price is less than the value at the time of the gift, loss is calculated by using that value. If the price is between the donor's basis and the value at the time of the gift, there is no gain or loss. These rules are designed to prevent low bracket taxpayers from transferring losses to higher bracket taxpayers. Regardless of the basis for gain or loss, however, the donee's basis for depreciation is always the donor's basis.

> **Example:** Assume in the above example that Weaver's basis for the property is $120,000 and the market value at the time of the gift is $100,000. If the daughter sells the property for $125,000, the gain is $5,000 ($125,000 less Weaver's basis of $120,000). If the price is $90,000, the loss is $10,000 ($90,000 less the value of $100,000). If the price is $110,000, there is no gain or loss because the price falls between the donor's basis ($120,000) and the value at the time of the gift ($100,000). If the daughter uses the property for business or investment, her basis for depreciation is $120,000, the same as that of the donor.

For gifts of property between husbands and wives, the basis of the donee spouse is *always* the same as that of the donor spouse, regardless of the value of the property at the time of the gift (see Chapter 6).[8]

### Inherited Property

Generally, the basis of inherited property is its fair market value at the date of the decedent's death.[9] The decedent's basis for the property is irrelevant. The "step-up" in basis to market value means that pre-death appreciation in value is never subject to income tax. This opportunity to avoid tax on all gains highlights the importance of tax deferral (see Chapter 2).

> **Example:** Assume in the above example that Weaver continues to own the property until his death, at which time its value is $200,000. The basis of his daughter, who inherits the property is $200,000. The pre-death gain of $80,000 ($200,000 less $120,000) will never be taxed.

The federal estate tax law permits an executor or administrator to value the estate's property at a date six months after the decedent's death. This is called the *alternate valuation date*. If this date is elected, the beneficiary's basis is the value at this date.

## Property Acquired as Compensation for Services

If you receive property as compensation for services, you must include its fair market value in income when you receive it. That value becomes your basis for the property.

## Basis of Property Received in Tax-Deferred Transactions

Generally, the basis of property you receive in a tax-deferred transaction is a *substituted basis*. This means that the basis of the property you give up (or sell) becomes the basis for the property you receive (or the reinvestment property). The substituted basis is adjusted for partially taxed gains, debt assumptions, debt relief, etc. The specific basis calculations are described in the chapters relating to the specific tax-deferred transactions as follows: home-sale rollovers (chapter 5), tax-deferred exchanges (Chapter 11), and involuntary conversions (Chapter 12).

## Acquisition Costs

Basis is increased by your costs of acquiring the property. These include most of the items on the buyer's side of the settlement statement. They include recording fees, transfer taxes, survey and appraisal costs, costs relating to searching and insuring title, and attorney fees. Real estate broker commissions add to basis if paid directly by the buyer, regardless of whether the buyer or seller signed the listing agreement.

You do not include in your basis prorated items such as insurance, utility charges and real estate taxes. However, a buyer may deduct real estate taxes relating to the portion of the year he owns the property (see Chapter 4). Items relating to the loan are not added to basis because they are costs of obtaining the loan rather than costs of acquiring the property. These charges include amounts a buyer pays for credit reports, credit insurance, appraisal fees, etc. Buyer *points* may be deductible under certain circumstances (see Chapter 4).

# DISPOSING OF REAL ESTATE

When you sell or exchange property, there are three steps for determining the tax consequences. First, you calculate the amount of the gain or loss. In tax terms, this is the difference between the *amount realized* from the transaction and the *adjusted basis* of the property.

Second, you determine whether the gain or loss has current tax consequences. Generally, the law taxes gains (*recognition*) in the year when the transaction takes place (*realization*). As discussed in Chapter 2, sometimes taxation is deferred until a later year. If a transaction results in a loss, tax consequences depend upon why you own the property. If you own it for personal use (such as your home or vacation home), losses have no tax consequences. They cannot be deducted, and cannot be offset against gains from other transactions. Investment and business property losses, however, can be used for tax purposes as discussed below.

Third, you determine whether the gains or losses are ordinary or capital. Under prior law, you got preferential tax treatment for long-term capital gains. Since the Tax Reform Act of 1986 (1986 TRA), the differential between long-term capital gains and ordinary income has been minimal. Although planning for capital gains is not as important as it was before, there are still limitations for using capital losses. The capital gain and loss rules continue to be relevant. See Appendix B for a discussion of capital gains and losses.

## SALES AND EXCHANGES

A sale is a transfer of property for money (cash or cash equivalent, such as a bank check). An exchange is a transfer of property for anything other than money. Sales and exchanges make it possible for you to measure the amount of the gain or loss. Sometimes, however, when you transfer an interest in property, it isn't a sale or exchange. Examples are sales of options and sales of easements.

### Options

An option is a contract to acquire or sell property at a specified price during a specified period. Usually you must pay something to acquire an option. The tax consequences of this payment depend upon what you do with your option rights. For tax purposes, the option is an open transaction until you exercise it, let it lapse, or sell it.

**Exercise of an Option**. If you exercise an option to acquire property, the amount you paid for the option is added to the amount you pay for the property to determine your basis. The person who granted the option adds this amount to the sale price. This will increase his gain or reduce his loss.

> **Example:** Kummer purchases a three-year option to acquire an investment townhouse from Randall for $90,000. She gives Randall $4,000 for the option. One year later, she exercises the option and buys the house. Her basis for the house is $94,000 ($90,000 purchase price + $4,000 option consideration). Randall's amount realized from the sale is also $94,000.

**Lapse of an Option**. If you fail to exercise an option, its lapse is treated as a sale of the option on the day it expires. The nature of the loss from the forfeited option consideration depends on the nature of the optioned property.[10] If the property would be a capital asset if you acquire it, the loss is a capital loss. Your holding period for the option determines whether the loss is long-term or short-term (see Appendix B). The forfeited option payment is ordinary income for the person who granted the option.[11]

> **Example:** Assume in the above example that Kummer fails to exercise the option, and that after three years it expires. Since the rental house would have been a capital asset if acquired, the $4,000 forfeited is treated as a long-term capital loss. The $4,000 is ordinary income for Randall.

If you intended to use the optioned property for personal purposes (such as for a principal residence or a second home), you can't use the loss for any tax purpose.

> **Example:** Assume in the above example that Kummer intends to live in the townhouse if she exercises the option. If she lets the option lapse, she cannot use the forfeited option consideration for any tax purpose. However, the $4,000 is ordinary income for Randall, even though Kummer has no tax benefit from the forfeiture.

**Sale of an Option**. Your gain or loss from the sale of an option has the same character as gain or loss from sale of the optioned property. Thus, if the property would be a capital asset if you acquire it, gain or loss from sale of the option is a capital gain or loss. The holding period depends upon how long you held the option.

**Example:** Assume in the above example that after one year Kummer sells the option for $5,500. The $1,500 gain is a long-term capital gain. Kummer's sale of the option has no tax consequences for Randall.

**Example:** Assume in the above example that the sale price for the option is $3,500. If Kummer intended to use the townhouse for investment, the $500 loss is a long-term capital loss. If she intended to live in the townhouse, however, she cannot use the loss for any tax purposes. The sale has no tax consequences for Randall.

### Easements

An easement is a right to use someone else's property in a manner inconsistent with the owner's normal property rights. Property subject to an easement is called *servient property*. Easements may be created when the servient property is transferred, or at some later time. Generally, when you acquire an easement you pay the servient property owner for the rights. Payment for an easement created when the property is transferred is an adjustment of the sale price.

**Example:** Losey sells to Mass the rear portion of his property. At the time of sale, there is no road into this portion from the main road fronting Losey's property. Losey agrees to set aside a strip of his retained property for a right-of-way for Mass. The sale price is increased $10,000 to compensate for this. The easement is created in the deed transferring title to Mass. The $10,000 is added to Losey's selling price, increasing his gain and Mass's basis by that amount.

When you sell an easement, the tax treatment of the payment you receive depends upon whether the easement deprives you of the beneficial use of the property. If you cannot continue to use the property affected by the easement, the transaction is treated as a sale of that part of the property. The basis of the property must be allocated between the part of the property subject to the easement, and the part retained (see discussion of apportionment of basis below). This is normally the tax treatment for easements permitting roads to be built for a right-of-way to adjacent property.[12]

**Example:** Assume in the above example that two years after Mass acquires the land, Losey agrees to sell, for $10,000, an easement to build a road across his property into Mass's property. Losey's basis for his property is $100,000, and the value of the land affected by the easement is 2% of the property's total value. The allocated basis is $2,000 (2% of $100,000). Losey's gain is $8,000 ($10,000 less $2,000). The basis for the remainder of Losey's property is $98,000 ($100,000 less $2,000).

If the easement doesn't deprive you of beneficial use of the land, the payment is treated as a reduction of the basis of your property.[13] This is often the case for payments for utility easements.

**Example:** McCoy sells an easement to Consolidated Gas Co. for the latter to install a gas pipeline ten feet below the surface of McCoy's land, which is currently used for growing strawberries. After the installation, McCoy can resume growing strawberries over the pipeline. Consolidated pays $30,000 for the easement, and McCoy's basis for his property is $90,000. Because he is not deprived of the beneficial use of his land, McCoy's basis for the entire property is reduced from $90,000 to $60,000.

If you are not deprived of beneficial use, but the payment for the easement is more than your basis for the entire property, you have gain equal to the excess.

**Example:** Assume in the above example that Consolidated pays $95,000 for the easement. McCoy has a taxable gain of $5,000 ($95,000 payment for the easement less $90,000, the basis for the entire property).

## CALCULATING THE AMOUNT OF GAIN OR LOSS

You determine your gain or loss from the sale or exchange of property by subtracting the property's *adjusted basis* from your *amount realized* in the transaction. If the adjusted basis exceeds the amount realized, you have a loss, and if the amount realized exceeds the adjusted basis, you have a gain.[14] The terms *amount realized* and *adjusted basis* have technical tax definitions that you must understand for effective tax planning. Often, tax laypersons equate the term *selling price* with *amount realized*, and the term *cost* with *adjusted basis*. These terms are inadequate to describe the tax dynamics of gains and losses.

## What is Amount Realized?

You determine the amount realized by looking at what you receive in a transaction, not the selling price you attach to the property conveyed. Thus, the amount realized may be more or less than the selling price, and this difference can have important tax impact on the gain or loss.

The amount realized is the total of the cash you receive, the fair market value of any property you receive, and the amount of your debts discharged as a result of the transfer. This amount is reduced by transaction costs you incur when you dispose of the property.[15]

Cash includes money (currency and checks) plus money equivalents such as treasury notes, certificates of deposit, etc. Notes you take from a buyer or notes of third parties given to you by a buyer are treated as property, not cash.

The fair market value of property you receive is defined as the value at which a willing buyer and a willing seller, acting at arm's length, would transfer property in without a forced sale. Thus, the fair market value may be less than the cash selling price or face value of property you receive.

Suppose you take a note from a buyer (secured by a second mortgage or deed of trust) as part of the selling price of a house. For purposes of calculating the amount realized, the note is treated as property. It is doubtful that the market value of the note is equal to its face value. Depending upon the credit rating of the buyer, the terms of the note, and market conditions, the note's market (or discount) value may be considerably less than its face value. This means that the amount realized calculated by using the market value is less than the selling price calculated by using the face value. The amount of gain is correspondingly less, and the difference between the market value and the face value is deferred until the note is paid. Tax planning for such *deferred payment* reporting is discussed in Chapter 10. Alternatively, you can include the note at its face value, and report the gain under the installment method, also discussed in Chapter 10.

The amount of your mortgages and other debt discharged as a result of a transaction is added to your amount realized. Thus, if a buyer assumes a mortgage, or pays real estate taxes or other assessments in arrears, your gain is increased accordingly. The tax law treats the discharge of your debts as if the buyer pays you cash, you pay off the debt, and then you transfer the property free of the debt. Thus, debt relief is treated the same as if you receive cash. It is immaterial whether you have personal liability for the debt (*recourse* financing), or whether the debt is secured only by the property itself without personal liability (*nonrecourse* financing). You include the full amount of the debt discharged in the amount realized even if the amount of the debt exceeds the value of the property you convey.[16]

Any costs you pay in connection with the property's disposition reduce the amount realized. Such include real estate commissions, legal fees, survey fees, etc. If you pay *points* related to the buyer's mortgage, these also reduce your amount realized (see Chapter 4).

You can see, then, that *selling price* is not an adequate substitute for the more technical tax term *amount realized*, because selling price:

o Assumes that the transaction is a sale. There are other types of property transfers, such as exchanges, where gain or loss must be calculated.

o Includes property you receive at its cash value or face value. If you include the property at fair market value, the tax results may be different.

o Does not take into account transaction costs you pay to dispose of the property.

**Example:** Cleary sells his house to Apperson. The house is subject to a $30,000 FHA mortgage that Apperson assumes. Cleary receives $5,000 cash and takes Apperson's note for $15,000 secured by a second mortgage on the house. His banker tells him that the note may be discounted at 50% of its face value. Cleary pays a real estate broker commission of $3,500 and legal fees of $500. The *selling price* and *amount realized* are determined as follows:

*Selling Price:*

| | |
|---|---:|
| Cash received | $ 5,000 |
| Notes of buyer | 15,000 |
| Mortgage assumed by buyer | 30,000 |
| Selling price | $50,000 |

*Amount Realized:*

| | |
|---|---|
| Cash received | $ 5,000 |
| Fair market value of notes | 7,500 |
| Mortgage assumed by buyer | 30,000 |
| | $42,500 |
| Less: Transaction costs | 4,000 |
| Amount realized | $38,500 |

The $7,500 discount in Apperson's note will be taxed when the note is paid in full. As an alternative, Cleary could include the note at its face value and use the installment method for reporting gain.

### What is Adjusted Basis?

You increase or decrease the basis of your property (as determined under the rules discussed above) to reflect events while you own the property. The basis of the property after these increases and decreases is called the "adjusted basis.[17]

Basis is increased by capital improvements. Noncapital repairs do not affect your property's basis, but might be deductible for investment property. The sometimes difficult distinction between capital expenditures and repairs is discussed in Chapter 7.

You decrease the basis by the depreciation allowed or allowable. Allowed depreciation is the amount deducted on your tax returns and not disallowed by the Internal Revenue Service. Allowable depreciation is the amount you were permitted to deduct, even though you did not actually deduct it. Basis is also decreased by casualty losses that you deduct. In a sense, such losses are treated as "instant" depreciation. Expenditures to restore the property after a casualty increase its basis.

There are many other adjustments to basis in special situations. For example, you reduce basis for returns of capital such as severance damages in condemnation proceedings (see Chapter 12), and amounts you receive as compensation for granting an easement (see discussion above).

The amount you pay for an option to acquire property increases the basis when you exercise the option (see discussion above). Costs of defending the property's title or removing a cloud on title also increase the basis.[18] Other basis adjustments are discussed throughout the book where appropriate.

### Allocation of Adjusted Basis When You Sell Part of a Property

If you sell only part of the property, the adjusted basis must be allocated between the part sold and the part retained. You do this in the ratio of the fair market value of the property sold to the fair market value of the entire property.[19]

> **Example:** Bergin owns a home located on twenty acres of land with a total value of $300,000 and an adjusted basis of $100,000. He sells five acres to Boynton who plans to build a home. The sale price is $60,000. The basis allocated to the five acres is $20,000 ($60,000/$300,000 x $100,000), so the gain is $40,000 ($60,000 less $20,000)

### Conversion of Property From Personal to Business or Investment Use

If you convert property from personal use to business or investment use, your personal basis becomes your basis for depreciation, gain, and loss if the fair market value of the property at the time of conversion exceeds your basis.

> **Example:** Bonham moves out of his principal residence and converts it into a rental property. At the time of conversion, the building (excluding land) has a fair market value of $150,000, and an adjusted basis of $100,000. Because the market value of the house at the time of conversion exceeds Bonham's basis, the basis for depreciation, gain, and loss is $100,000. He rents the house for three years, deducting $24,800 of depreciation. He sells the house for $120,000. His gain is calculated as follows:
>
> | | | |
> |---|---|---|
> | Amount realized | | $120,000 |
> | Less adjusted basis: | | |
> |     Basis at conversion | $100,000 | |
> |     Less depreciation | 24,800 | 75,200 |
> | Gain realized | | $44,800 |

If the market value at the date of conversion is less than your basis, however, the market value is the basis for depreciation and for determining loss.[20] This is to prevent you from using a personal, nondeductible loss indirectly by deducting depreciation on the higher basis.

> **Example:** Assume in the above example that the market value of the property at the time of conversion is $80,000. Since this is less than the basis of

$100,000, it becomes the basis for depreciation and calculation of loss. Bonham rents the house for three years and deducts depreciation of $19,800. He then sells the property for $60,000. His loss is calculated as follows:

| | | |
|---|---|---|
| Amount realized | | $60,000 |
| Less adjusted basis: | | |
| Basis at conversion | $80,000 | |
| Less depreciation | 19,840 | 60,160 |
| Loss | | $ 160 |

If you subsequently sell the converted property for a gain, your adjusted basis is the basis at the time of conversion less the depreciation you have deducted, calculated by using the fair market value at the time of conversion.

**Example:** Assume in the above example that Bonham sells the house for $110,000. His gain is calculated as follows:

| | | |
|---|---|---|
| Amount realized | | $110,000 |
| Less adjusted basis | | |
| Basis at conversion | $100,000 | |
| Less depreciation | 19,840 | 80,160 |
| Gain realized | | $ 29,840 |

## NATURE OF THE GAIN OR LOSS

The final step in determining the tax consequences of a sale or exchange is to identify the nature of the gain or loss recognized in the year of the transaction. Generally, this is the distinction between capital gains and losses and ordinary gains and losses. Before 1987, this distinction was very important for gains because only 40% of long-term capital gains were taxed. After 1986, as discussed above, the tax advantages of long-term capital gains are severely limited.

The 1986 TRA did not materially change the treatment of capital losses. As under prior law, an individual taxpayer may use capital losses to offset capital gains, and, in addition, you may deduct up to $3,000 from ordinary income. Thus, capital losses continue to be less useful than ordinary losses. Losses incurred in a trade or business are ordinarily fully deductible, but the limitations on using capital losses remain unchanged.

Other than limiting the long-term capital gain advantage for individuals, and making a few changes in the use of capital losses, the 1986 TRA left intact the prior provisions relating to capital gains and losses. The retention of the overall capital gain and loss structure is intentional. If income tax rates are increased, it probably will be necessary to increase the tax preference for long-term gains. This will be easy since all of the mechanics are in place.

Because we must still use the old system to determine tax consequences for capital losses, and because the old capital gains preference may be restored, the details of the capital gain and loss structure are further discussed in Appendix B.

## FOOTNOTES

1. *Estate of Boyd v. Comm'r.*, 28 TC 564 (1957).

2. *Tracy v. Comm'r.*, 25 BTA 1055; *Powell v. Comm'r.*, TC Memo 1967-32.

3. Internal Revenue Code (IRC) §1012.

4. *Crane v. Comm'r.*, 331 U.S. 1 (1947).

5. Reg. §1.1012-1(b).

6. IRC §1015.

7. IRC §1015(d)(6); Reg. §1.1015-5.

8. IRC §1015(e) and IRC §1041(b)(2).

9. IRC §1014.

10. IRC §1234(a)(1).

11. Reg. §1.1234-1(b).

12. Rev. Rul. 72-255, 1972-1 CB 221.

13. *Conway v. U.S.*, 31 AFTR 2d 73-1028; *Inaja Land Co.*, 9 TC 727 (1947), Acq. 1948-1 CB 2.

14. IRC §1001(a); Reg. §1.1001-1(a).

15. IRC §1001(b); Reg. §1.1001-1(b).

16. *Comm'r. v. Tufts*, 459 US 941 (1983).

17. IRC §1016.

18. Reg. §1.263(a)-2(c).

19. Reg. §1.61-6(a); see particularly Example 2.

20. Reg. §1.165-9(b)(2); Reg. §1.167(g)-1.

# TAX BREAKS FOR HOME OWNERSHIP

## CHAPTER 4

*Tax Breaks While You Own
Your Home*

## CHAPTER 5

*Tax Breaks When You Sell
Your Home*

## CHAPTER 6

*Buying and Selling A Home:
Husbands, Wives, Marriages,
and Divorces*

*part*

# Chapter

# FOUR

## TAX BREAKS WHILE YOU
## OWN YOUR HOME

The government's ongoing commitment to home ownership has emerged as one of the few "sacred cows" of the tax law and has resisted continuous attempts for reform. The two most important tax breaks for homeowners are the deductions for real estate taxes and for mortgage interest. Real estate taxes continue to be fully deductible. The mortgage interest deduction, however, was wounded by tax reform, and contains tax traps for the unwary. Other homeowner tax benefits include the deductions for business use of your home, personal casualty losses, and moving expenses.

### THE INTEREST DEDUCTION –
### GENERAL RULES

Interest has been deductible since the first tax law in 1913. It has always been a controversial deduction, however. In a continuing response to the controversy, Congress has made the interest deduction rules some of the most confusing in the tax law.

Interest is rent accruing over time for the use of money. Other charges or fees, although related to a loan, are not tax deductible interest. Examples are loan processing fees, survey and appraisal fees for the collateral securing a loan, legal and accounting fees, etc. Although not deductible as interest, some of these expenses may be deductible under other provisions of the tax law. You are permitted to deduct only interest on a bona fide debt for which you are liable. You are not permitted to deduct interest you pay on someone else's debt. Regardless of your tax accounting method (see Chapter 2), you are allowed to deduct interest only for the period to which it relates. Thus, if you prepay interest on a loan, your deduction is delayed until the interest accrues, even if you are a cash basis taxpayer.[1]

### Classifications of Interest

Interest is classified into several categories depending upon the collateral for the loan, how you use the borrowed funds, or both. Generally for tax deduction purposes, interest falls into one of the following categories:

o  Business interest,

o  Personal or consumer interest,

o  Home mortgage interest,

o  Passive activity interest, or

o  Investment interest.

There are also several types of interest subject to special deduction restrictions. These include interest to support tax-exempt income, interest on loans to purchase single premium annuity contracts, and interest incurred during construction of a building. This chapter discusses business, personal, and home mortgage interest. Passive activity and investment interest are discussed in Chapter 7.

### Business Interest

Interest expense that is incurred or paid to carry on a trade or business is deductible in full, and is not subject to any interest deduction limitations.[2] The business interest deduction is applicable only if the loan is incurred in an active trade or business where you *materially participate* in the management (see Chapter 7 for a discussion of material participation). If you don't materially participate in management, or if the activity is any rental activity, the loan is classified as a loan for a passive activity, and the interest deductions are governed by the rules discussed in Chapter 7.

Interest on a business loan is deductible from gross income to arrive at adjusted gross income (see Appendix A for a discussion of the individual tax calculation). Thus, you may deduct business interest even when you don't itemize deductions.

### Personal or Consumer Interest

Before 1987, you were permitted to take an itemized deduction for interest on debts incurred for personal expenditures. Personal or consumer interest includes interest on personal automobile loans, student loans, personal credit cards, etc. Now, such interest is nondeductible. The disallowance also applies for interest on tax underpayments other than deferred payments of estate taxes.[3]

## HOME MORTGAGE INTEREST DEDUCTION

Home mortgage interest indebtedness is divided into two categories: acquisition indebtedness, and home equity indebtedness. Deductions are permitted only for interest on loans in these two categories, regardless of the cost (and improvements) of the home.[4] Home mortgage interest is an itemized deduction (see Appendix A).

To qualify, the loan must be secured by a principal residence or a qualifying second home. Thus, the interest deduction depends upon the collateral for the loan and ignores how you use the loan proceeds. If you own a housing cooperative unit, debt secured by your stock held as a tenant-stockholder is treated as being secured by the residence.[5]

### Acquisition Indebtedness

Acquisition indebtedness is a loan incurred to acquire, construct, or substantially improve a principal residence or a second home. For an amortizing loan, acquisition indebtedness is reduced as payments of principal are made, and cannot be increased by refinancing. Thus, if you borrow $85,000 to buy your principal residence, and pay the debt down to $60,000, your acquisition debt cannot thereafter be increased above $60,000 unless you borrow to substantially improve the home.

If you refinance, the new loan is treated as acquisition debt only for the amount of the principal of the acquisition debt immediately before the refinancing. The bottom line (at least for tax purposes) is that you should borrow as much of the purchase price as possible, and pay it off as slowly as possible.

The maximum amount of acquisition debt that qualifies for an interest deduction is $1,000,000. This limit applies cumulatively for both your principal residence and a second home. Interest on acquisition debt in excess of $1,000,000 is nondeductible personal interest. The limit is $500,000 for married persons filing separately.

### Home Equity Indebtedness

The law permits deductions for interest on up to $100,000 of loans in excess of acquisition indebtedness, as long as the total acquisition and home equity indebtedness doesn't exceed the fair market value of the property. Like acquisition indebtedness, home equity debt qualifies only if it is secured by a principal residence and/or a qualifying second home.[6] The $100,000 cap applies cumulatively for both the principal residence and a second home. The limit is $50,000 for married persons filing separately. The home equity debt may result from refinancing in excess of the acquisition debt, by a second mortgage, or by a home equity line of credit. Unlike prior law, there are no special deductions for interest on amounts borrowed for medical or educational purposes. However, if the total home equity indebtedness is $100,000 or less, the interest is deductible regardless of how you use the proceeds.

The total amount of your home equity debt for a principal residence and a second home, when combined with the amount of your acquisition debt for the same properties, may not exceed a $1,100,000 overall limit ($1,000,000 maximum acquisition debt plus $100,000 home equity debt). The limit is $550,000 for separate filers.

### What is a Principal Residence?

The definition of a principal residence is the same as that for the home-sale rollover and over-55 exclusion discussed in Chapter 5. Generally, it is the home where you live most of the time. You can only have one principal residence at any time.[7]

## What is a Qualifying Second Residence?

If you use a second home exclusively for personal purposes and don't rent it out at any time during the year, it qualifies as a second residence. If you have more than one second residence, you must choose one of them.

However, if you rent your second residence to tenants at any time during the year, it qualifies only if it is treated as a residence under the vacation home limitation rules (discussed in Chapter 7).[8] Generally, this means that you must occupy the residence for more than the greater of (1) fourteen days, or (2) ten percent of the total number of days the property is rented.

If you occupy the property for less than fifteen days, it is treated as a passive rental activity, and the interest allocable to the rental period, along with all other rental deductions, are subject to the passive loss limitation (see Chapter 7). Since in this situation the home doesn't qualify as a second residence, the interest allocated to the period it is not rented is personal interest and is nondeductible.

The decision of whether to qualify the property as a residence under the vacation home limitation can be complex. The purpose for doing so is to maximize the home mortgage interest deduction for a second residence. However, the desirability of avoiding or qualifying under the vacation home rule also depends upon your situation with passive gains and losses. Factors for making the decision are discussed in Chapter 7.

## Points

It is common for lending institutions to make charges in connection with granting a loan. These charges are payable in advance when the loan is granted. The charges may have various names such as loan processing fees, premium charges, loan place-ment fees, loan origination fees, discount fees, etc. Regardless of the name attached to the charges by the lending institution, they are usually called *points,* if the charge varies with the amount of the loan. Each point equals one percent of the amount of the loan. Thus, if a "discount fee" is stated as 3% of the loan amount, it is three points.

The tax treatment of points depends upon whether the charges are part of the cost of borrowing (interest), or are charges for some other service performed for the borrower.

If the points represent extra interest, they are classified as prepaid interest, and you must allocate the deduction over the life of the loan. There is one important exception to this rule, however. If you meet certain requirements, you may deduct points charged on a loan for the purchase or substantial improvement of your *principal residence* in the year you pay them.[9]

The Internal Revenue Service (IRS) has ruled that, as a matter of administrative practice, it will permit a deduction for points paid during a taxable year if you meet the following five requirements:[10]

**Designation on Uniform Settlement Statement.** This statement, required by the Real Estate Settlement Procedures Act of 1974 (Form HUD-1) must clearly designate the amounts as points incurred in connection with the loan. For example, they may be called *loan origination fees, discount points,* or *points.*

**Computed as a Percentage of the Amount Borrowed.** The amounts must be computed as a percentage of the stated principal amount of the loan. This means that they must represent some identifiable percentage (e.g., 1%, 2.5%, 3%, etc.), not just a flat fee.

**Charged Under Established Business Practice.** The amounts paid must conform to an established business practice of charging for principal residence financing in the area where the property is located. The amount charged cannot exceed the amount generally charged in that area. Thus, amounts designated as points, but paid in lieu of amounts that are ordinarily stated separately on the settlement statement, are not deductible as points. These include appraisal fees, inspection fees, title fees, attorney fees, property taxes, mortgage insurance premiums, etc.

**Paid to Acquire a Principal Residence.** The amounts must be paid in connection with the acquisition of a principal residence, and the loan must be secured by the residence.

**Paid Directly by the Taxpayer.** You must pay the points directly to the lender, using funds that you did not borrow as part of the overall transaction. It was well settled before the IRS guidelines that points are not deductible in the year of purchase if you pay them from the proceeds of the mortgage loan. This is because a note you give for points (part of the total loan) is not *payment.* The direct payment requirement is satisfied if you provide, from funds that have not been borrowed as part of the overall transaction, cash at least equal to the amount of points charged. The cash can be used for down payments, escrow deposits, earnest money applied at the closing, and funds paid over at closing.

The IRS guidelines do not apply for the following types of points:

**Home Improvement Loans.** Points paid for loans where you use the proceeds for the improvement (not acquisition) of a principal residence. However, if the loan is for improvements that are *substantial*, it probably qualifies as acquisition indebtedness, and the points are deductible if you satisfy the requirements described above.

**Loans for Other Residential Property.** Points paid for loans where you use the proceeds to purchase or improve a residence that is not your principal residence. This includes loans related to a second home, vacation property, investment property, or business property.

**Refinancing.** Points paid on a refinancing loan, home equity loan, or line of credit, even though the indebtedness is secured by a principal residence. However, if the proceeds are used for *substantial* home improvements, it probably qualifies as acquisition indebtedness, and the points are deductible if you satisfy the requirements described above. Otherwise, the IRS position is that points for refinancing may only be deducted ratably over the life of the refinanced loan. The reasoning is that refinancing an existing loan does not fall within the statutory prepaid interest exception allowing immediate deduction for points to *purchase* a principal residence.

> **Example:** Sirangelo has an outstanding mortgage of $60,000 on his home which has a fair market value of $200,000. He refinances the home for $120,000, and spends $30,000 for *substantial* improvements. He pays three points, amounting to $3,600 (3% of $120,000). He may deduct only $900, the points relating to the improvements ($30,000/$120,000 x $3,600). The remaining $2,700 is deductible ratably over the life of the loan.

Points you pay as a seller are never deductible because the loan is not your legal obligation. Such points reduce the amount realized from the sale for calculating your gain or loss.[11] In some situations, you might be able to deduct seller points as moving expenses (see below).

### Prepayment Penalties

Most mortgage loan agreements contain a provision permitting you to prepay the principal amount in whole or in part. In most situations, homeowners prepay their mortgages because they sell their homes before loan's term expires. For the privilege of prepayment, lenders usually charge a fee called a prepayment penalty. For the borrower, the prepayment penalty is treated as additional interest, and is an itemized deduction in the year paid.[12]

Prepayment penalties follow a rule similar to that for points when they are paid from the loan proceeds. If you refinance with the same lender, and the penalty is deducted from the refinancing proceeds, it is not *paid*, and you may not deduct it. To insure a deduction, either refinance with a different lender (with the penalty being forwarded to the lender being paid off) or pay the penalty with a separate check from separate funds.[13]

### Prepayment of a Mortgage Loan at a Discount

If you prepay your mortgage for less than its outstanding balance, you will get an unpleasant tax surprise. You have income for the amount of the discount.[14] It does not matter whether you have personal liability for the loan. Thus, if your bank offers to let you pay off your low-interest loan at a discount, and you have the cash to do so, you should consider using the money for an investment yielding a larger return than the interest you are paying on the loan.

> **Example:** To reduce the number of its low-interest mortgages, Wagner's bank offers a 10% discount to each individual with an existing 7% home mortgage who prepays the balance. Wagner pays the bank $18,000 in full settlement of his $20,000 mortgage loan. Wagner has $2,000 of income from the prepayment. Instead of repaying the loan, Wagner should consider investing the $18,000 in another investment which yields more than 7%, after taking into consideration the extra income tax that is payable if the old loan is paid.

## REAL PROPERTY TAXES

You are allowed an itemized deduction for real property taxes on your home. These are taxes imposed on interests in real property levied for the public welfare. Charges for improvements allocated to the specific property owners benefited are not deductible taxes. Such special assessments are discussed below.[15] The deduction is allowed for real property taxes imposed by state, local, and foreign governments.

You may deduct real property taxes imposed on you personally, or imposed on your property. The deduction is permitted even if you have a partial beneficial interest in the property (joint tenant, tenant in common, etc.), and even if you pay an amount larger than your partial interest.[16] If your lender requires you to make monthly payments into a *tax escrow* account, the deductible amount is what is paid by the lender to the government, not what you pay into the account. In effect, the lender is acting as your agent for paying the tax.

### Allocating Real Estate Taxes in the Year of Sale

Usually contracts for the sale of real estate provide that the real estate taxes are prorated between the buyer and the seller according to the portion of the year the property is owned by each. The tax law also adopts the proration approach for property tax deductions.

The law allows you (as buyer or seller) to deduct only the amount of property taxes applicable to the number of days during the year you own the property. For the seller, the period begins on the first day of the tax year and ends on the day before date of sale. For the buyer, the period begins on the date of sale and ends on the last day of the tax year. Thus, even though you pay the entire tax and don't provide for a proration, your deduction is limited to the amount applicable to the part of the tax year you own the property. The tax year is the period specified by the taxing jurisdiction.[17]

> **Example:** The real property tax year is April 1 to March 31. Ms. Tippy, the owner on April 1, 19X1, sells the property to Mr. Mittens on June 30, 19X1. Mr. Mittens owns the property from June 30, 19X1 through March 31, 19X2. The real property tax for the tax year April 1, 19X1 - March 31, 19X2 is $3,650. Ms. Tippy's deduction is limited to the amount deemed to be imposed on her, or $900 (90/365 x $3,650). $2,750 (275/365 of $3,650) is deemed to be imposed on Mr. Mittens, and his deduction is limited to this amount.

If your sale contract doesn't provide for proration of real estate taxes, you (either as buyer or seller) may be in a position where you have paid taxes exceeding the amount you are permitted to deduct. If you are the buyer, the nondeductible tax is a capital expenditure that you must add to your basis for the property.[18] If you are the seller, treatment of the nondeductible tax depends on when you pay the tax. If you pay it in the year of sale, you add the nondeductible portion to your basis for determining your gain or loss on the sale. If you paid and deducted the tax in a prior year, you must report the nondeductible part as ordinary income in the sale year and add it to your basis of the property to determine your gain or loss from its sale.[19]

If your sale contract provides for proration of real estate taxes, the reimbursement from the buyer to the seller (or vice versa) has no effect on the amount realized from the sale by the seller or the basis of the property for the buyer. The payment of taxes deemed to be imposed upon the other party are treated as loans for the amount reimbursed, and the reimbursement is treated as repayment of the loan. The following examples, adapted from the Income Tax Regulations illustrate how these rules work.[20]

**Example:** Assume that the contract price is $50,000 and that property taxes of $1,000 for the property tax year when the sale occurs are paid by Seller. $750 of the taxes are deemed to be imposed upon Buyer and Buyer reimburses Seller in that amount in addition to the selling price. The amount realized by Seller is $50,000. Similarly, $50,000 is Buyer's cost. If Buyer makes no payment other than the contract price of $50,000, the amount realized by Seller is $49,250, since the sales price is deemed to include $750 paid to Seller in reimbursement for real property taxes imposed upon the Buyer. Similarly, $49,250 is Buyer's cost.

**Example:** Assume that Buyer in the above example pays all of the real property taxes. Assume that $250 of the taxes are treated as being imposed on Seller. The amount realized by Seller is $50,250. Similarly, $50,250 is Buyer's cost, regardless of the taxable year in which Buyer makes actual payment of the taxes.

### Special Assessments

Often when government agencies install improvements that increase the value of adjacent property, they charge the benefited property owners their ratable share of the cost. Such improvements include installation of sidewalks or sewers, paving streets, planting trees, etc. These charges are called *special assessments,* and are not deductible as real estate taxes.[21] You capitalize nondeductible special assessments as part of your basis for the property. For the tax treatment of special assessments in connection with condemnation awards, see Chapter 12.

### Transfer and Recording Fees

Transfer and recording taxes paid in connection with the purchase of your home are not deductible real estate taxes, but add to your basis for the property. If paid in connection with the sale of your home, they are treated as selling expenses, and reduce your amount realized for determining gain or loss (see Chapter 3).[22] In some situations, recording and transfer taxes paid by a seller might be deductible as moving expenses (see below).

As a property owner, government agencies might charge you for many other items. If the charges are for specific services rendered to you (as distinguished from charges for services allocated among all property owners in the jurisdiction), the charges are not deductible. Examples are sewer charges and sewer hook-up fees. Charges which aren't based on real estate ownership aren't deductible. For instance, the New York *renters' tax* is not a real estate tax since it is based on rent rather than on real estate ownership. It is additional nondeductible rent.

### Housing Allowances for Ministers and Members of the Armed Forces

Ministers who receive tax-free parsonage allowances and members of the armed forces who receive tax-free off-base housing allowances do not lose their deductions for home mortgage interest and real property taxes.[23]

## COOPERATIVE HOUSING CORPORATIONS

If you own a cooperative house or apartment, you don't own your unit directly (see Chapter 3). You are entitled to rent your unit because you own stock in the corporation that owns the property. You do not directly pay the interest on the corporation's mortgage or real estate taxes on the corporation's property.

The tax law permits you to deduct your ratable share of the mortgage interest and real estate taxes of a qualifying cooperative housing corporation if you are a tenant-shareholder. To qualify, the corporation must meet several technical requirements. You achieve tenant-shareholder status if you own stock in the corporation and your stock ownership entitles you to live in a unit owned or leased by the corporation. You need not occupy the unit, as long as you have the right to do so. This provision applies not only to individuals, but also to corporations, trusts, and other entities that are shareholders.[24] The corporation may elect to permit you to deduct separately allocated amounts (not necessarily based on your percentage of stock ownership) if the allocation reflects the corporation's actual cost attributable to your unit.

## CASUALTY LOSSES TO YOUR HOME

You are allowed a limited deduction for losses caused by casualties to your home. Casualty losses arise from such events as "fire, storm, shipwreck, or other casualty, or from theft."[25] Although this statutory list is not exhaustive and not necessarily relevant (probably you won't have destruction by shipwreck unless you live on a houseboat), the general message is that to qualify, the damage must be the result of an identifiable event caused by an unexpected and sudden destructive force. Losses resulting from floods, earthquakes, vandalism, bursting boilers, and bombardment have qualified as *other* casualties. Gradual deterioration of property because of a steadily operating cause does not qualify as a casualty. These events include slow erosion, rusting, corrosion and contamination.

There are many court cases and IRS rulings discussing borderline casualties. Many involve insect damage (such as termite and beetle damage) and damage from droughts. The results of these cases turn on their facts. For instance, there are "fast" termite cases (where the deduction is allowed), and "slow" termite cases (where it is not allowed). Some of the reasoning and arguments in these cases becomes esoteric, to say the least. Incidentally, the IRS position is that there is no such thing as "fast" termites, and that the casualty loss deduction will be denied for any termite damage.[26]

For the tax treatment for casualty losses for business or investment property, see Chapter 8.

**What is the Amount of the Loss?**

The amount of a casualty loss is the *lesser* of:

o The difference between the fair market values of the property immediately before and immediately following the casualty, or

o The adjusted basis of the property for determining loss (see Chapter 3).

For theft or total destruction of property, the amount of the loss is the fair market value immediately before the casualty (limited to the amount of the property's basis).

For a partial destruction, you should determine the before-and-after fair market values by competent appraisal. The cost of repairs determines the amount of the loss if you actually make them. Otherwise, estimated repair costs to restore the property to its prior condition are only evidence of the loss in value.[27]

The amount of the loss is reduced by insurance recovery. No nonbusiness casualty loss deduction is allowed unless you file a timely insurance claim for a loss covered by an insurance policy. If there is a reasonable prospect of insurance recovery, the loss is not deductible until you determine with reasonable certainty whether you will receive the reimbursement.

**How Much is the Deduction?**

You must reduce the loss by two amounts. First, you reduce each loss by $100 per casualty. Second, you reduce the combined losses (after reduction by the $100 floor amounts) by 10% of your adjusted gross income (see Appendix A for the calculation of adjusted gross income).[28] The excess of the losses over these amounts is an itemized deduction.

**Example:** Five years ago Goopdad purchased a residence for $90,000. After the purchase, she planted trees and ornamental shrubs on the grounds surrounding the home at a cost of $1,200. In 19X1 the land, building, trees, and shrubs are damaged by a hurricane. At the time of the casualty, the adjusted basis of the property is $91,200. The value of the property immediately before the hurricane was $90,000. After the hurricane the value is $70,400. Goopdad's adjusted gross income is $30,000. She receives $5,000 insurance recovery. The amount of the casualty loss deduction is $11,500, determined as follows:

| | |
|---|---|
| Value before | $90,000 |
| Less: Value after | 70,400 |
| Loss of value | $19,600 |

*Amount of casualty loss:*

| | | |
|---|---|---|
| Lesser of decrease in value or basis of property | | $19,600 |
| Less: Insurance | $5,000 | |
| Floor amount | 100 | |
| 10% of AGI | 3,000 | 8,100 |
| Amount of deduction | | $11,500 |

## DEDUCTION FOR AN OFFICE IN YOUR HOME

You are allowed to deduct otherwise nondeductible home maintenance expenses if they are related to an area of your home used for specified business purposes and if you meet certain other requirements. Such expenses include utilities, repairs, insurance and depreciation.

To qualify for deduction, you must use the portion of your home *exclusively* and on a regular basis for one of the purposes specified in the tax law.[29] If you also use the area for personal use, you don't get allocated deductions. This would be the case, for example, if you carry on your qualifying activities at a desk in the corner of a den or family room that you otherwise use for recreation. The IRS has indicated that it will accept a separately identifiable area as long as it is exclusively used for the specified purposes. It need not be a separate room or permanently partitioned.

If you are an employee, the deductions are available only if the qualifying use of your home is for the convenience of your employer. You cannot circumvent the employee rule by leasing your home office to your employer.[30]

The law specifies four ways you can use your home so that you can deduct allocated expenses. The otherwise nondeductible expenses are allowed if you *exclusively* use the area of the home as:

o The principal place for conducting any business in which you are engaged, whether or not it is your principal business, o A place where you meet patients, clients, or customers in the normal course of your business, whether or not it is the principal place for such meetings, or

o A place where you store inventory which you sell at retail or wholesale if your home is the sole fixed location of such business, or

o A place where you conduct a licensed day care center for children or the elderly.

In addition, you may deduct expenses related to a structure used in your business if it is not physically attached to your home. An artist's studio, a florist's greenhouse, and a carpenter's workshop are examples of structures that qualify.

### Principal Place of Business

If you engage in a single business at more than one location, you must determine which is the *principal* place in the light of all facts and circumstances, which include the following:

o The portion of total income from the business attributable to activities at each location,

o The time you spend in activities related the business at each location, and

o The facilities available to you at each location.

**Example:** An outside salesperson has no office space except at home and spends a substantial amount of time on paperwork at home. The office in the home qualifies as his principal place of business.

The IRS historically has adopted a *focal point* test to determine the principal location of your business. This is the most visible place to the public. For example, the IRS contends that the principal place of business for a laundromat is where the washers and dryers are located, even if the owners spend most of their time in a home office doing paperwork. The courts are moving away from this position, and are determining the principal place of business by considering other factors.[31] At the present time, the law in this area is developing rapidly. You are deemed to have a principal place of business for each separate business you conduct.

### Place You Meet Patients, Customers or Clients

Although it is not required that your home office is the *principal* place where you meet patients, customers or clients, it must be used exclusively and regularly for this purpose. The patients, customers or clients must be physically present in the home office. Conversations by telephone do not qualify as a meeting. In addition, the use must be substantial and integral to the conduct of your business. Occasional meetings are not sufficient.

### Place Where You Store Inventory

The area of your home qualifying for this purpose includes only the space actually used for storage. Thus, if you store inventory in one portion of a basement, the storage unit includes only that portion, even if you make no use of the remainder of the basement. In addition, your home must be the only fixed location of the business, and the space used must be a separately identifiable space suitable for storage.

### Day Care Center

Qualifying day care services must be primarily custodial in nature and provided for only certain hours during the day. You may provide educational, developmental, or enrichment activities which are incidental to the primary custodial services. If the services are primarily educational in nature, however, they do not qualify.

### Limitations on Home Office Deductions

The total deductions for business use of your home cannot exceed the gross income produced in the home. In other words, you are allowed to offset your taxable income from the home business activities, but you cannot create a loss to offset income from other sources.

If you operate your business in more than one location, you must allocate the income to the different locations on a reasonable basis. You can only offset expenses related to the operation of your home against the income allocated to the business operation in your home. The factors for allocating income include the amount of time you work at each location, the capital investment at each location, and other relevant circumstances.

Gross income is defined as the gross receipts derived from activities in your home and reduced by expenses required for the business, but not applicable to the use of the home itself. For example, expenses for supplies and compensation paid to other persons fall into this category. If any expenses related to the home are disallowed after applying the gross income rule, you may carry the disallowed deductions forward and deduct them in future years, subject to the same gross income limitation.[32]

Next, you allocate general home maintenance expenses to the home office using any method that is reasonable. If the rooms in the home are of approximately equal size, you may allocate the general expenses according to the number of rooms used for the business. You also may allocate according to the percentage of the total floor space that is used for the business. Expenses attributable to defined portions of the home (such as repairs for kitchen appliances), are allocated in full to those portions.

You take deductions for the business use of you home in the following order:

o The allocable portions of home mortgage interest, real estate taxes and casualty losses allowable without regard to how you use the property,

o Cash expenses, such as repairs, utilities, insurance, etc., related to the business,

o Depreciation and other amounts that cause a reduction in the basis of the home.

If you use the office to conduct a business as an unincorporated proprietor, you take the allowable deductions *from* gross income to arrive at adjusted gross income. If you are an employee, and your home office is maintained for the convenience of your employer, you take an itemized deduction subject to the 2% of adjusted gross income floor for employee and miscellaneous deductions (see Appendix A for a discussion of the 2% limitation).

The deductions and limitations are illustrated by the following example adapted from the Proposed IRS Regulations:[33]

> **Example**: Benedict, a self-employed individual, uses an office in her home on a regular basis as a place of business for meeting with clients of her consulting service. She makes no other use of the office and uses no other premises for the consulting activity. She has a special telephone line for the office and occasionally employs secretarial assistance. She also has a gardener to care for the home's lawn. Benedict determines that 10% of the general expenses for the home are allocable to the office. On the basis of the following figures, Benedict determines that the sum of the allowable business deductions for the use of the office is $1,050.

| | | |
|---|---|---|
| Gross income | | $1,900 |
| | | |
| Expense for secretary | $500 | |
| Business telephone | 150 | |
| Supplies | 200 | |
| Non-office expenses | | 850 |
| Gross income from office | | $1,050 |
| | | |
| Deductions allowable regardless of the use of the unit: | | |
| | | |
| Mortgage interest (10%) | $500 | |
| Real estate taxes (10%) | 200 | |
| Amount allowable | | 700 |
| Limit on further deductions | | $ 350 |
| | | |
| Cash deductions related to the unit: | | |
| | | |
| Insurance (10%) | $ 60 | |
| Utilities (10%) | 90 | |
| Lawn care | 0 | |
| Amount allowable | | 150 |
| Limit on further deductions | | $ 200 |
| | | |
| Deduction for depreciation: | | |
| | | |
| Depreciation $3,200 @ 10% = $320 | | |
| Amount allowable | | $ 200 |

> No portion of the lawn care expense is allocable to the business use of the home. Benedict may claim the remaining $6,300 paid for mortgage interest and real estate taxes as itemized deductions. The $120 of depreciation which is disallowed is carried forward.

**Example:** Assume in the following year, Benedict's income from her consulting practice is $2,500, and all other expenses remain the same. Her home office deductions are calculated as follows:

| | |
|---|---:|
| Gross income - consulting | $2,500 |
| Less: Non-home expenses | 850 |
| Gross income | $1,650 |
| | |
| Less: Interest & taxes | 700 |
| Limit on other deductions | $ 950 |
| | |
| Less: Cash deductions | 150 |
| Limit for depreciation | $ 800 |
| | |
| Less: Allocated depreciation | 320 |
| Net income | $ 480 |
| | |
| Less: Carryover | 120 |
| Net income | $ 360 |

## MOVING EXPENSES

Often when you sell your home it is because you must move to a new location to take another job. Sometimes your new employer reimburses you for some or all of your moving expenses. If so, the entire amount of the reimbursement is included in your income.[34]

The tax law allows you to deduct qualified moving expenses. Strictly speaking, this deduction is not a tax break because of owning a home, since home ownership is not required. You get the deduction whenever you move to a new place of employment (or self-employment) if you meet the requirements. It does not matter whether you were working before the move. Thus, if you are a non-working student, you may deduct the expenses of moving to the location of your first job. Similarly, if you are already working, you may deduct the expenses of moving to a new job for the same or another employer, or to a new location where you are self-employed. The deduction is not allowed, however, if you are working and move to a place where you do not work, such as a move to your retirement home.

In line with the above guidelines, you must meet two requirements before you are permitted to deduct your moving expenses. First, you must work at the new location for a specified period of time. Second, the distance you move must exceed a specified minimum.

### Post-Move Work Time Requirements

If you are an employee, you must be employed full-time for at least thirty-nine weeks during the twelve-month period following the move. If you are self-employed, you must work full-time for at least seventy-eight weeks during the twenty-four month period following the move (of which the first thirty-nine weeks must be during the first twelve-month period).[35] The time requirement is waived if you die or become disabled, or if you are laid off (but not because of willful misconduct), or if you are transferred for the benefit of your employer.

Note that you are not required to have a job at the new location at the time of the move. As long as you are employed (or become self-employed) within thirteen weeks after the move (52 weeks less 39 weeks), you qualify for the deduction.

If both you and your spouse are employed (or self-employed) at the new location and file a joint return, either of you can qualify for the post-move work requirement. However, either you or your spouse must satisfy the requirement on your own. Weeks worked by one of you cannot be added to weeks worked by the other.

### Distance Requirement

The distance requirement denies the deduction for short moves, moves where you buy a new home in the same general area without changing your employment, and moves because you accept new employment in the same general area and move for personal reasons.

To qualify for the deduction, your new principal work location must be at least thirty-five miles farther from your old residence than the old residence was from the former work location. If you are moving to your first work location, it must be at least thirty-five miles from your former residence.[36]

This requirement is not a problem if you move to a distant location. You must be careful, however, if you accept a new job in the same general vicinity and move closer to the new work location. The rule is designed to insure that the new work location is far enough away from your old home to justify a move. In essence, you compare the commuting distances to the old and new jobs. The distance between the old and new homes doesn't matter.

**Example:** Jarvis works in the Virginia suburbs of Washington, D.C., and commutes 15 miles each day to his job. He accepts a new job in the northern suburbs of Baltimore, Md., which is 60 miles from his old home. He doesn't want to contend with Washington traffic, so he moves to a closer location between Washington and Baltimore which is only 30 miles from his old home. Even though his old and new homes are not at least 35 miles apart, he qualifies for the deduction because his new job is 45 miles farther from his old home than was his former job (distance between old home and new job - 60 miles, less distance between old home and old job - 15 miles, equals a difference of 45 miles)

## What Expenses Qualify as Moving Expenses?

The main reason you might not maximize the moving expense deduction is that you are not aware of the range of expenses that qualify. You probably know that the cost of the moving van and the cost of transporting you and your family qualify. However, there are other qualifying expenses that you might not be aware of.

There are five classifications of qualifying moving expenses.[37] Two of these classifications (called direct moving expenses) are deductible without limitation as long as they are reasonable.

**Cost of Moving Personal and Household Goods**. This includes fees paid to moving companies for transporting, packing and storing household possessions, including the cost of moving pets. If you move yourself, it includes the amount of rental for the truck and gasoline, etc.

**Cost of Travel to the New Home**. This includes the cost of transportation, meals, and lodging for you and the members of your household en route to the new home. If you drive your car, you may deduct the actual expenses or deduct the standard mileage rate. If you have more than one car, the deduction is allowed for each car. The travel expenses must be reasonable. Thus, if it takes you the months of December and January to move from New York to Cleveland with stopovers in Miami and New Orleans, you are deemed to be taking a vacation in connection with your move, and you cannot deduct the expenses related to the vacation.

The total deduction for next two types of indirect moving expenses cannot exceed $1,500 regardless of how much you spend:[38]

**House Hunting Trips.** If you have already secured a job you may deduct (subject to the limitation) the amount of the cost of traveling to the new work site to find a place to live. Included are costs of transportation, meals, and lodging. You aren't required to be looking for a home to buy. The deduction is also available for trips to find a house or apartment to rent.

**Temporary Living Expenses.** If you incur meals and lodging expenses in the new location while waiting to move into your new home, you can deduct those costs incurred during the first thirty days (subject to the above limitation). Here again, the expenses are deductible only if you have already secured your new job.

The deduction for the final category of indirect expenses, together with any deductions in the preceding two categories of indirect expenses cannot exceed $3,000.

**Costs of Disposing of the Old Residence or Acquiring the New One.** These are buying and selling expenses of the new and old homes.[39] Included are costs which you, as a seller, would normally deduct from the amount realized to determine your gain or loss. Examples are real estate commissions, escrow fees, legal expenses, points paid to help the buyer secure a mortgage, and recording or transfer taxes.

To the extent that you deduct such costs as moving expenses, you cannot reduce your amount realized. However, if you cannot deduct some of these costs because of the limitation, you may reduce your amount realized by the excess (see Chapter 3).

These expenses also include those that a buyer would add to the basis of his property. Again, if you deduct these costs as moving expenses, you do not add them to your basis. Any excess not deducted as moving expenses add to basis. You also may deduct the cost of settling a lease on your old home, such as a forfeited security deposit.

Some expenses in connection with a move do not qualify under any of the above categories. They are either capital expenditures or nondeductible personal expenditures. Such costs include the cost of refitting fixtures, drapes, etc., for the new home; new carpeting; losses from cancellation of club memberships; private school tuition; expenses of fixing up the old home for sale (see Chapter 5), etc.

**Example:** Rann is transferred by his employer from San Francisco to New Orleans. The bill for moving his household furniture to the new location is $2,400. The travel expenses for himself and his family are $3,000. In addition, he spends $200 to transport his pet pig, Priscilla. After being notified of the new job, Rann traveled to New Orleans to locate a new home. The cost of this trip was $700. He pays a real estate broker $5,000 to sell his home in San Francisco. After arriving in New Orleans, he finds that the new home is not ready for occupancy. He and his family move into a motel for 45 days, and incur $100 per day for lodging. After moving into the new home, Rann pays $800 to a decorator to refit the antique drapes from his San Francisco home. His employer reimburses him for the moving company fee. Rann includes the reimbursement of $2,400 in his income. He calculates his moving expense deduction as follows:

| | | |
|---|---:|---:|
| Moving company fee | | $2,400 |
| Travel for the family | | 3,000 |
| Pet transportation | | 200 |
| House hunting trip | $ 700 | |
| Temporary living | 3,000 | |
| Total | $3,700 | |
| Amount deductible | | 1,500 |
| Disposition expenses | $5,000 | |
| Less: Expenses deducted | 1,500 | |
| Deductible selling expense | | 1,500 |
| Total deduction | | $8,600 |

The cost of refitting the drapes is a nondeductible personal expense.

### When Do You Take the Deduction?

You might not be able to meet the post-move work test (39 or 78 weeks) before the end of the year you move. Accordingly, there are two ways to take the deduction.[40]

o You can take the deduction in the year you move even if you have not met the post-move work test. If you subsequently fail to meet the test, you add the amount you deducted to your income for the following year (or the second following year for failing the self-employment work test), or o You can wait until you meet the test, and file an amended return for the year you moved.

As a cash basis taxpayer, you deduct the expenses in the year when you pay them. If you receive reimbursement in the year after you pay the expenses, you can elect to deduct the expenses in that following year. If you receive reimbursement in the year you move, you can deduct expenses in the following year that you pay them.

The reimbursement is included as salary income on the IRS Form 1040. You use the IRS Form 3903 to show the detailed calculations of the amount of the deduction.

### Military Personnel and Foreign Moves

Special, more liberal rules apply for members of the armed forces [41] and taxpayers who make job-related moves to foreign countries. [42]

Military personnel making mandatory moves for less than thirty-nine weeks, or for less than thirty-five miles may deduct moving expenses without regard for the post-move work time and minimum mileage requirements. Further, in-kind moving and storage services furnished by the U.S. Government provided in connection with a permanent change of station aren't included in income.

If your move is in connection with beginning work outside the U.S., the deductions for indirect moving expenses are modified as follows:

o Temporary living expenses include those for the first ninety days (rather than thirty days) at the new location,

o The dollar limitation for temporary living expenses and house hunting expenses is increased from $1,500 to $4,500, and

o The overall dollar limitation for house hunting, temporary living, and acquisition and disposition expenses is increased from $3,000 to $6,000.

In addition, your moving expenses back to the U.S. from a residence and work place outside the U.S. are deductible even if you don't meet the post-move work requirement.


## MEDICAL EXPENSES

Generally, capital improvements to your home are not deductible, but add to the basis of the property.

However, if you make the improvements upon the advice of a physician as being a medical necessity for your health or the health of your spouse or dependents, they might be deductible as medical expenses for the excess of their cost over the increase in the value of your home. To qualify, the person for whom the facility is installed must be the primary person who uses it, and the expenditure must be reasonable.[43]

> **Example:** Higgins, who is afflicted with heart disease, is advised by her physician to install an elevator in her home so that she will not be required to climb stairs. The cost of installing the elevator is $10,000. An appraiser determines that because the home is in an area inhabited by elderly people, the elevator increases the value of the property by $7,000. Higgins may deduct the excess cost of $3,000 as a medical expense (subject to the limitation on medical expense deductions). If it is determined that the value of the residence is not increased, the entire amount of the expenditure is deductible as a medical expense.

In addition to the capital expenditure, costs associated with installation of the facility, such as appraiser fees, and extra expenses associated with the facility are deductible.

> **Example:** In the above example, the appraisal fee to determine the amount of Higgins' property value, and any extra utility costs associated with the elevator are deductible as medical expenses.

The amount of any home-improvement medical expenses, together with other qualifying medical expenses are an itemized deduction, but only to the extent that they exceed 7.5% of adjusted gross income (see Appendix A).

## FOOTNOTES

1. Internal Revenue Code (IRC) §461(g).

2. Sen. Rept. 99-313, 99th Cong., 2d Sess., p. 805.

3. IRC §§163(h)(1) & (2); H. Rept. 99-841, 99th Cong., 2d Sess., p. II-154.

4. IRC §163(h)(3)(A).

5. IRC §163(h)(4)(B).

6. IRC §163(h)(3)(C).

7. IRC §163(h)(4)(A)(i)(I).

8. IRC §163(h)(4)(A)(i)(II).

9. IRC §461(g)(2).

10. Rev. Proc. 92-12, IRB 1992-3.

11. Rev. Rul. 68-650, 1968-2 CB 78.

12. Rev. Rul. 57-198, 1957-1 CB 94; in accord, Rev. Rul. 73-137, 1973-1 CB 68.

13. *England, Jr.*, 34 TC 617 (1960); *Thomason*, 33 BTA 576 (1937); *Lichtman*, 44 TCM 1536 (1982).

14. Rev. Rul. 82-202, 1982-2 CB 35.

15. IRC §164(a)(1); Reg. §1.164-3(b).

16. *Lulu L. Powell*, TC Memo 1967-32; *Theodore Milgroom*, 31 TC 1256; *Nicodemus*, 26 BTA 125.

17. IRC §164(d)(1); Reg. §1.164-6(c).

18. IRC §1012; Reg. §1.1012-1(b).

19. Reg. §1.164-6(d)(5); Reg. §1.1001-1(b).

20. IRC §1001(b)(1) & (b)(2); Reg. §1.1001-1(b)(4), Examples 1 and 2.

21. IRC §164(c)(1); Reg. §1.164-4

22. Rev. Rul. 65-313, 1965-2 CB 47.

23. IRC §265(a)(6).

24. IRC §216; Reg. §1.216-1.

25. See generally IRC §165(c)(3).

26. Rev. Rul. 63-232, 1983-2 CB 97.

27. Reg. §1.165-7(a)(2).

28. IRC §165(h).

29. Generally, see IRC §280A(c); Prop. Reg. §1.280A-2.

30. IRC §280A(c)(6), reversing *Feldman*, 84 TC 1 (1985).

31. *Meiers v. Comm'r*, 782 F2d 75 (CA 7, 1986); *Drucker v. Comm'r*, 715 F2d 67 (CA 2, 1983); *Weissman v. Comm'r*, 751 F2d 52 (CA 2, 1984); *Soliman v. Comm'r*, 933 F2d 52 (CA 4, 1991).

32. IRC §280A(c)(5)(B), reversing *Scott*, 84 TC 683 (1985).

33. Prop. Reg. §1.280A-2(i)(7).

34. IRC §82.

35. IRC §217(c)(2); Reg. §1.217-2(c)(4).

36. IRC §217(c)(1); Reg. §1.217-2(c)(2) & (c)(3).

37. IRC §217(b)(1); Reg. §1.217-2(b).

38. IRC §217(b)(3); Reg. §1.217-2(b)(9).

39. IRC §217(b)(2); Reg. §1.217-2(b)(7) & (b)(8).

40. IRC §§217(d)(2) & (d)(3); Reg. §1.217-2(d)(2).

41. IRC §217(g); Reg. §1.217-2(g).

42. IRC §217(h); Reg. §1.217-2(h).

43. Reg. §1.213-1(e)(1)(iii).

# Chapter

# FIVE

## TAX BREAKS WHEN YOU SELL YOUR HOME

The income tax law has special tax breaks to help you sell your home. Before signing any listing agreements or contracts for sale, you should be careful to structure the transaction to maximize these opportunities. In this chapter, we examine the rules for two important tax breaks:

    o  The home-sale *rollover*, that permits you to postpone payment of tax on your gain, and

    o  The over-55 *exclusion*, that allows up to $125,000 of gain to escape income tax altogether.

A third important tax break, the moving expense deduction, is sometimes available if you sell because of a work-related move to a new location. We discuss this deduction in Chapter 4.

Circumstances surrounding home sales and purchases are numerous and varied. It is impossible to address every conceivable situation. In the Tax Planning Ideas sections of this chapter we discuss some common situations where court cases, Income Tax Regulations or rulings provide guidance.

Sales and purchases of homes by husbands and wives before, during, and in termination of a marriage create special tax problems.

Tax rules for these situations are sufficiently extensive to warrant separate treatment. We discuss the law relating to these matters in Chapter 6.

## ROLLOVER OF TAX ON GAIN FROM THE SALE OF YOUR PRINCIPAL RESIDENCE

Usually, the tax law requires you to pay tax on a gain in the year of the sale. However Congress enacted a special tax break permitting you to postpone (defer) payment of tax on your home sale gain if you reinvest the sale proceeds in a new home. We usually call this provision the home-sale *rollover*.[1] There is a twofold reason for the rollover. First, your gain is often illusory, resulting largely because of inflation. Second, if tax were imposed on your gain you would have less to reinvest, which might reduce your standard of living. We discuss the economic impact of tax deferral as an "interest-free loan from the government," in Chapter 2.

To qualify for tax deferral, the home must be your *principal residence*, and you must reinvest the entire *adjusted sales price* of the old home within a specified period of time. The terms *principal residence* and *adjusted sales price* have special definitions which we discuss below.

If your sale and reinvestment transactions fit within the tax law definition for the rollover, tax deferral is mandatory. If you have losses to offset the gain, you may want to avoid the rollover and cause your gain to be taxed. In this event, you must deliberately violate the rollover's requirements. You may do this by purchasing the new home outside the specified reinvestment period, or by disqualifying the property by converting it to a rental property or a second home. The rollover applies only for gains. Losses from home sales never have any tax consequences. You cannot deduct them or offset them against gains from sales of other property.

### What is Your Gain from the Sale?

Gain from the sale of your home is calculated the same way as gain from the sale of any other asset: the difference between the *amount realized* and the *adjusted basis*. These terms have special meanings in the tax law (see Chapter 3).

The amount realized is the selling price less expenses related to the sale. The selling price is the total of cash you receive, the fair market value of property you receive, and the amount of your liabilities assumed by the buyer. These liabilities might include your existing mortgages or delinquent real estate taxes. Selling expenses include your real estate commissions, costs of advertising the property for sale, costs of preparing the deed, and other legal services in connection with the sale.[2]

> **Example**: Bartfeld sells his home for $120,000. The terms of sale require the buyer to pay Bartfeld $40,000 cash and assign to him stock in XYZ Corporation having a fair market value of $10,000. In addition, the buyer agrees to assume an existing FHA mortgage with an outstanding balance of $70,000. Bartfeld pays a real estate commission of $8,000, and legal fees of $2,000. The amount realized is determined as follows:

| | | |
|---|---|---|
| Cash received | | $ 40,000 |
| Fair market value of stock | | 10,000 |
| Mortgage assumed by buyer | | 70,000 |
| Selling price | | $120,000 |
| Less: Selling expenses | | |
| Commission | $8,000 | |
| Legal fees | 2,000 | 10,000 |
| Amount realized | | $110,000 |

The adjusted basis of your first principal residence is its cost. This includes the cash down payment, the amount of any purchase money mortgage, and any expenses associated with the purchase. The purchase loan can come from either an institutional lender or the seller. The basis of any subsequent home you buy after taking advantage of the rollover is determined under special rules discussed below.

### What is Your "Principal Residence?"

Both the home you sell and the reinvestment home must be your *principal residence*. Your principal residence is the place where you live most of the time. This is a physical presence test, and is not the same as the legal concept of *domicile*, which is the place where you *intend* to make your home, regardless of where you physically reside.

For purposes of the rollover, you may have only one principal residence. If you have two or more residences (such as summer and winter homes), only one qualifies. In such a case, the facts and circumstances determine which is your *principal* residence. Your principal residence may be a house, cooperative apartment, condominium, houseboat or mobile home. The law doesn't require it to be real estate. If you convert your home permanently for rental or business, it doesn't qualify. See the Tax Planning Ideas section below for tax planning problems in situations where you must rent the old residence before its sale, or where you use the property for more than one purpose.

You must own both the old and the new residences. If someone else takes title to the new home, even though closely related to you (such as your son or daughter), the transactions do not qualify for the rollover. In Chapter 6, we discuss special rules for taking title in sales and reinvestments by spouses.

## How Much Must You Reinvest?

To postpone the entire gain, you must reinvest at least the amount of the *adjusted sales price* of your old home. If the amount you reinvest is less than the adjusted sales price, your gain is taxed for the excess of the adjusted sales price of your old home over the cost of the new one.

The adjusted sales price is the amount realized from the sale less expenses for work you do to help sell the home (fixing-up expenses).[3] Fixing-up expenses do not include selling expenses (such as real estate commissions) or amounts that you may otherwise deduct. In addition, fixing-up expenses must meet three tests:

o You must complete the work during the ninety day period ending on the day when you enter into a contract to sell your old home,

o You must pay for the expenses on or before the thirtieth day after the date you sell (close) the old home, and

o The work must be a repair, and not a capital expenditure.

See the Tax Planning Ideas section below for further discussion.

You are not required to reinvest all the cash you receive from the sale of your old home. Don't worry about how the old and new homes are financed. As long as the cost of the new home is at least as much as the adjusted sales price of the old one, you qualify for total tax deferral. Thus, if the new home is highly leveraged, you can take tax-free cash from settlement of your old home, and still qualify.

> **Example:** Brenner sells his home for $75,000. The property is subject to a $30,000 mortgage. At settlement he receives cash of $45,000 after payment of the mortgage. He immediately purchases a replacement home for $100,000, giving a $20,000 down payment. These transactions qualify for tax deferral even though Brenner pockets the $25,000 excess of the cash received from the old home sale ($45,000) over the cash put into the new home purchase ($20,000).

The rollover is only available for a sale of *one* principal residence, followed by reinvestment in *one* principal residence. Thus, if you sell two homes, each of which you used as a principal residence, you cannot match the proceeds of both sales with the purchase of a single replacement home.[4]

> **Example:** On May 15, 19X1, DiBacco sells, at a gain, Home A that has been his principal residence for the preceding two years. Following this sale, DiBacco moves to Home B that was previously a rental property, and uses it as a principal residence until shortly before November 15, 19X2, when he purchases and uses Home C as a principal residence. He purchased and used Home C within two years after selling Home A. He sells Home B at a gain, shortly after November 15, 19X2. DiBacco's cost of purchasing Home C exceeds the adjusted sales prices of both Homes A and B. For the rollover, the cost of Home C is matched against the adjusted sales price of Home A. Since his cost for Home C exceeds his adjusted sales price for Home A, no gain from Home A is taxed. However, the entire gain from his sale of Home B is taxed.

Similarly, you don't qualify if you sell a single residence and reinvest in two principal residences.[5]

> **Example:** Edelman sells his principal residence at a gain and within the reinvestment period purchases a new home in New York, and a new home in Florida. During the reinvestment period, he lives in each of the homes at various times. For the rollover, you look only at the cost of the home qualifying as the principal residence at the expiration of the reinvestment period. You ignore any amount reinvested in the other home.

If you provide financing for the buyer by taking back installment notes when you sell your home, you report any gain under the installment method. This delays the tax until you receive payment on the notes (for details about making the calculations, see Chapter 10).

## When Must You Replace Your Home?

In most instances, your replacement period begins two years before you sell your old home and ends two years later. The sale and purchase occur on the date when you *close* the old and new home sales. Contracts to sell the old home or to purchase the replacement home are irrelevant. For tax rollover purposes the contract to sell your old home is relevant only to measure the time to qualify fixing-up expenses as discussed above.

The law also requires that you must physically occupy both homes as a principal residence at some time during the replacement period. Thus, if you do not both *close* and *occupy* the new home within the four-year replacement period, you do not qualify for the rollover. Similarly, you must occupy the old home as a principal residence within the two years before its sale even if you live elsewhere at the time of its sale.

Sometimes you may continue to live in the old home after buying the new one. The rollover permits you to rent out the new home until you move in, as long as you sell the old home and move into the new one within two years after you purchase the new home.[6]

Construction or reconstruction of a new home is treated as a purchase, as long as you occupy it within the replacement period. However, you take into account only the construction or reconstruction costs you incur during the replacement period to determine how much you have reinvested. The Internal Revenue Service (IRS) has ruled that reconstruction of a home you previously used as vacation home qualifies if the reconstruction expenses during the replacement period exceed the adjusted sales price of the old home.[7] These expenditures must be for *reconstruction*, or additions to the vacation home, and not merely for improvements such as a swimming pool, new roof, landscaping, etc.

The timing of your purchase and sale transactions is crucial. If you don't close and occupy within the reinvestment period, you are denied tax deferral. No extensions of time are permitted, regardless how compelling your reason for the delay.[8] The courts have consistently denied the rollover despite overwhelming homeowner hardships including sickness, bad weather, slow contractors, and sellers who default.

**Members of the Armed Forces.** If you are a member of the Armed Forces on full-time active duty when you sell your home, the replacement period after the sale is suspended for a maximum of four years, if you remain on active duty during this period.[9] This gives you a maximum reinvestment period of six years: two years before sale, and four years thereafter.

There are two situations where the replacement period following the old home's sale is suspended for a maximum of eight years (thus allowing you a maximum ten-year replacement period).[10] To qualify, you must be on full-time active duty in the Armed Forces both at the time of sale and during the suspension period. The eight year suspension period applies where:

o  You are stationed outside the United States during the suspension period, or

o  After returning from duty outside the U.S., you are required to live in government quarters during the suspension period.

**Homeowners Who Establish Foreign Residences.** If you establish a residence (tax home) in a foreign country after you sell your old home, and you remain abroad during the entire suspension period, the reinvestment period after sale is extended to four years.[11]

### How Many Times May You Use the Rollover?

There is no limit to the number of times you may use the tax-free rollover. This rule is subject to one important limitation, however. Generally, you may not use the rollover more than once during any two-year period.[12] This limitation is inapplicable, however, if the reason you sell the home is that you must begin work as an employee or self-employed person at a new principal work location, and you qualify for the moving expense deduction (see Chapter 4.)

If you sell and purchase more than two homes during a two-year period, you compare your reinvestment in the last home to the adjusted sales price of the first home you sold to determine how much of the first home's gain is taxed. Gains from sales of any intermediate homes are taxed.

> **Example:** Hampton sells his old home (Home #1) on January 15, 19X1, and purchases another home on February 15, 19X1 (Home #2). On March 15, 19X1, he sells Home #2 and purchases another home on April 15, 19X1 (Home #3). The gain from sale of Home #1 is recognized only if Hampton's adjusted sales price of Home #1 exceeds the cost of purchasing Home #3. Gain on the sale of Home #2 is taxed.[13]

### What is Your Tax Basis for the New Home?

The most misunderstood aspect of the rollover is how you calculate the tax basis of your replacement home. Many homeowners assume that the new home's tax basis is its cost. However, basis (or adjusted basis) is a technical tax term, and is not always the cost. The basis of the new home after using a home-sale rollover is such a situation. At this point, you should review the general tax basis rules discussed Chapter 3.

The law achieves tax deferral by reducing the basis of the replacement home by the untaxed gain from sale of the old home. The adjusted basis of a replacement home is its cost reduced by the old home's deferred gain.[14]

> **Example:** Martyn sells his home for $60,000. His basis for the home is $25,000, so his gain is $35,000 ($60,000 less $25,000). Within the replacement period, he purchases a new home for $65,000. Since the reinvestment exceeds the adjusted sales price of the old home, none of the $35,000 gain is taxed. The basis of the replacement home is $30,000 (its cost of $65,000 less the $35,000 untaxed gain from the old home). Suppose the new home does not appreciate and is sold for $65,000, the amount of its cost, and Martyn doesn't reinvest in another home. The taxable gain from its sale is $35,000 ($65,000 less the basis of $30,000). This is the deferred gain from the sale of the first home that is triggered by sale of the second home.

Note that the old home's gain includes the deferred gains from sales of all previous homes (since the basis of the old home and all previous homes were, in turn, reduced by such deferred gains). Thus, the deferred gains from all prior homes are reflected in the basis of the current home. Therefore, although the value of your home might be no more than its cost (or indeed, it might be less), if you don't reinvest, you pay tax on all postponed gains. You might get relief from this harsh result if you are eligible to elect the over-55 exclusion discussed below.

Your basis is increased by the expenses of acquiring the new home (see Chapter 3). The basis is also increased by *capital* improvements you make while you own the home. Capital improvements are those that increase the value of the home, or that extend its useful economic life. For example, they include costs of permanent landscaping, addition of structural components such as a garage or a room, or construction of an improved roof. Repairs that merely maintain your home's current value or economic life are not capital improvements. Repairs have no tax consequences for a homeowner. They do not increase your basis for the property, and they are not deductible. The distinction between capital improvements and repairs is sometimes difficult, and is discussed in Chapter 8.

### Illustrations of Rollover Computations

To summarize, you take the following steps to determine how much gain from sale of your home is taxed and the adjusted basis of your new home:

o  Calculate the gain from sale of your old home - Amount realized less adjusted basis,

o  Calculate the *adjusted sales price* of your old home - Amount realized less *fixing-up expenses,*

o  Determine how much gain is taxed - Adjusted sales price of the old home less the cost of the new home,

o  Determine how much gain is postponed - Total gain less the amount taxed because of insufficient reinvestment.

o  Determine the adjusted basis of your new home - Cost of the new home less the postponed gain from sale of the old home.

These steps are illustrated by the following examples, that are adapted from examples in the Income Tax Regulations.[15]

**Example:** Owens sells his home on June 1, 19X5, for $75,000. Photias pays $30,000 cash and assumes the outstanding FHA mortgage of $45,000. In 19X1, Owens purchased the home for $50,000. He had never owned a home before that time. In 19X2 he added a bedroom that cost $4,000. The real estate broker's commission for the sale is $4,500. Twenty days before the closing, Owens spends $2,000 to repaint the interior walls. He pays for this when the job was completed. In September of 19X5, Owens closes on his new home that costs $71,000. The tax consequences are as follows:

*Gain Realized:*

| | | |
|---|---:|---:|
| Cash received | | $30,000 |
| Mortgage assumed | | 45,000 |
| Gross selling price | | $75,000 |
| Less: Sales commission | | 4,500 |
| Amount realized | | $70,500 |
| Less: Adjusted basis | | |
| Cost of old home | $50,000 | |
| Bedroom (capital) | 4,000 | 54,000 |
| Gain realized | | $16,500 |

*Adjusted Sales Price:*

| | |
|---|---:|
| Amount realized (above) | $70,500 |
| Less: Fix-up expenses (painting) | 2,000 |
| Adjusted sales price | $68,500 |

*Gain Taxed:*

No gain taxed - Amount reinvested exceeds adjusted sales price.

*Basis of New Home:*

| | |
|---|---:|
| Amount reinvested (new home) | $71,000 |
| Less: Untaxed gain (old home) | 16,500 |
| Basis of new home | $54,500 |

**Example:** Assume the facts of the above example except that the amount Owens reinvests is only $50,000.

*Gain Taxed:*

| | |
|---|---:|
| Adjusted sales price (above) | $68,500 |
| Amount reinvested | 50,000 |
| Under-reinvestment | $18,500 |
| | |
| Gain taxed - Actual gain | $16,500 |

*Basis of New Home:*

| | |
|---|---:|
| Cost of new home | $50,000 |
| Less: Untaxed gain | None |
| Basis of new home | $50,000 |

**Example:** Assume the facts of the above example except that the amount Owens reinvests is $65,000.

*Gain Taxed:*

| | |
|---|---|
| Adjusted sales price (above) | $68,500 |
| Amount reinvested | 65,000 |
| Under-reinvestment (gain taxed) | $ 3,500 |

*Basis of New Home:*

| | |
|---|---|
| Basis of new home | $65,000 |
| Less: Untaxed gain on old home ($16,500 - $3,500) | 13,000 |
| Basis of new home | $52,000 |

## How Do You Report the Sale and Reinvestment?

Nitty-gritty mechanics for reporting the old home's sale and new home's purchase are tedious, but have considerable practical importance.

Regardless of whether you plan to reinvest, you must attach IRS Form 2119 to your income tax return for the year you sell your old home. If you aren't going to reinvest, you indicate this on the Form 2119, and report and pay tax on the full gain the year of sale. If, within the replacement period, you change your mind and buy a new home, you file an amended income tax return (IRS Form 1040X) to claim a refund for the tax you paid. You attach a new Form 2119 to this amended return.

If you reinvest before filing the return for the year of sale, the IRS Form 2119 attached to the return reports the details of the sale of the old home, the reinvestment in the new home, and the basis of the new home.

If you don't reinvest before filing your return for the year of sale, you attach Form 2119 to that year's return, but you only complete those sections of the form relating to the old home's sale.

If you purchase another home within the replacement period, and your reinvestment is enough to defer the entire gain, you should send notice of your reinvestment to the Director of the Internal Revenue Service Center where you filed your return in the year you sold the old home. In addition, you must file a new Form 2119 with the return for the year of reinvestment.

If you don't buy a replacement home, or if some of your gain is taxed because you don't reinvest enough, you file an amended return (IRS Form 1040X) for the year you sold the old home, and pay the additional tax. You attach a revised Form 2119 to this amended return. You will pay interest on the additional tax due.

### Statute of Limitations

The normal three-year period the IRS has to assess additional tax is automatically extended if you have gain from the sale of your home. The extension, however, applies only for the tax on any unreported gain from sale of the home, and not for other items in the return.[16]

The extension allows the IRS to assess tax on unreported gain within three years after receipt by written notice of:

o The cost of the new home that postpones all or part of your gain from sale of your old home,

o Your intention not to purchase a new home within the reinvestment period, or

o Your failure to purchase a new home within the reinvestment period.

You file the required notification with the IRS District office where you filed your return for the year when you sold the old home. Even though you reinvest enough to postpone the entire gain, it is important to file the notice of reinvestment to start the running of the statute of limitations. See Chapter 2 for a discussion of the normal rules for the statute of limitations.

## TAX PLANNING IDEAS FOR
## THE HOME-SALE ROLLOVER

Court cases, and IRS rulings and regulations provide guidance for tax planning in some common home-sale situations. The footnotes at the end of the chapter contain the appropriate citations for your tax advisor to check.

### How the Rollover Works When You Use Only Part of Your Home as a Principal Residence

If you use part of a home as a principal residence and part for another purpose (such as a home office or a rental apartment) you must allocate the sale price and the home's basis for purposes of the rollover. You may defer the part of the gain allocable to the residence portion, and you are taxed on the remainder.[17]

**Example:** Sachs owns a four-story townhouse. He rents the first story, an English basement, as an apartment, and lives in the upper three stories. His adjusted basis for the house is $40,000. He sells the house for $100,000, and incurs selling expenses of $8,000. His gain for purposes of the rollover is calculated as follows:

|  | 3/4 Principal Residence | 1/4 Rental Apartment |
|---|---|---|
| Selling Price | $75,000 | $25,000 |
| Less: Sale exp. | 6,000 | 2,000 |
| Amount realized | $69,000 | $23,000 |
| Adjusted basis | 30,000 | 10,000 |
| Gain | $39,000 | $13,000 |

Sachs may defer the gain of $39,000 from the principal residence portion if he reinvests at least $69,000 in a replacement home. He pays tax on the $13,000 gain from the rental unit.

### Planning When You Use Part of the Home as an Office

As discussed in the preceding section, if you use part of your home as an office at the time of sale, gain from that part does not qualify for the rollover. You must pay tax on the part of the gain allocated to the home office. However, if, at the time of sale, the office no longer qualifies for the home office deduction (see Chapter 4), gain from sale of the entire home qualifies for the rollover.[18] To make the rollover available, you should deliberately disqualify the office for the home office deduction. The easiest way is not to take home office deductions such as depreciation, utilities, repairs, etc., on your tax return for the year of the sale. Better yet, if you know in advance that you are going to sell your home, you should cease such deductions in your tax return for the year *prior* to sale. Otherwise, you must establish by other evidence that you abandoned the office.

### Renting the Old Home After You
### Buy the New Home

Since the rules permit replacement within the two year period before you sell the old home, you might buy and occupy your new home before you sell the old one. In recent years, many homeowners have been placed into this position because interest rates and other market conditions have made it difficult to sell the old home. Often, the financial burden of paying two mortgages makes it necessary to rent the old home while you wait for its sale.

Does such rental disqualify the old home as your principal residence and disallow the tax-free rollover? The happy answer is that you aren't disqualified if the rental is temporary and you continue to market the home actively while you rent it. Active marketing requires, at the minimum, that you maintain an active real estate listing during the rental period. It is also helpful to show that the rental began only after you tried unsuccessfully to sell. In any event, the normal reinvestment period rules discussed above require that you sell the old home within two years after you buy the new home.

### Renting the Old Home Before You
### Buy the New Home

Suppose you must temporarily move to another location, but you intend to return to your old home. During your absence you rent the old home. At the temporary location you rent a place to live. If you return to the old home and reestablish it as your principal residence, the interim rental does not disqualify the old home for the tax-free rollover.

What if after relocating, you decide that because of changed circumstances you cannot return to the old home, and you sell it? Does failure to reoccupy the old home disqualify it for the rollover? There is judicial authority that the old home is not disqualified if:

o You buy a new home and occupy it within the appropriate reinvestment period,

o You can prove that you intended to return to the old home, and o Your failure to reoccupy the old home is due to circumstances unknown to you when you rented the old home.

**Example:** Ralph Trisko, a federal employee, received a temporary overseas assignment for a minimum of one year and a maximum of four years. During the absence, he rented his house in the Washington, D.C., area where he had lived with his family. The lease was for a period of one year, subsequent rentals being on a month-to-month basis. When Ralph returned to the United States, rent control and other complications made it impossible for him to move back into the old home. Ralph purchased a new home within the reinvestment period, and financed it by selling his old one. The court concluded that rental during the temporary absence did not transform the home into an investment or business property and allowed him to defer the gain under the home-sale rollover.[19]

**Example:** Arthur Barry was required to move because of a military transfer, but intended to return to his old home when his current enlistment was finished. He received a job offer at the new location that he could not refuse. He sold the old home and purchased another one at the new location within the reinvestment period. The court allowed a tax-free rollover.[20]

**Example:** Seldin received a two-year assignment in another city and rented his old home during his absence. When he returned, he discovered that the local high school had been closed, and the children would be forced to travel an unacceptable distance to a new high school if the family reoccupied the original home. Within the reinvestment period, he sold the old home and purchased a new one closer to the school. The IRS ruled that the old home was not disqualified as a principal residence, and permitted the tax-free rollover.[21]

Although the courts and IRS have been liberal in permitting homes that have been rented to qualify for the tax-free rollover, it is not entirely clear exactly what facts and circumstances are acceptable to prove the intent to return to the old home. You may be in trouble, however, if the facts show that at the time you rent the old home it is clearly unlikely that you will be able to return.[22]

**Example:** Sood, on active duty in the military service, receives a three-year assignment abroad. Other military personnel in his position are usually transferred to a different duty post when they return from an overseas assignment. Sood knows that he can sell his home and that he would have time after his return to purchase a new one and qualify for the tax-free rollover. However, because the home is in an area experiencing high appreciation and a strong rental market, he decides not to sell, but to rent it during his absence. As expected, he is assigned to a different duty post when he returns, and is unable to reoccupy the old residence. To finance the purchase of a new home within the reinvestment period, he sells the old home. These facts probably would disqualify the old home for the rollover, since Sood was aware at the time of renting the old home that he would be unable to return. Thus, his decision to rent probably will transform the home into an investment property.

### Rental Deductions While You Wait to Sell Your Old Home

Suppose you want to have the best of all possible worlds and claim rental deductions during the temporary rental period (depreciation, utilities, repairs, etc.). The IRS has always taken the position that a property is either a principal residence (qualifying for the rollover) or a rental property (qualifying for rental deductions), but it can't be both at the same time. Thus, its view has been that you must make a choice, and choosing to take rental deductions precludes you from using the rollover.

One court decision,[23] however, held that both rental deductions and the rollover are available if you can demonstrate that you:

o  Actively continued to market the property during the rental period,

o  Charged fair market rent, and

o  Sold the old residence within two years after purchasing the new one.

The IRS has not formally reacted to this decision, but it is probable that it will continue to adhere to its prior position (disallowing either the rollover or rental deductions) outside the Ninth Federal Judicial Circuit where it is required to follow the decision (Alaska, Arizona, California, Nevada, Idaho, Montana, Oregon, Washington, Hawaii). Therefore, if you do not live in this area, prudence suggests that you should forego rental deductions during the rental period to ensure that the rollover is available.

## Planning for Fixing-up Expenses

You should plan in advance how you will fix up your property to help sell it. No deductions are allowed for such expenses, and they have no effect on the amount of gain. They merely reduce the amount you must reinvest to defer tax. Thus, if you plan to reinvest more than your adjusted sales price, the fixing-up expenses give you no tax benefit. Also, the ninety-day limitation means that if you don't enter into contract for sale within that period after you complete the work, the expenses are non-deductible personal repairs, and you have no tax benefits.

If you plan to reinvest the entire adjusted sales price, you should qualify the fix-up work as capital expenditures (see Chapter 8). This is because capital expenditures increase your basis for the home, thereby reducing the amount of your gain from its sale. It also reduces the gain from any future reinvestment home sale. Your increase in tax basis is permanent, and doesn't disappear within ninety days. This is important when you sell a replacement home without reinvesting the proceeds.

## Documentation for Your Home's Basis

As discussed above, the basis for your principal residence is usually not its cost. You must maintain adequate records to prove what the basis is. The tax law says that if you cannot prove your basis, it is zero. This could be a disaster if you sell your last home and don't reinvest. In such a case, if you can't prove its basis, the entire sales price is taxed as gain.

Your starting point for home basis documentation is the IRS Form 2119 for the year you bought the home. The form calculates the initial basis for the new home. Because capital expenditures increase your property's basis, you should keep, in a safe place, all receipts and cancelled checks for any work you do on the property while you own it. You don't need to distinguish between non-deductible repairs and capital expenditures at the time you do the work. Your tax advisor can make this distinction when you sell the home.

## Direct Exchanges of Principal Residences

The home-sale rollover is designed for a sale of a home

followed by reinvestment in a new home. This is usually how homeowners move from one home to another. However, the rollover also applies where you directly exchange your old home for a new one. There is no taxable gain if the value of the home you receive exceeds the value of the home you transfer. Gain from exchange of the old home is taxed if you receive any cash because the value of your old home exceeds that of the new home. In general, the basis of the old home becomes the basis of the new home received in the exchange. See Chapter 11 for a complete discussion of tax-deferred exchanges.

### How You Determine the Cost of a Reinvestment Cooperative Apartment

The cost of a cooperative apartment includes both your cash purchase price for the co-op stock, and your ratable share of the cooperative corporation's indebtedness on the property.[24]

**Example:** Whitley sells his old home for $120,000. Its basis is $80,000, and the gain realized is $40,000 ($120,000 less $80,000). He purchases a cooperative apartment for cash of $90,000, which represents 10% of the corporation's stock. The corporation has mortgage debts of $500,000 outstanding on the building. Whitley's share of the indebtedness is $50,000 (10% of $500,000). For purposes of the rollover, his reinvestment is $140,000 ($90,000 cash plus $50,000, his 10% share of the corporation's debts). He therefore qualifies for the rollover.

## EXCLUSION OF GAIN FROM SALE OF A PRINCIPAL RESIDENCE

As indicated in the previous discussion, the basis of your current residence is reduced by all gains from all prior homes where you used the tax-free rollover. Hence, the sale of your current home without reinvestment triggers taxation of all previous deferred gains. This is harsh for older home sellers who plan to rent a home, or to purchase a smaller and less expensive one.

Congress provided limited relief for a homeowner who meets certain qualifications. The provision permits qualifying homeowners over age 55 to exclude from income up to $125,000 of gain from sale of a principal residence.[25] As an exclusion, the provision ensures that the gain escapes taxation permanently. In this respect, it differs from the home-sale rollover which only defers gain until you sell a home without sufficient reinvestment.

Unlike the mandatory home-sale rollover, the over-55 exclusion is elective, and the election is available only once in your lifetime. Thus, if you elect the exclusion when your gain is less than $125,000, you lose the exclusion for the difference between the amount of your gain and $125,000.

### Requirements to Elect the Exclusion

To elect the exclusion, you must meet two requirements:

o Attain the age of 55 years before the date of sale. You are considered to be age 55 on the first moment of the day preceding your 55th birthday, and

o Own and use the property as your principal residence for periods aggregating three years or more during the five year period before sale.

The definition of *principal residence* is the same as that discussed above for the home-sale rollover.

### Three-Year Ownership and Use Requirements

You satisfy the three-year requirement if you show that you owned and used the property as your principal residence for 36 full months or for 1,095 days (3 x 365) during the five year period preceding its sale. Short, temporary absences such as those for vacations are counted as periods of use, even though you rent the home during such absences.

There is no requirement that you occupy the home as a principal residence at the time of sale, as long as the three-year period is otherwise satisfied.[26]

**Example:** Abramson has owned and used his house as his principal residence since 19X0. On January 1, 19X8, when he is over 55, he retires and moves to another state. He leases his house from then until September 30, 19X9, when he sells it. He may elect the exclusion since he owned and used the house as his principal residence for three of the five years preceding the sale.

**Example:** Assume the facts of the above example, except that during the three summers from 19X5 through 19X7, Abramson left the home for a two month vacation each year. Although, in the five year period preceding the sale, the total time spent away from his home on such vacations (6 months) plus the time spent away from the home from January 1, 19X8 to September 30, 19X9 (21 months) exceeds two years, he may make the election since the two-month vacations count as periods of use.

**Example:** Biles, a college professor, purchased and moved into a house on January 1, 19X1. He used the house as his principal residence continuously until February 1, 19X3, when he went abroad for a one-year sabbatical leave. During a portion of the period of leave the property was unoccupied and it was leased during the balance of the period. On March 1, 19X4, one month after returning from the leave, he sold the house. His leave is not considered a short temporary absence, so the period of such leave is not included to determine whether Biles used the house as his principal residence for periods aggregating three years during the five year period ending on the date of the sale. Thus, Biles may not elect the exclusion.[27]

There must be *both* three years of occupancy *and* three years of ownership during the five year period. Three years of occupancy without three years of ownership is insufficient.[28]

**Example:** Butts lived in a house owned by his son from 19X0 through 19X7. On January 1, 19X8, he purchases the house and on July 31, 19X9, he sells it. Although he used the property as his principal residence for more than three years, he did not own the home for a period aggregating three years during the five year period. Therefore, he may not elect the exclusion.

Ownership and occupancy need not be concurrent. During the five years before sale, periods of occupancy without ownership count for the occupancy test, and periods of ownership without occupancy count for the ownership test.[29]

**Example:** On January 1, 19X1, Gorman, who was 51 years old, moved into a rental apartment as his principal residence. The building was subsequently converted to a condominium, and on January 1, 19X3, he bought his apartment. In 19X4, he became seriously ill, and on February 2, 19X4, he moved to a convalescent home, and rented the apartment. On February 15, 19X6, while still at the home, he sells the apartment. Since Gorman occupied the apartment for three years (January 1, 19X1 to February 2, 19X4) and owned the apartment for three years (January 1, 19X3 to February 15, 19X6), he qualifies for the exclusion.

### Relationship of the Over-55 Exclusion to the Rollover

Suppose your gain from the sale of your home is more than $125,000, and you plan to reinvest in a smaller home. Can you defer the gain in excess of $125,000 by using the tax-free rollover? The answer is yes.

The effect of the exclusion is to reduce your normal rollover adjusted sales price by $125,000. The replacement period and other requirements of the rollover apply as if you had not elected the exclusion. The interplay between the exclusion and the rollover is illustrated as follows:[30]

**Example:** Holmberg, who meets the requirements for the exclusion, sells his home for $320,000. His basis is $75,000. He incurs qualifying fix-up expenses of $3,000. His gain from the sale is $245,000 ($320,000 less $75,000). Under the normal rollover rules, the reinvestment required to defer that gain (the adjusted sales price) is $317,000 (amount realized of $320,000 less fixing-up expenses of $3,000). Holmberg elects to exclude $125,000 of gain. If he doesn't reinvest, $120,000 of his gain is taxed (total gain of $245,000 less exclusion of $125,000). To defer this remaining $120,000, Holmberg must reinvest $192,000 (the original adjusted sales price of $317,000 less $125,000 excluded). If he reinvests less than this amount, all or part of the remaining $120,000 is taxed according to the normal rollover rules. For instance, suppose Holmberg only reinvests $140,000. His taxable gain and basis for the new home are calculated as follows:

| | |
|---|---:|
| Reinvestment required | $192,000 |
| Amount reinvested | 140,000 |
| Gain taxed - Under-reinvestment | $ 52,000 |

The basis of the new home is calculated under the rollover rules as follows:

| | |
|---|---:|
| Taxable gain after exclusion | $120,000 |
| Gain taxed - above | 52,000 |
| Untaxed gain | $ 68,000 |

| | |
|---|---|
| Cost of new home | $140,000 |
| Less: Untaxed gain | 68,000 |
| Basis of new home | $ 72,000 |

### How You Elect the Exclusion

You elect the exclusion by filing IRS Form 2119 with your tax return for the year of sale, or by filing the Form 2119 with an amended return during the period for making a claim for refund of tax due (see Chapter 2).[31] If you are married at the time of sale, your spouse at that time must join in the election (see Chapter 6 for more details). The Income Tax Regulations also provide rules for revoking the election.[32]

## TAX PLANNING IDEAS
## FOR THE OVER-55 EXCLUSION

### Exclusion Where Only Part of the
### Property is Used as a Home

Consistent with the rule for the home-sale rollover, only the gain applicable to the part of your home you use as a principal residence qualifies for the exclusion. Gain attributable to a part of the home you use for rental or business is taxed.[33]

However, if you use the entire home as a principal residence for a period aggregating three out of the five years before sale, you may exclude the entire gain even though a portion of the home was used for rental or business at some time during the five-year period.

**Example:** Ivison purchased his home on January 1, 19X1. During the period from January 1, 19X1, until January 1, 19X3, he used one-third of the home as an office. At that time, he converted the office back for personal use, and he used it as such until he sells the home on January 1, 19X6. Gain from the entire home qualifies for the exclusion because he used it as a principal residence for three years (January 1, 19X3 - January 1, 19X6). The gain also qualifies for the home-sale rollover because he uses the entire home as a principal residence at the time of sale.

**Example:** Assume the facts of the above example except that he used the entire home as a principal residence until January 1, 19X4, when he converted one-third into an office, and used it as such until January 1, 19X6, when he sells the home. The gain still qualifies for the exclusion, because the entire home was occupied as a principal residence for three years (January 1, 19X1 - January 1, 19X4). However, only the gain applicable to the residential portion of the home qualifies for the home-sale rollover unless the office is abandoned before its sale (see discussion above).

### Exclusion for Unmarried Co-owners

The exclusion is available if you own an undivided interest in your principal residence.[34] Thus, any co-owner (such as a joint tenant or a tenant in common) who qualifies may exclude his or her allocable share of the total gain.

> **Example:** Sadie and Sarah, sisters, ages 60 and 66 respectively, inherited their home from their father twenty years ago, and have occupied it as their principal residence since that time. They hold title as tenants in common. Their basis for the home is $40,000 ($20,000 each). They sell the home for $400,000 and move to a nursing home. The total gain is $360,000 ($180,000 each). Since each sister meets the age and residence requirements, each may exclude $125,000 (for a total exclusion of $250,000), and each must pay tax on only $55,000 ($180,000 less $125,000 excluded).

### Election When You Reinvest Less Than the Adjusted Sales Price

If you have taxable gain because you reinvest less than the adjusted sales price in a new home, you should consider the election, even though your gain is less than $125,000. Although this means that you must forgo exclusion of the difference between the gain you exclude and $125,000, the "bird-in-hand" approach may save you taxes in the long run. If you die while you own the replacement home, all gain will go untaxed anyway because of the step-up of basis at death (see Chapter 3).

### Election When the Amount of Reinvestment is Uncertain

When you don't intend to reinvest in another home, it is usually appropriate to elect the exclusion. When your reinvestment plans are uncertain, or are contingent upon a future event, you have the entire period under the statute of limitations to make (or revoke) the election. This gives you some time to decide what to do. This period is usually three years from the date you file the return for the year of sale or two years after you pay the tax for that year, whichever is later (see Chapter 2). Thus, you don't need to make the decision immediately at the time of sale.

### Election When You Reinvest the Entire Adjusted Sales Price

Normally, if you can roll over your gain by reinvesting the proceeds from sale, should not elect the exclusion. However, suppose you plan to live in the new home for a few years, and later convert it to a rental property, after which you plan to move to a rented home or to a nursing home. If these circumstances are probable, it might be wise to elect the exclusion, because the basis of the replacement home will not be reduced by the untaxed gains from all prior homes. This permits greater depreciation deductions when you rent the replacement home.

> **Example:** Kokus, who qualifies for the exclusion, sells his home for $150,000. His basis is $30,000, so the sale produces a realized gain of $120,000 ($150,000 less $30,000). He plans to reinvest $160,000 in a new home within two years. If he does not elect the exclusion, the basis for the new home under the rollover rules is $40,000 (cost of $160,000 less the untaxed gain of $120,000). However, if he elects to exclude the $120,000 gain, the basis of the new home is its cost, $160,000. If he later rents the new home, the basis for depreciation is $160,000 (less the portion allocable to the land).

This strategy also applies if you give the new home to a child or other donee. Here, the donee uses your basis for the home. Therefore, by electing the exclusion, you give the donee a higher basis than would be the case if you used the rollover, as demonstrated in the above example. See Chapter 3 for a discussion of the basis of gift property.

## FOOTNOTES

1. See generally Internal Revenue Code (IRC) §1034.

2. Reg. §1.1034-1(b)(4).

3. IRC §§1034(b)(1) and (2).

4. Rev. Rul. 77-371, 1977-2 CB 308.

5. Rev. Rul. 66-114, 1966-1 CB 181.

6. Reg. §1.1034-1(c)(3)(i).

7. Ltr. Rul. 8548027.

8. Rev. Rul. 75-438, 1975-2 CB 334; *James A. Henry*, ¶82,469 P-H MemoTC (1982).

9. IRC §1034(h)(1); Reg. §1.1034-1(g).

10. IRC §1034(h)(2).

11. IRC §1034(k).

12. IRC §§1034(d)(1) and (2).

13. Reg. §1.1034-1(d)(2).

14. IRC §1034(e).

15. These illustrations are adapted from the examples in Reg. §1.1034-1(c)(2).

16. IRC §1034(j); Reg. §1.1034-1(i)(1).

17. Reg. §1.1034-1(c)(3)(ii).

18. Rev. Rul. 82-26, 1982-1 CB 114.

19. *Ralph L. Trisko*, 29 TC 515 (1957); Rev. Rul. 59-72, 1959-1 CB 203.

20. *Arthur R. Barry*, ¶71,179 P-H MemoTC (1971).

21. Rev. Rul 78-146, 1978-1 CB 260.

22. For situations where it was held that the intention to return was not adequately established, see the following:

    *William C. Stolk*, 40 TC 345, aff'd 326 F2d 760 (CA 2, 1964).
    *Robert L. Young*, ¶85,127 P-H MemoTC (1985).
    *Rene A. Stiegler*, ¶64,057 P-H MemoTC (1964).
    *Richard T. Houlette*, 48 TC 350.
    *Armand F. Roberge*, ¶66,001 P-H MemoTC, aff'd 377 F2d 558 (CA 9, 1967).
    *Ann K. Demeter*, ¶71,209 P-H MemoTC (1971).
    *Rudolph M. Stucchi*, ¶76,242 P-H MemoTC (1976).
    *R. Joe Rogers*, ¶82,718 P-H MemoTC (1982).

23. *Bolaris*, 81 TC 840 (1983), rev'd 776 F2d 1428 (CA 9, 1985).

24. Rev. Rul. 60-76, 1960-1 CB 296.

25. See generally IRC §121.

26. Reg. §1.121-1(c).

27. Reg. §1.121-1(d), Examples 1,5, and 4.

28. Reg. §1.121-1(d), Example 3.

29. Rev. Rul. 80-172, 1980-2 CB 56.

30. Reg. §1.121-5(g).

31. Reg. §1.121-4.

32. Reg. §1.121-4(c).

33. Reg. §1-121-5(e).

34. Rev. Rul. 67-234, 1967-2 CB 78; Rev. Rul. 67-235, 1967-2 CB 79.

# Chapter

# SIX

## BUYING AND SELLING A HOME: HUSBANDS, WIVES, MARRIAGES, AND DIVORCES

Married people usually give little thought to how they should hold title to their home. They may not even be aware that there are alternatives, or that different alternatives can have significant legal and tax consequences.

For personal reasons, you may feel that the title should be held jointly rather than by only one of you. Generally, the joint ownership provides for survivorship, so that when you die, your interest automatically passes to your surviving spouse. This allows you to avoid probate. You can get this important non-tax feature by titling the home as joint tenants, as tenants by the entireties, or (in the nine states where applicable) as community property. Occasionally, married people hold title as tenants in common. Here, you have no survivorship. When you die, your interest passes through your estate to your heirs rather than directly to your surviving spouse. See Chapter 3 for a complete discussion of the legal aspects of taking title to property.

Your form of ownership makes little difference for income tax purposes as long as you and your spouse file joint returns. Deductions for mortgage interest and real estate taxes apply the same way for homes owned by only one spouse and for homes owned jointly. Similarly, the home-sale rollover and over-55 exclusion are not affected. The form of ownership, however, may affect your estate and gift tax consequences.

When your marriage ends by divorce or by the death of your spouse, or when you sell an old home before marriage, the form of ownership has income tax consequences. In these situations, both the home-sale rollover and the over-55 exclusion are affected by whether you hold title to the home jointly.

## TRANSFERS BETWEEN HUSBANDS, WIVES, EX-HUSBANDS AND EX-WIVES

### Transfers Between Husband and Wife During Marriage

A special tax rule applies when you transfer any property, including your principal residence, to your spouse. It also applies if you transfer property to your ex-spouse pursuant to a divorce.[1] The divorce aspect is discussed below. The rule includes all transfers between husbands and wives, regardless of the type of transaction. Thus, it applies equally for gifts, sales, and exchanges.

The rule specifies that no gain or loss is taxed for transfers between husbands and wives. The basis of the spouse receiving the property is the same as the basis of the spouse transferring it. The *carryover* basis applies regardless of whether the fair market value is more or less than the donor's basis at the time of the transfer. Thus, this inter-spousal transfer rule differs from the usual gift basis rule. See Chapter 3 for a complete discussion of basis. The non-recognition of gain, coupled with a carryover basis for the property results in tax deferral.

> **Example:** George and Sylvia are married and file a joint return. George is the sole owner of their home with a fair market value of $60,000 and an adjusted basis of $46,000. George gives a one-half interest in the home to Sylvia. No gain is taxed for George, and Sylvia's basis for her new interest is $23,000 (one-half of $46,000).

> **Example:** Assume in the above example that Sylvia, from her separate funds, purchased her one-half interest for its full market value of $30,000. There is no gain taxed to George, and Sylvia's basis is $23,000.

### Transfer to a Spouse or Former Spouse in a Separation or Divorce

What if the terms of your divorce or separation agreement require that you transfer your interest in the home to your ex-spouse? This is common if your ex-spouse has custody of your children.

The deferral rule for transfers between spouses during marriage also applies for transfers related to a divorce if:

o The transfer is required in a divorce or separation agreement, *and* it occurs not more than six years after the date when the marriage ceases, or

o The transfer is within one year after the date when the marriage ceases, whether or not the transfer was connected with the divorce.

**Example:** Jack and Jill own their home as tenants by the entirety. Its fair market value is $90,000 ($45,000 for each one-half interest). The adjusted basis is $20,000 ($10,000 for each one-half interest). As required by their divorce decree, Jack transfers his one-half interest to Jill. Jack's $35,000 gain ($45,000 less $10,000) is not taxed, and Jill's basis for the one-half interest she receives is $10,000.

**Example:** Assume in the above example, that the transfer was required by the divorce decree, but that it is not to take place until Jack and Jill's daughter reaches age 21 ten years from the date of the divorce. Since the transfer will occur more than six years after the divorce, Jack is taxed on his gain (calculated by using the fair market value of the property at the time of transfer ten years later). Jill's basis for the one-half interest she receives is its fair market value when she receives it.

The rule also applies if one spouse purchases the other spouse's interest for its full market value. This scenario is becoming more common, particularly where both spouses have substantial income. As in a gratuitous transfer discussed in the above example, the selling spouse has no gain, and the selling spouse's basis becomes the basis of for the purchasing spouse. This causes a tax problem for the purchasing spouse. Even though he or she pays full value for the other spouse's interest, the basis for the interest is the basis of the selling spouse. This means that upon sale, the purchasing spouse pays tax on the selling spouse's gain.

**Example:** Assume in the above example that the divorce decree requires Jill to pay Jack $45,000, the fair market value, for his interest. Jack is not taxed on the sale, and Jill's basis for his interest is $10,000. If she sells the property for $90,000, her gain is $70,000 ($10,000 less the combined basis of $20,000). This amount represents the gain on her original one-half of the property plus Jack's gain on the half that she purchased.

## MARRIAGE, DIVORCE, AND THE HOME-SALE ROLLOVER

If you have a gain when you sell your home, tax on the gain is deferred if you reinvest an amount at least equal to the old home's *adjusted sales price* in a new home within the applicable reinvestment period. In most cases, this reinvestment period begins two years before the old home's sale, and ends two years after its sale (See Chapter 5). The rules become more complex, however, if you get married or divorced before, during, or after either the sale or reinvestment transactions.

### Taking Title to a New Home During Marriage

If you and your spouse both occupy the old and new homes as your principal residences, you may take title to the new home differently from that of the old, as long as:

o You take title to both the old and the new homes in the names of one or both of you, and

o You and your spouse both consent to have the basis of the new home reduced by the deferred gain from sale of your old home.[2]

**Example:** Dick sells the principal residence of himself and his wife, Jane, for $80,000. Dick owns the home in his name only, and his adjusted basis is $45,000. Within the reinvestment period, he and Jane each contribute $40,000 from their separate funds to buy their new home. They take title to the new home as tenants in common, each owning an undivided one-half interest. If Dick and Jane file the required consent, he won't pay tax on the gain of $35,000. Dick and Jane's total basis for the new home is $45,000 (its cost of $80,000 less the old home's untaxed gain of $35,000). Dick's adjusted

> **basis for his one-half interest is one-half of that amount, or $22,500. Jane's basis for her one-half interest is also $22,500.**
>
> **Example:** Dick and his wife, Jane, sell their home for $80,000. They own the home as joint tenants, and their total adjusted basis is $45,000 ($22,500 each). Within the reinvestment period Jane spends $80,000 of her funds to purchase a new home for herself and Dick, and she takes title in her name only. If Dick and Jane file the required consent, Jane's adjusted basis for the new home is $45,000 (its cost of $80,000 less the old home's untaxed gain of $35,000), and Dick's gain of $17,500 (one-half of the total $35,000 gain) is deferred. Jane's half of the gain is also deferred.

You make the required consent on IRS Form 2119 filed with your income tax return for the year you sell or reinvest. The instructions to Form 2119 indicate that you do this by writing the following statement in the margin at the bottom of the form: "We consent to reduce the basis of the new residence by the gain from selling the old residence." You and your spouse must each separately sign this consent.

### Sale of Separate Homes Before Marriage

What happens if you and your spouse-to-be sell your separate homes before your marriage, and use the proceeds of both sales to buy your new home? The good news is that you can roll over the gains of both homes, if, within the reinvestment period:

o You buy a new home costing at least as much as the combined adjusted sales prices of both your old homes,

o You each contribute an amount more than the adjusted sales price of your respective old homes, and

o You take title to the new home jointly.[3]

> **Example:** Ricky, before his marriage to Lucy, owns his principal residence. Lucy also owns her principal residence. Ricky and Lucy are married in January 19X6, and in March they purchase a new home for $90,000, and use it as their principal residence. Ricky and Lucy each contribute one-half of the purchase price of the new home ($45,000) and they take title as tenants by the entireties. Ricky completes the sale of his former home in March, 19X6 for an adjusted sales price of $40,500. Lucy

sells her former home in April, 19X6, for an adjusted sales price of $40,000. Each has gains from the sales of their former homes. Since each reinvests an amount more than the adjusted sales price of their respective old homes during the applicable reinvestment period, neither is taxed on the gains.

### Sale of a Home As Part of a Divorce Settlement

If your divorce or separation agreement requires that you sell your home, your tax consequences can become complex. Tax results depend, among other things, upon:

o  The marriage and divorce law of your home state,

o  The terms of your property settlement, separation agreement and/or divorce decree, and

o  The period between the sale of your old home and your divorce decree.

**Where Sale Proceeds are Split According to the Share of Ownership.** If you split the home's sale proceeds with your ex-spouse in proportion to your ownership interests, and each of you buy and occupy a separate replacement home, the rollover applies separately to each of your gains.[4]

Example: Jim and Marylou purchased their first home in 19X0 for $50,000 and held title as tenants by the entireties. On July 1, 19X6, they agree to live apart, and execute a contract to sell the home for $110,000. They continue to occupy the home until the closing on September 1, 19X6. Each realizes a $30,000 gain from the sale of the home (one-half to total gain of $60,000). During the period between the execution of the sales contract and the closing of the sale of their home, Jim and Marylou individually execute purchase contracts for separate new homes. The cost of each new home exceeds $55,000, their respective shares of the adjusted sales price of the old home (one-half of the total adjusted sales price of $110,000). The purchases are closed and the new homes are occupied as separate principal residences by Jim and Marylou before the end of 19X6. The rollover applies separately to defer the gains realized by both spouses.

What if you and your spouse decide to separate or divorce after having sold your home, and one of you doesn't reinvest your share of the adjusted sale price?

> **Example:** Murry and Fran file a joint return without reporting the gain from the sale of their jointly-owned home because they expect to purchase a new home within the reinvestment period. The next year they decide to split up, and are divorced. Murry purchases a new home for himself within the reinvestment period, in an amount sufficient to defer his half of the gain. Fran however, does not purchase a new home. Her half of the gain is taxed.

As discussed in Chapter 5, if you don't reinvest enough to defer tax on your home-sale gain, you must file an amended return for the year when you sell the old home. What if your spouse refuses to sign an amended joint return? In this situation, you must file an amended joint return, using the tax rates for the year of the old home's sale, and pay the tax on your half of the gain. You should attach a letter to the amended return explaining why your spouse's signature cannot be obtained.[5]

**Where Sale Proceeds are Split Differently From the Share of Ownership.** What happens in the above example if your home's sale is required by your divorce settlement and you must pay the proceeds from your half to your ex-spouse? This is called a *transfer on behalf of a spouse* and is treated as two separate transactions:[6]

o A transfer of your one-half interest in the home to your ex-spouse, followed by

o A sale by your ex-spouse of the entire home to the third party.

Your ex-spouse gets your basis for the one-half deemed to have been transferred by you. Therefore, in the example above the entire $60,000 gain from the home's sale belongs to Marylou. The gain may be postponed under the home-sale rollover she reinvests the old home's adjusted sale price of $110,000 in a new principal residence. As an alternative, if she qualifies, she may exclude the gain under the over-55 exclusion. See the discussion below of the effects of marriage and divorce on the exclusion election. Since you are deemed to have disposed of your interest before the sale, you cannot use the home-sale rollover or the over-55 exclusion.

This treatment applies in any situation where you sell your home pursuant to a divorce settlement and you split the proceeds with your ex-spouse in a ratio different from your respective shares of ownership in the home. The treatment also applies in two other situations that don't involve divorces:

o Where you transfer the home to a third party pursuant to the written request of your spouse (or ex-spouse), or

o Where you receive from your spouse (or ex-spouse) a written consent or ratification of your transfer to the third party stating that you both intend the transfer to be treated in this manner.

## MARRIAGE, DIVORCE AND THE OVER-55 EXCLUSION

Generally, to elect the $125,000 exclusion, you must be over 55 years old, and have occupied your home as a principal residence for three of the five years before the sale (see Chapter 5). However, for marital changes such as divorces, separations or remarriages, surprising results may occur if you don't carefully plan the timing of your sale.

### Election of the Exclusion Where Only One Spouse Qualifies

What happens if you qualify as to age and occupancy, but your spouse does not? In this situation, you are both treated as satisfying the requirements if:[7]

o You own the home as joint owners, and

o You file a joint income tax return for the year of sale.

**Example:** Neal and Barbara sell their jointly owned home that they have owned and used as a principal residence for seven years. At the time of sale, Neal is age 60, and Barbara is age 45. Both spouses qualify under the occupancy test, but Barbara does not pass the age test. However, if Neal and Barbara file a joint return, Barbara is considered to have passed the age test.

One spouse must meet *all* the requirements. Thus, if you meet the age test but not the occupancy test, and your spouse meets the occupancy test but not the age test, you can't use the exclusion.[8]

**Example:** Fernande, age 50, has owned and occupied her home for the past ten years. This year she marries Rudy, age 60, who, after the marriage, lives with her in her home for six months, after which they sell the home and move to an apartment. The exclusion is not available since neither spouse meets *both* the age and occupancy requirements.

It is important to note that the non-qualifying spouse who joins in the election is a "tainted spouse," and disqualifies any subsequent spouse from making an election (as discussed below).

### Election for Property of a Deceased Spouse

If you otherwise don't qualify for the exclusion, you are treated as satisfying the age and/or occupancy tests if:[9]

o  Your spouse is deceased at the date you sell the home, and

o  Your deceased spouse had satisfied the age and occupancy requirements during the five-year period before your sale of the home.

o  You are unmarried when you sell the home.

**Example:** Warren and Louisa are married on January 1, 19X4. They move into a home which Warren has owned and occupied since January 1, 19X0. Warren dies on January 1, 19X6, when he is 70. Louisa inherits the property and continues to live there. She sells the home on August 31, 19X6, when she is 62 and unmarried. Even though she does not satisfy the occupancy test (having lived in the home for only two years and eight months), she may elect the exclusion because Warren had satisfied all the requirements.

### The "Tainted Spouse" Trap

Suppose you qualify for the exclusion, but you marry someone who has elected to exclude gain on another home before your marriage. Your "tainted spouse" disqualifies you from making the election.[10]

> **Example**: While Charlie and Doris are married, Charlie sells his separately owned home and elects to exclude the gain. Doris joins in the election as required. Subsequently, Charlie and Doris are divorced and Doris marries Vernon. While Doris and Vernon are married, Vernon, who qualifies under the age and occupancy tests, sells his home. Vernon is not entitled to elect to exclude the gain, since his wife, Doris, had made an election. It does not matter that Doris didn't have any personal benefit from her former husband's election.

> **Example**: Assume the facts of the above example, except that after Vernon sells his home, Charlie and Doris revoke their election within the required period (see Chapter 5). Doris and Vernon may then elect to exclude gain from the sale of Vernon's home.

> **Example**: Assume the facts of the first example except that Vernon marries Doris after he sells his home, but before he elects to exclude the gain. Vernon, if he has never made a prior election, may elect with respect to this sale since Doris is not required to join with him in the election.

### Sale of Separate Residences Owned Before Marriage

**Where Spouses Do Not Buy a New Home After Marriage**. If you and your spouse own homes before your marriage, and you each qualify for the exclusion, you each may separately elect to exclude the gain from your respective homes if you sell the homes before your marriage.[11]

> **Example**: Gordon, age 58, and Katherine, age 56, each own homes that they have occupied for ten years. They decide to sell their old homes, and after their marriage to move into a rented apartment. If they sell their homes before their marriage, each may elect to exclude up to $125,000 of gain.

If, however, you sell your old homes after you are married, you can elect to exclude gain for only one of the homes, even if the two homes are sold as part of a single transaction.

> **Example**: Assume the facts of the above example except that Gordon and Katherine get married, move into the apartment, and then sell their old homes.

> In this case they can elect to exclude the gain from only one of the homes.

If you sell one of the homes before your marriage, and the other after, the spouse who makes an election before the marriage is "tainted," and precludes the other spouse from excluding the gain from the home sold after the marriage.

> **Example:** Assume the facts of the above example except that Katherine sells her home before the marriage and elects to exclude her gain. After they are married, Gordon sells his home. Since Katherine has made an election, her *"taint"* precludes Gordon from excluding gain from sale of his home.

**Where Spouses Reinvest in a New Home After Marriage**. Suppose you and your spouse owned homes before marriage, and plan to sell both old homes and reinvest the proceeds in a new home. If the new home costs as much as the combined sales prices of your old homes, you can defer both gains under the home-sale rollover as discussed above. What, however, if you don't reinvest enough in a new home to defer the entire gain. The Internal Revenue Service issued a private ruling permitting one spouse to use the rollover to defer her gain and the other spouse to elect the over-55 exclusion for his gain.[12] Although the IRS is not bound to follow private rulings in subsequent cases, this approach seems to make sense in view of the legislative purposes for the two provisions.

> **Example:** Macy, age 58, owns a home he has occupied for ten years, and sells for $80,000 immediately before marrying Marjorie. Marjorie, age 40, sells her home for $95,000 six months before marrying Macy. Three months after they are married, they purchase a new home for $100,000, and occupy it as their principal residence. If Macy and Marjorie were required to reinvest their aggregate adjusted sales prices of $175,000 ($80,000 + $95,000), they would not qualify for deferral of their respective home-sale gains. However, the ruling allows Macy to exclude his gain under the over-55 exclusion, and Marjorie to defer her gain under the home-sale rollover, as long as they reinvest at least the amount of the adjusted sales price of *her* old home ($95,000).

**Exclusion Where Husband and Wife
File Separate Returns**

Consistent with other provisions dealing with the filing of separate returns by married taxpayers, the maximum amount that you may exclude if you file a separate return is $62,500, or one-half of the maximum amount allowed on a joint return.

## Determination of Marital Status

For purposes of the over-55 exclusion, your marital status is determined as of the date of the sale (closing) of the home. An individual who is legally separated from his spouse under a decree of divorce or a decree of separate maintenance is not considered as being married.[13]

## FOOTNOTES

1. IRC §1041; Temp. Reg. §1.1041-IT.

2. IRC §1034(g); Reg. §1.1034-1(f) Examples 1 & 2.

3. Rev. Rul. 75-238, 1975-1 CB 257.

4. Rev. Rul. 74-250, 1974-1 CB 202.

5. Rev. Rul. 80-5, 1980-1 CB 284.

6. Temp. Reg. §1.1041-IT (c).

7. IRC §121(d)(1); Reg. §1.121-5(a).

8. Ltr. Rul. 8352023.

9. IRC §121(d)(2); Reg. §1.121-5(b).

10. Reg. §1.121-2(b)(2).

11. Reg. §1.121-2(b)(1)(ii).

12. Ltr. Rul. 8302032.

13. IRC §121(d)(6).

# TAX BREAKS FOR
# RESIDENTIAL RENTAL PROPERTY

## CHAPTER 7

*Limitations on Tax Benefits for Rental Property*

## CHAPTER 8

*Tax Deductions for Rental Property*

## CHAPTER 9

*The Alternative Minimum Tax for Individual Taxpayers*

*part*

*3*

# Chapter
# SEVEN

## LIMITATIONS ON TAX BENEFITS FOR RENTAL PROPERTY

The Tax Reform Act of 1986 (1986 TRA) revolutionized tax planning for rental real estate. Generally, it retained tax benefits for homeowners (see Chapter 4). However, it severely curtailed tax benefits for investment property.

A primary thrust of the attack was to curtail traditional tax shelter syndicates. These are investment vehicles, usually organized as limited partnerships, that are designed to generate tax losses to offset income such as compensation, interest, and dividends. Often these losses are caused by non-cash deductions such as depreciation. This can put your investment into the best of all possible worlds: non-cash tax losses combined with positive cash flow. The positive cash flow is enhanced by tax savings (see Chapter 1). Thus, though an investment isn't economically viable on its merits, Uncle Sam might foot the bill for its negative cash flow by giving you extra tax savings.

Uncle Sam decided that he no longer wanted to subsidize economically questionable projects. However, his attack on tax shelter syndicates is an example of legislative overkill. The restrictions spill over to affect many rental property owners who never had anything to do with traditional tax shelter syndicates, and whose investments make economic sense apart from tax benefits.

The 1986 TRA used the back-door for its anti-tax shelter attack. Except for the depreciation deduction, it did little to redefine the scope of deductions for rental property. Instead, it created a maze of limitations and restrictions on how you may use the deductions. This approach reflects opposing Congressional forces at work as the 1986 TRA developed. The strong support for eliminating many tax "loopholes" was opposed by equally strong support for retaining them. The solution was to retain the tax benefits, but to restrict how you may use them.

The centerpiece of the anti-tax shelter legislation is the limitation on how you may use losses generated from *passive activities*. In addition, the *at-risk* limitation, formerly applicable only for personal property investments, was, under some circumstances, extended to real estate activities. Also, you must continue to cope with the old rules that limit losses from rental of vacation homes, and losses from the operation of businesses classified as hobbies.

When there are alternative ways to handle a deduction (such as depreciation), your choice may hinge on whether one of the overall limitations precludes you from using the deduction currently. This chapter discusses the loss limitations as a background for tax planning for deductions. Chapter 8 explores the specific deduction rules for repairs, insurance, supplies, casualty losses, and depreciation.

## LIMITATION ON DEDUCTION OF LOSSES FROM PASSIVE ACTIVITIES

The purpose of the passive loss limitation is to prevent you from using losses (and tax credits) from one type of activity to reduce income from another type of activity. You must divide your income and expenses into separate compartments that are classified according to the nature of the activity. You may deduct expenses only from income in the same compartment, and may not use them to reduce income from another compartment. The law specifies three different compartments or types of activities: *active*, *portfolio*, and *passive*.

The limitation does not completely disallow deduction of excess expenses for a given compartment. It merely postpones the time you may take the deductions. The idea behind the limitation is that the income and expenses of a single year do not reflect the true economic result of an activity. Therefore, if expenses exceed income in a given year, the deduction allowed for the excess loss is postponed until you dispose of the activity and recognize all possible income (both current income such as rents, as well as gain from disposition). At that point, you can determine the overall economic outcome of the activity, and you are permitted to deduct all postponed losses relating to the activity.[1]

The postponed deductions are not limited to losses resulting from non-cash expenses such as depreciation. You also may be required to postpone losses created by out-of-pocket cash expenses. In this respect the passive loss limitation differs from the *at-risk* and investment interest limitations, both of which permit you to deduct cash losses.

The limitation also applies for tax credits produced by passive activities. This has little impact on small-unit residential investors, however, because the only remaining tax credits for residential property are those for low-income housing and for rehabilitation of historic structures. As a practical matter, both credits are more likely to be used by investment syndicates than by residential investors, so they are not discussed in this book. The complex passive loss rules for tax credits are also omitted. The passive loss limitation applies for the Alternative Minimum Tax (AMT) which is discussed in Chapter 9.

### Who is Subject to the Passive Activity Rules?

The rules apply for individuals, estates, and trusts. Passive losses of general partnerships and S Corporations are allocated to their partners or shareholders, and applied at the owner level. Special rules apply for closely-held corporations (other than S Corporations), and for personal service corporations. The characteristics of these corporations are specifically defined in the law.[2] Because the rules for entities other than individual taxpayers are complex, and do not generally affect small-unit residential investors, this discussion is limited to the application of the passive loss rules to individual taxpayers.

### What is Active Income?

Active income is compensation for performing services or income from a business where you materially participate in the management. Compensation includes salaries, wages, commissions, bonuses, and other benefits derived from employment.

Business income includes only income from your activities as a sole proprietor, general partner, or shareholder of an S Corporation where you materially participate in the business activity. Business income of other corporations (even if you are the only shareholder) is not active income at the shareholder level. The nature of income distributed by a corporation depends upon how it is distributed. If you receive it as compensation for services, it is active income. If it is distributed as a dividend, it is portfolio income (see below). If the corporation pays you rent for property you own individually, it is passive income (see below).

Two activities are specifically defined as active, and losses resulting from them are not subject to the passive loss limitation. The first is the construction and operation of certain low-income housing projects placed into service or under binding contract before August 17, 1986.[3] The second is ownership of certain oil and gas working interests.[4]

### What is Portfolio Income?

Portfolio income is derived from investment securities such as stocks, bonds, and other interest-producing investments such as money market funds and certificates of deposit. It includes dividends, interest, REIT dividends, annuities, and royalties (other than those received in the ordinary course of business). It also includes net gains from the sale of portfolio investments.[5] Unimproved real estate, such as a residential lot, is also a portfolio investment.

Portfolio income that is *directly connected* to another activity is characterized by the nature of that activity. Thus, just because income is from dividends, interest, annuities, etc., it isn't automatically classified as portfolio income. You must look at its relationship to the other activity. For instance, interest produced as a direct result of an active business is active income.[6]

> **Example:** Hayes is a real estate developer who builds tract housing projects. His usual business practice is to finance the sale of new homes by carrying back a loan until the buyer can obtain institutional financing. The interest on these loans is *directly connected* with his business, and is active income.

Similarly, temporary investments of the excess working capital of a business are not *directly connected* with the business, and therefore they produce portfolio income.[7]

> **Example**: Seyah owns a real estate brokerage office. During April, an unusual number of closings generate $120,000 cash that she doesn't need for immediate business operations. However, she plans to use the funds in the following year to expand the business. Meanwhile, she invests the funds in stocks and bonds. The investments are not *directly connected* to the business, so income from the investments is portfolio income.

### What is Passive Income or Loss?

Passive income or loss results from ownership of a passive activity. The law defines passive activities as:

o Any business activity where you do not *materially participate* in the management.[8]

o Any rental activity regardless of whether you *materially participate*.[9]

### Business Activities Where You Don't "Materially Participate"

The passive loss rules are designed to prevent you from reaping tax benefits from businesses (as distinguished from rental activities) that produce losses. Any trade or business where you do not materially participate is a passive activity. Material participation requires that you are regularly, continuously, and substantially involved in the operations of the activity. The law does not elaborate on exactly what is *regular, continuous,* or *substantial.*[10] However, the Internal Revenue Service (IRS) has issued extensive temporary Regulations setting forth further guidelines to determine whether you *materially participate* in a business.[11] These guidelines are based on your current and prior participation in the business. Participation includes any work you do in an activity that you own. It does not include work that is not customarily done by owners if one of the principal purposes of the work is to avoid the disallowance of passive losses. Also excluded is work done in your capacity as an investor (such as reviewing financial statements in a nonmanager capacity). Participation by your spouse counts as work done by you.

**Tests Based on Current Participation.** These quantitative tests measure the number of hours you participate in the business during the year. You are considered a material participant if you satisfy any one of the tests. Specifically, your participation in the activity must:

o Be more than 500 hours during the year,

o Constitute substantially all of the participation in the activity of all individuals (including non-owner employees) during the year,

o Be for more than 100 hours during the year, and not less than the participation of any other individual (including non-owner employees) for the year, or

o Be a *significant* activity, and your aggregate participation in all significant activities during the year must exceed 500 hours. A significant activity is one where your participation exceeds 100 hours during the year.

**Tests Based on Prior Participation.** Under these tests, a person who no longer participates in the business may continue to be classified as a material participant. These tests are based on the presumption that if you have materially participated in an activity for a long period, it probably is your principal livelihood, rather than a passive investment. Thus, you are classified as a material participant if:

o You materially participated in the activity for any five taxable years during the ten preceding taxable years, *or*

o The activity is a personal service activity and you materially participated in the activity for any three preceding taxable years.

The Temporary Regulations contain examples of how these quantitative tests are applied. In addition, there is a catchall test providing that you materially participate if, based on all the facts and circumstances, you participate in the activity on a regular, continuous and substantial basis during the taxable year. The Temporary Regulations do not elaborate on this test, but the IRS plans to issue further guidelines in the future. Meanwhile, you should rely on the quantitative tests described above.

Under these tests, an activity can be active for one investor, and passive for another, depending upon the degree of involvement of each in the activity.

> **Example**: Valjean's daughter wants to open a restaurant, but doesn't have the cash to make the necessary investment. Valjean agrees to provide the money and become an equal general partner in the venture. He doesn't have any managerial role, and never visits the restaurant because he doesn't like the food it serves. His daughter has full responsibility for operating the venture. This is a passive activity for Valjean because he doesn't materially participate. On the other hand, any income or loss allocated to the daughter is *active*.

Generally if you are a limited partner, you are not a material participant unless you participate for more than 500 hours per year, or qualify under one of the past participation rules. However, a general partner may qualify under any one of the tests. If you own both general and limited partnership interests in the same activity, you are treated as a general partner.[12]

## What is a Rental Activity?

All rental activities are passive regardless of whether you materially participate in managing the property. Under the tax law, there is no longer any such thing as a *business* of renting property. However, there is a limited exception permitting certain small investors to deduct up to $25,000 of losses from nonpassive income (discussed below). Passive rental activities include rental of any type of real estate or personal property. It does not matter whether real estate is residential or commercial. There is a very limited exception for real estate where you provide *significant services* in connection with the rental, and the lease term is short when compared to the useful life of the property. The Temporary Regulations provide six exceptions to general definition of rental activity based upon the concept of *significant services*.[13] If you materially participate in such an activity, income or loss from the activity is active. Otherwise the income or loss is passive.

**Average Rental Period for Customer is Seven Days or Less**. This rule is based on the presumption that if you rent property for seven days or less, you generally are required to provide *significant services*. This classifies it as a service business rather than a rental business. Examples are short-term rentals of hotel rooms.

**Average Rental Period for Customer is 30 Days or Less, and You Provide Significant Personal Services.** Here the presumption that you provide significant services is not automatic. You must prove that you provided such services in connection with the rental of the property. The services must be provided by individuals, and the following services do not qualify:

o Telephone and cable television services,

o Services necessary to permit the lawful use of the property,

o Services in connection with repairs lasting longer than the average customer rental period,

o Services in connection with capital improvements,

o Services similar to those commonly provided in connection with long-term rentals of high-grade commercial or residential property (e.g., trash collection, elevator service, and security).

**You Provide Extraordinary Services Without Regard to the Average Period of Customer Use.** This is where the use of the property is incidental to the performance of services. Examples are the use of a hospital bed incidental to medical care, or the use of a dormitory incidental to academic services received.

**Rental is Incidental to a Nonrental Activity.** The Temporary Regulations provide that the following activities are not passive activities:

o Property held primarily for investment, where the gross rental income is less than 2% of the lesser of (1) the property's unadjusted basis or (2) the fair market value of the property,

o Property is used in a trade or business,

o Property held for sale to customers (dealer property),

o Lodging rented to employees for the convenience of the employer, o Property rented by a partner to a partnership for use in the partnership's business.

**Property Made Available Only During Defined Business Hours for Nonexclusive Use by Various Customers.** Examples are owner-operated golf courses or commercial parking lots.

**Property Provided for Use in an Activity Conducted by a Partnership, S Corporation, or Joint Venture in Which You Own an Interest.**

### What is a Passive Activity?

The passive loss rules substantially increase your accounting burden. If you have more than one passive activity, you must account for each activity separately. This requires identification of each separate passive activity.

Identifying the separate activities is important for several reasons. First, you must offset the income from each activity by the deductions relating to the same activity before you may use losses from other activities. Second, if the activity has suspended losses, you must account for them separately so that you may deduct them when you dispose of the activity (see below).

The IRS has issued extensive Temporary Regulations providing guidance for identifying an activity.[14] These Regulations include many examples of how to apply the guidelines. These examples should be consulted if you are involved in large business or investment operations. For small-scale residential real estate investments, however, the rules are relatively straightforward and flexible. Therefore, only a brief explanation of the structure of the rules is included here.

The first step is to identify each of your *undertakings*. An undertaking is the smallest unit that can be an activity. An undertaking may be a single rental house or may include widespread and diverse business and rental operations. The most important factors for identifying an undertaking are *location* and *ownership*. Generally, business or rental operations that you own at the same location are considered a single undertaking. Similarly, your business or rental operations at separate locations are separate undertakings.

If you have both business *and* rental operations at the same location, the rental and business operations are treated as separate undertakings. The rental operations are passive, and the business operations are active only if you materially participate.

**Example:** Gibbons owns a building where she rents apartments and operates a restaurant. 60% of her income comes from the apartments and 40% from the restaurant. The rented apartments and the restaurant operation are treated as two separate activities. The apartment undertaking is a passive activity. The classification of the restaurant undertaking depends on whether Gibbons is a material participant.

A special exception treats rental and nonrental activities as a single undertaking if either is a predominant part of the undertaking. This exception applies if less than 20% of the gross income from an undertaking is attributable to either activity.

**Example:** Assume in the above example that 85% of Gibbons' gross income is from the apartment rentals and 15% is from the restaurant. Because less than 20% of the gross income is from the nonrental operation, the rental operation and restaurant operation are considered a single activity. Since the entire operation is classified as a rental undertaking, it is a passive activity.

If you have rental activities at different locations, the rules are more flexible. You are permitted to treat the real estate activities at different locations as separate undertakings, or to aggregate them in any manner you desire as separate undertakings. Generally, you should fragmentize your rental activities into as many separate undertakings as possible. This is because the sale of an undertaking triggers the deduction of suspended passive losses relating to that undertaking from nonpassive income (see below). Thus, if you have seven rental houses in the same town, you should treat them as seven separate undertakings.

### How to Apply the Passive Activity Loss Limits

After you determine which of your activities are passive, you calculate the net gain or loss from each. You then offset the net gains and losses from the passive activities against each other. If the result is a net gain, you are not subject to the passive loss limits. If the result is a loss, the loss is suspended as described below (subject to the small investor exception).[15]

**Example:** Javert acquires and places into service four rental houses on January 1, 19X1. Each house is a separate passive activity. The operating results for the houses for 19X1 are as follows:

|  | House A | House B | House C | House D | Total |
|---|---|---|---|---|---|
| Income | $11000 | $ 1000 | $4000 | $ 7000 | $23000 |
| Deductions | ( 6000) | (10000) | (1000) | ( 8000) | (25000) |
| Income (loss) | $ 5000 | $(9000) | $3000 | $(1000) | $(2000) |

Assuming the $25,000 rental real estate exception is not applicable, the disallowed passive loss to be suspended and carried forward is $2,000. You allocate the net suspended loss only among those activities that produce losses. You do not allocate any loss to the activities that produce income. You allocate the total loss in the ratio that each loss activity contributes to the total losses.[16]

**Example:** In the above example, Houses B and D generated total losses of $10,000. The $2,000 net loss is allocated to these two houses in the ratio of each of their losses to the total as follows:

| House B (9/10 x $2,000) | $1,800 |
|---|---|
| House D (1/10 x $2,000) | 200 |
| Loss carried forward | $2,000 |

You carry forward the suspended losses indefinitely. However, you cannot carry the losses back to offset passive income from prior years. In the following year, you add the suspended loss for each activity to the current deductions for that activity to determine the activity's income or loss for that year.[17]

**Example:** In 19X2, Javert's income and losses for each rental house are determined as follows:

|  | House A | House B | House C | House D | Total |
|---|---|---|---|---|---|
| Income | $10000 | $ 1300 | $ 1000 | $2800 | $15100 |
| Deductions | (4600) | (1500) | (11000) | (2000) | (19100) |
| Loss fwd. |  | (1800) |  | ( 200) | ( 2000) |
| Income (loss) | $ 5400 | $(2000) | $(10000) | $ 600 | $(6000) |

The suspended net loss to be carried forward is $6,000. The losses generated by Houses B and C are $12,000 ($2,000 + $10,000). The net loss is allocated to Houses B and C as follows:

House B (2/12 x $6,000)          $1,000
House C (10/12 x $6,000)          5,000
Total loss forward               $6,000

### Special $25,000 Exception for Rental Real Estate

In some situations, you are permitted to deduct up to $25,000 per year of passive losses from active and portfolio income ($12,500 if you are married and file separately). This special rule applies only for losses from renting real estate (either residential or commercial) where you *actively participate* in management of the property.[18]

The special deduction is only available for individual taxpayers and their estates. It isn't available for corporations, trusts, or for individually owned property subject to the vacation home or hobby loss limitations (see below). If you are married, you get no special deduction if you file separately and live with your spouse at *any* time during the year. This strange rule is to discourage married people who live together from filing separate returns.[19]

The degree of involvement in management of a rental activity to qualify for *active participation* is not as great as that required for *material participation* in a trade or business activity (see above). The primary difference is that active participation does not require "regular, continuous, and substantial involvement," as long as you participate in making management decisions. The day-to-day operations of your rental properties may be delegated to a managing agent if you participate in decisions relating to:[20]

o  Approving new tenants,

o  Deciding and approving the terms of rental agreements,

o  Approving repairs and capital expenditures, and

o  Other similar management decisions.

If you die while actively participating in management of rental properties, your estate may continue to take advantage of the special rule for the two years following your death.

In addition to active participation in management, you must own at least 10% (in value) of the activity during the entire taxable year (or shorter period if you acquire your interest after the beginning of the year).

To determine the amount deductible under this rule, you first offset the income and losses from all rental real estate activities where you actively participate in management. If the result is a net loss, you subtract income from passive activities other than rental real estate (such as a business where you don't materially participate). If the resulting net passive losses from rental activities exceed $25,000 in any year, the excess is allocated to the individual activities according to the rules discussed above.

**Example:** Stutts has three rental houses (passive activities) where he actively participates in management. His adjusted gross income before considering passive activities is $68,000. The three houses produce total losses of $60,000, as follows:

| | |
|---|---|
| House A | $12,000 |
| House B | 16,000 |
| House C | 32,000 |
| Total losses from rental real estate | $60,000 |

In addition, Stutts is a general partner in a restaurant business where he does not materially participate. His share of the partnership's income for the year is $20,000. His net loss from rental activities is $40,000 ($60,000 rental losses less $20,000 non-rental passive income). He may deduct $25,000 of the passive rental losses from his active and portfolio income. The remaining $15,000 of rental passive losses ($40,000 less $25,000) are suspended and carried forward for the three houses in the ratio of the contribution of each house to the total rental passive losses, as follows:

| | |
|---|---|
| House A (12/60 x $15,000) | $ 3,000 |
| House B (16/60 x $15,000) | 4,000 |
| House C (32/60 x $15,000) | 8,000 |
| Excess loss carried forward | $15,000 |

The special $25,000 deduction is intended only for relatively low income taxpayers who own rental property to provide economic security. The assumption is that high income taxpayers provide for their financial security by other means, and do not need the special relief.

Accordingly, the $25,000 deduction is phased-out when your adjusted gross income is between $100,000 and $150,000.[21] The

$25,000 deduction is reduced by 50% of the amount by which your adjusted gross income exceeds $100,000. For this purpose, adjusted gross income is calculated without taking into account the passive losses, taxable social security benefits, and Individual Retirement Account contribution deductions.

> **Example:** Scott has adjusted gross income of $120,000 before considering her passive activities. She has passive rental losses of $30,000 for rental houses where she actively participates in management. Her special deduction is reduced by one-half of the excess of her adjusted gross income over $100,000, or $10,000 ($120,000 less $100,000 x 50% = $10,000). The amount she may deduct from active and portfolio income under the special exception is $15,000 ($25,000 less $10,000).

### Taxable Disposition of a Passive Activity

When you dispose of your entire interest in a passive activity in a taxable transaction (such as a sale), you are permitted to deduct fully all suspended passive losses relating to that activity. This is in line with the underlying concept that you may use your losses when you finally determine the economic outcome of your investment activity by closing it out. If you dispose of the activity in a transaction that is not fully taxable, special rules apply as discussed below.

Suspended passive losses first offset any gain from the disposition of the passive activity. If the suspended losses relating to the activity exceed the gain, the excess offsets other income in the following order:[22]

o Income from the passive activity for the tax year,

o Net income or gain for the year from all other passive activities,

o Active and portfolio income.

> **Example:** Dunn has a rental house with a basis of $58,000, and suspended passive losses carried forward of $6,000. In addition, he has income for the year from other passive activities of $1,000. He sells the house for $60,000 cash. He uses the suspended passive loss as follows:

| | |
|---|---:|
| Amount realized from sale | $60,000 |
| Less: Adjusted basis | 58,000 |
| Gain from sale of house | $ 2,000 |
| Less: Suspended passive loss | 6,000 |
| Excess suspended losses | $ 4,000 |
| Less: Other passive income | 1,000 |
| Losses deducted from active income | $ 3,000 |

If the passive activity is a capital asset, and its sale results in a loss, the loss is subject to the limitation on capital losses before taking into account the suspended passive loss. Generally, this means that you may offset the loss from the activity's sale against your capital gains plus $3,000 of other active or portfolio income. The excess capital loss is subject to the normal capital loss carryforward rules (see Appendix B).[23]

> **Example:** Assume in the above example that the sale price is $48,000. The loss from the sale is $10,000 ($48,000 less $58,000). If there are no capital gains, Dunn may deduct $3,000 of the loss. The remaining $7,000 is carried forward to offset future capital gains, etc. The $6,000 suspended passive loss first offsets the $1,000 passive income, and the remaining $5,000 may be deducted from active and portfolio income.

For treatment of suspended passive losses in a sale where you use the installment method of reporting, see Chapter 10. For treatment of suspended passive losses in a tax-free or partially taxable like-kind real estate exchange, see Chapter 11.


### Sale to a Related Party

The law has a provision to discourage you from selling a passive activity to a related party merely to trigger deduction of suspended passive losses. Essentially, you are required to continue to postpone suspended losses until the property is transferred to someone outside your related group. The rule applies even if the transaction is otherwise fully taxable.

Related parties include your spouse, brothers and sisters, ancestors, and lineal descendants. You are also related to entities (corporations, trusts, partnerships) where you have certain levels of ownership (generally more than 50%).

When you transfer property to a related party, its suspended losses remain with you until your related party transfers the property to an unrelated party in a taxable transaction. Then, you may use the suspended losses as described above.[24]

### Transfer of a Passive Activity at Death

Generally, the basis of inherited property is the fair market value at the date of the decedent's death (see Chapter 3). Suspended passive losses for property transferred at death are first reduced by the amount that the basis of the property is stepped-up (the difference between the decedent's basis and the fair market value). Any excess suspended loss is reported as described above on the decedent's final return.[25]

> **Example:** Stewart dies when she owns an investment house with a basis of $90,000, a fair market value of $110,000, and suspended passive loss of $15,000. The basis for the beneficiary is $110,000 and the amount of the step-up is $20,000 ($110,000 less $90,000). None of the suspended loss may be deducted since it is less than the basis increase.

> **Example:** Assume in the above example that Stewart's basis is $105,000. $5,000 of the passive loss is absorbed by the basis increase and is therefore nondeductible ($110,000 less $105,000). The remaining $10,000 is deducted on Stewart's final income tax return as described above.

### Gift of a Passive Activity

Suspended passive losses are not triggered when you give a passive activity to someone else. They are added to your basis for the property. This means that you get no benefit from the suspended losses. The benefit goes to the donee, who gets an increased carryover basis (see Chapter 3).[26]

> **Example:** Brandeis gives an investment house with a basis of $45,000, and suspended passive losses of $3,000 to his nephew. The nephew's basis for the property after the gift is $48,000 ($45,000 + $3,000). Brandeis gets no tax benefit from the suspended losses.

If you give a partial interest in a passive activity, you allocate the suspended losses between the part transferred and the part retained. Those allocated to the part transferred increase the donee's basis. You keep the suspended losses allocated to the interest you retain.

## LIMITATION ON DEDUCTIONS
## FOR VACATION HOMES

The *vacation home* limitation was enacted in 1976 to frustrate taxpayer attempts to get unwarranted tax deductions for property used part of the year for personal purposes, and rented to tenants for part of the year. The approach is similar to that for the passive loss and home-office limitations: it permits deductions only to the extent of the income generated, and does not permit you to create losses to offset income from other sources.

The application of the limitation, however, goes far beyond the abuse it was intended to correct. It applies not only for leisure-time property, but also for any other property you occupy for personal use. The wide net of the limitation might ensnare bona-fide rental properties when the wrong people live in them.

### How Are You Caught by the Vacation
### Home Rules?

The vacation home rules define property as a *residence* when you occupy it for personal purposes for too many days during the year. Thus, if you occupy the property for more than the greater of (1) fourteen days, or (2) 10% of the number of days the home is rented during the year, you are subject to the vacation home rules.[27] The latter test applies only if you rent the property for more than 140 days per year. For instance, if you rent the home for 200 days, you may occupy it for twenty days without getting caught. The rules apply not only for houses, but also for condominiums, boats, mobile homes, apartments, etc.

Many unsuspecting taxpayers are trapped because they don't understand how the vacation home rules define *personal use*. Under a set of *constructive occupancy* rules, days of occupancy by other people might be counted as days of occupancy by you. Thus, if the wrong people live there, you could be subject to the limitation even though you never set foot in your rental property.

Occupancy by the following people is considered occupancy by you:[28]

o Certain members of your family. These include your spouse, brothers and sisters, ancestors, and lineal descendents. This rule applies even if your family member pays full market rent. The rule doesn't apply, however, for family members who pay fair rent *and* occupy the property as a *principal residence* as defined for the home-sale rollover and over-55 exclusion (see Chapter 5).

o Anyone else who has an interest in the property or members of the family (as defined above) of anyone else with an interest in the property (for example, a co-owner as a tenant in common),

o Anyone with whom you have an arrangement permitting you to use another dwelling unit (even if you pay fair rent for the other unit),

o Anyone who is not paying fair market rent (determined by the facts and circumstances).

In addition, any day of occupancy by any shareholder, partner, or beneficiary of any S corporation, partnership, estate, or trust that owns the property is considered a day of occupancy by every other shareholder, partner, or beneficiary.[29]

Any day you spend at the property performing repair or maintenance work doesn't count as a personal use day, even if someone else who isn't helping is with you.[30] Also, occupancy by a co-owner under a qualified *shared equity financing agreement* doesn't count as occupancy by you (see Chapter 11).[31]

Suppose you convert your home into a rental property. Your occupancy won't disqualify the property for the subsequent rental period during the year of conversion if you rent it for twelve consecutive months after the conversion.[32]

### How the Limitation Works

Your deductions for a property caught under the vacation home trap may not exceed the gross rental income from the property for the year. Gross rental income is the total rents collected from the property, less expenses to obtain tenants. These expenses include fees, advertising costs, etc.[33]

First, you allocate the expenses between the personal and rental use in the ratio of the number of days the property is used for each purpose to the total number of days the property is used for any purpose. Mortgage interest and real estate taxes allocated to the personal use days are itemized deductions.[34] Mortgage interest is deductible only to the extent permitted under the home mortgage interest rules (see Chapter 4).

Before the 1986 TRA, the courts had held that interest and real estate taxes are allocated based on the entire tax year rather than the number of days the property is used. The result was that interest related to days of non-use was allocated to personal use, leaving a larger amount for deduction of other expenses related to rental days. The 1986 TRA seems to reject this approach and adopt the IRS position illustrated below.[35]

' You deduct the expenses allocated to the rental days in the following order:[36]

o Allocated interest and real estate taxes,

o Other allocated cash expenses, such as repairs, utilities, insurance, etc.,

o Depreciation.

If any expenses are disallowed after applying the gross income rule, you may carry the disallowed deductions forward and deduct them in future years, subject to the same gross income test.[37] These rules are illustrated by the following example adapted from the Proposed Regulations:[38]

**Example:** O'Hara owns a lakeside home that he rents at a fair rental for ninety days during the year. He uses the home for personal purposes on twenty other days during the year, and rents it to a friend at a discount for ten days. Thus, the home is used for some purposes for 120 days during the year (90 + 20 + 10). The days he rents the home at a discount are treated as personal use days. Therefore, the rental allocation fraction is 90/120. He calculates his tax results for the year as follows:

Gross receipts from rental:

| | | |
|---|---|---|
| 90 days at $25 | $2,250 | |
| 10 days at $15 | 150 | $2,400 |
| Less: Advertising, realtor | | 200 |
| Gross rental income | | $2,200 |

| Gross rental income | | $2,200 |
|---|---|---|

Less: Allocated interest and real estate taxes:

| | 90/120<br>*Allocated*<br>*to Rental* | |
|---|---|---|
| Mortgage interest | $ 750 | |
| Real estate taxes | 600 | |
| Amount allowable | | 1,350 |
| Limit for further deductions | | $ 850 |

Less: Cash expenses:

| | | |
|---|---|---|
| Insurance | $ 300 | |
| Utilities | 450 | |
| Amount allowable | | 750 |
| Limit for depreciation | | $ 100 |
| Depreciation | $1,125 | |
| Amount allowable | | $ 100 |

If he itemizes his personal deductions, O'Hara may claim the other $250 of mortgage interest and the other $200 of real estate taxes as itemized deductions. The disallowed depreciation of $1,025 is carried forward.

## Rental for Less Than Fifteen Days

If you rent property for less than fifteen days during a year, you get no deduction for any allocated expenses other than mortgage interest and real estate taxes. However, you don't report the rent you receive. This, in effect, gives you two weeks of tax-free income.[39]

**Example:** Simms owns a townhouse in Washington, D.C. During the summer while she is on vacation, she rents the house for fourteen days to out-of-town friends visiting Washington for their vacation. Her friends pay her $800 rent, that Simms does not include in her income. She may not deduct any expenses (other than interest and real estate taxes) allocated to the two rental weeks.

## Tax Planning for a Second Home

Before the 1986 TRA, tax planning strategy was to avoid the vacation home limitation so that excess rental deductions could reduce income from other sources. Now, planning strategy is much more complex. There is an intricate interplay between the vacation home limitation, the passive loss limitation, and the home mortgage interest deduction.

If your rental property is not subject to the vacation home rules, it is subject to the passive loss rules, and the special $25,000 deduction exception may be available for the losses allocated to the time the property is rented (see above). However, the mortgage interest allocated to the time you use the property for personal purposes is nondeductible because it is personal consumer interest (see Chapter 4). Thus, if you rent the property for most of the year, creating passive losses that you may offset with the $25,000 exception or with passive income from other activities, it might be advisable to sacrifice the deduction for the interest allocated to personal use days.

If the property is subject to the vacation home rules, it is not subject to the passive loss rules, but deductions are suspended in a similar manner, and the special $25,000 passive loss deduction exception is not available. However, if the property qualifies as a second home, mortgage interest is deductible in full subject to the limitations discussed in Chapter 4. If the rental time is small compared to the personal use time, you might want to save the mortgage interest deduction by deliberately subjecting the property to the vacation home rules. To do this, you need not occupy the property yourself. You can have tenants (such as those paying less than fair rent) whose occupancy is treated as your personal use.

Thus, your decision whether you want to avoid or embrace the vacation home limitation depends upon the interplay of a variety of factors including:

o The amount of rental losses generated by the property, and the extent that they may be offset by passive income from other activities,

o The amount of time the property is rented compared to the amount of time you use it for personal purposes,

o The amount of total mortgage interest you pay compared to potential rental losses,

o The amount of mortgage interest allocated to rental days compared to the amount allocated to personal use days.

Your tax situation regarding your second home must be reexamined every year.

## LIMITATIONS ON INVESTMENT INTEREST

As summarized in Chapter 4, deductibility of interest depends upon how you use the proceeds of the loan. Of the five broad categories of interest, those for personal interest, business interest, and home mortgage interest are discussed in Chapter 4. Passive interest is discussed above in connection with the more general limitations on passive losses. This section describes the rules for deduction of investment interest.

The limitation applies for all non-corporate taxpayers (individuals, estates and trusts). Investment interest of partnerships and S corporations passes through to the partners or shareholders who then apply the limitation at the individual level.[40]

Investment interest is defined as interest incurred on loans to support portfolio investments. These investments include stocks, bonds, certificates of deposit, money market funds, real estate investment trusts, etc. In addition, the limitation applies to interest on loans to finance unimproved land that is not used in your business. The limitation doesn't apply for interest on business loans, home mortgage interest, or interest relating to passive activities.[41]

### How the Limitation Works

Your deduction for investment interest in any tax year may not exceed your net investment income. Net investment income is the excess of your investment income over your investment expenses. Investment income is interest, dividends, etc., from your portfolio investments and gains from dispositions of investment assets.[42]

Investment expenses are those that are directly connected with investment income. Examples are fees for financial planning services, investment newsletters, safe-deposit box rentals for storage of securities, etc. These expenses, when added to certain unreimbursed employee expenses are deductible only to the extent they exceed 2% of adjusted gross income (see Appendix A). In computing the amount of expenses that exceed the 2% floor, expenses that are not investment expenses are disallowed before any investment expenses are disallowed.[43]

> **Example:** In 19X1, Hamilton borrows to purchase securities and unimproved land for speculation. His adjusted gross income (AGI) is $60,000. The securities produce income of $8,100, and the interest on the loans is $10,000. Hamilton has unreimbursed employee entertainment expenses of $900 incurred in his job as an electrical engineer. In addition, he subscribes to an investment advisory newsletter that costs $500. He computes his net investment income as follows:

| | | |
|---|---:|---:|
| Investment income | | $8,100 |
| Less: Investment expenses | | |
| Employee expenses | $ 900 | |
| Investment expenses | 500 | |
| Total subject limitation | $1,400 | |
| Less: 2% of AGI | 1,200 | |
| Investment expenses | | (200) |
| Net investment income | | $7,900 |

> Thus, Hamilton may only deduct $7,900 of investment interest in the current year. The $2,100 excess interest is carried forward.

You carry forward any current interest disallowed under this rule and add it to investment interest incurred in the following year. You may carry forward disallowed interest indefinitely, but you may not carry it back to offset investment income in prior years. However, unlike the passive loss carryforward, you are not permitted to deduct suspended investment interest in excess of the gain on disposition of the investment. You continue to carry forward the excess suspended interest.[44]

> **Example:** Assume in the above example that Hamilton disposes of some corporate stock in 19X3 at a gain of $4,000. His other investment income in that year is $10,000, so that he may deduct $14,000 of investment interest in 19X3, as shown by the following calculations for 19X1 (calculations above), 19X2, and 19X3 (using assumed income and expenses):

| | *19X1* | *19X2* | *19X3* |
|---|---:|---:|---:|
| Interest on debt | $10,000 | $12,000 | $11,000 |
| Interest carried forward | | 2,100 | 4,100 |
| Total investment interest | $10,000 | $14,100 | $15,100 |
| Deductible (Net investment inc.) | 7,900 | 10,000 | 14,000 |
| Interest carried forward | $ 2,100 | $ 4,100 | $ 1,100 |

## OTHER DEDUCTION LIMITATION PROVISIONS

There are two other provisions limiting deductions for some real estate related activities. They only apply to non-corporate taxpayers and S Corporations. Although these limitations have little application for the type of residential real estate investments contemplated in this book, we include a brief summary.

### At-Risk Limitation

Until the 1986 TRA, the "at-risk" limitation was the principal provision attacking tax shelter syndicates. Real estate activities, however, were exempted from its scope. The 1986 TRA expanded the at-risk limitation to include real estate activities.[45]

The thrust of the provision is to disallow deductions for activities financed by non-recourse loans (see Chapter 10). The underlying idea is that you should only be allowed tax deductions to the extent that you have placed your personal assets *at risk* in the project. Because most individually-owned small-unit investments are financed by recourse loans, the expansion of the limitation should have little impact for small-unit residential rental investors.

The amount you have at risk is generally the total cash you have invested, the basis of any property you contributed to the activity, and the amount of any debt where the lender can levy against your other assets for payment of the loan (recourse or personal liability debt). Your amount at risk is increased by your share of income from the activity, and decreased by the losses you deduct.

You are not allowed to deduct losses of more than the amount you have at risk in any given year. The loss that is disallowed because it is more than your at-risk amount is suspended and carried forward indefinitely, and may be deducted in a future year when you increase your amount at risk. You can increase your amount at risk by further investments of money or property, or by incurring additional recourse debt.

### Hobby Loss Limitation

This rule is designed to distinguish between bona-fide

business activities and activities that, although having business elements, are primarily personal in nature. In the context of residential investment, it is applicable only for investments, such as farms, that have some business elements.[46]

The limitation creates a rebuttable presumption that an activity is a bona-fide business if it produces taxable income for three out of five consecutive taxable years (two out of seven years for activities involving horses). If you meet this test, the IRS has the burden of proving that your activity is not truly profit-seeking. If you don't meet the test, you must prove that the activity is a business and not a hobby. The Income Tax Regulations list factors relevant in making this determination.[47]

If you are subject to the limitation, you may deduct your expenses only to the extent of the income from the activity. The ordering of the deductions is similar to that for the home-office and vacation home limitations. First you deduct mortgage interest and real estate taxes. Next, you deduct cash operating expenses. Finally, you may deduct depreciation. Any expenses (other than mortgage interest and real estate taxes) in excess of income are disallowed completely, and there is no carryforward.

## FOOTNOTES

1. See generally Internal Revenue Code (IRC) §469; Sen. Rept. 99-313, 99th Cong, 2nd Sess., p.725.

2. IRC §469(a)(2); Temp. Reg. §1.469-1T(b).

3. Tax Reform Act of 1986, P.L. 99-514, §§502(a) and (d).

4. IRC §469(c)(3); Temp. Reg. §1.469-1T(e)(4).

5. IRC §469(e)(1); Temp. Reg. §1.469-2T(c)(3).

6. Temp. Reg. §1.469-2T(c)(3)(ii).

7. IRC §469(e)(1)(B).

8. IRC §469(c)(1); Temp. Reg. §1.469-1T(e)(2).

9. IRC §469(c)(2); Temp. Reg. §1.469-1T(e)(3).

10. IRC §469(h)(1).

11. Temp. Reg. §1.469-5T.

12. IRC §469(h)(2); Temp. Reg. §1.469-5T(e)(3).

13. Temp. Reg. §1.469-1T(e)(3)(ii).

14. Temp. Reg. §1.469-4T.

15. IRC §469(d)(1); Temp. Reg. §1.469-1T(f)(2).

16. Temp. Reg. §1.469-1T(f)(2)(D) Example 1.

17. IRC §469(b); Temp. Reg. §1.469-1T(f)(4).

18. IRC §469(i).

19. IRC §469(i)(5)(B).

20. IRC §469(i)(6).

21. IRC §469(i)(3).

22. IRC §469(g)(1)(A); Temp. Reg.§1.469-2T(c).

23. IRC §1211.

24. IRC §469(g)(1)(B).

25. IRC §469(g)(2).

26. IRC §469(j)(6).

27. IRC §280A(d)(1); Prop. Reg. §1.280A-1(d).

28. IRC §§280A(d)(2) and (d)(3).

29. Prop. Reg. 280A-1(e)(5).

30. IRC §280A(d)(2); Prop. Reg. §1.280A-1(e)(6).

31. IRC §280A(d)(3)(C).

32. IRC §280A(d)(4); Prop. Reg. §1.280A-1(e)(4).

33. IRC §280A(c)(5); Prop. Reg. §1.280A-3(d)(2).

34. IRC §280A(e)(1); Prop. Reg. §1.280A-3(c).

35. *Bolton v. Comm'r.*, 694 F.2d 556 (CA 9, 1982); disagreeing with Prop. Reg. §1.280A-3(d)(4).

36. Prop. Reg. §1.280A-3(d)(3).

37. IRC §280A(c)(5).

38. Prop. Reg. §1.280A-3(d)(4).

39. IRC §280A(g).

40. IRC §163(d)(1).

41. IRC §163(d)(3).

42. IRC §163(d)(4)(A).

43. IRC §163(d)(4)(C).

44. IRC §163(d)(2).

45. Generally, see IRC §465 and the Regulations thereunder.

46. Generally, see IRC §183 and the Regulations thereunder.

47. Reg. §§1.183-2(b)(1) through (9).

# Chapter

# EIGHT

# TAX DEDUCTIONS FOR
# RENTAL PROPERTY

In addition to mortgage interest and real estate taxes, a variety of deductions are available for rental property. Interest deductions are not subject to the limitations imposed on home mortgage and investment interest. You may also deduct all ordinary and necessary operating expenses, as well as depreciation for buildings and other eligible property.

If the deductions create a tax loss, availablilty of such losses to offset other income may be denied or postponed because of one (or more) of the loss limitations discussed in Chapter 7. If you determine in advance that one of the limitations will apply, you should arrange your expenditures and deduction elections to maximize tax benefits in the current year, and to preserve other benefits for future years.

You must also consider the impact of the Alternative Minimum Tax (AMT). Some deduction rules for the AMT are different from those for the income tax. Your income tax strategy might be useless in a year when you are subject to the AMT. Such analysis is particularly important for depreciation and interest on refinanced home mortgages (see Chapter 9). This chapter examines deductions for the most common operating expenses for small-unit residential rental investments, and the all-important deduction for depreciation. There also is a short examination of the tax aspects of rental agreements.

## OPERATING EXPENSES

Subject to the passive loss limitation (see Chapter 7) the tax law permits you to deduct ordinary and necessary expenses paid or incurred for the management, conservation or maintenance of a rental building even if there is no income from the property in the taxable year.[1] However, if your property is allowed to remain vacant for an extended period of years, the Internal Revenue Service (IRS) may disallow rental deductions, asserting that you no longer have a profit motive for owning the property. In one case, the IRS permitted rental deductions for an apartment that was vacant for ten years because the property was in a run-down, high crime area. However, when the taxpayer gave up trying to locate a tenant and boarded up the building, the IRS (and Tax Court) held that she had abandoned the property for rental, and denied rental deductions.[2]

You take deductions for rental property from gross income to arrive at adjusted gross income (see Appendix A). Deductions for nonrental property are itemized deductions.

### Repairs

You may deduct expenditures for incidental maintenance and repairs. You must capitalize improvements, and deductions (if any) are governed by the depreciation rules (see below). Thus, the distinction between repairs and a capital expenditures is crucial. The rules for making the distinction are deceptively simple. In general, an incidental repair does not materially add to the value of the property or appreciably prolong its life. It merely keeps the property in an ordinarily efficient operating condition. On the other hand, a capital improvement either increases the property's value, increases its economic life, or both.[3] This distinction can be difficult to apply in borderline situations, and there are many court cases that grapple with the factual distinction. The most concise and most often quoted statement of the distinction is in an early court decision:[4]

> "In determining whether an expenditure is a capital one, or is chargeable against operating income, it is necessary to bear in mind the purpose for which the expenditure was made. To repair is to restore to a sound state or to mend, while a replacement implies a substitution. A repair is an expenditure for the purpose of keeping the property in an ordinarily efficient operating condition. It does

not add to the value of the property, nor does it appreciably prolong its life. It merely keeps the property in an operating condition over its probable useful life for the uses for which it was acquired. Expenditures for that purpose are distinguishable from those for replacements, alterations, improvement or additions which prolong the life of the property, increase its value, or make it adaptable to a different use. The one is a maintenance charge, while the others are additions to capital investment which should not be applied against current earnings."

If the expenditure changes the nature of the property, it is usually a capital expenditure. For example, covering a wood shingle roof entirely with composition shingles is a capital expenditure.[5] The cost differential between spot repairs and replacement doesn't matter. An entire roof resurfaced with asphalt felt at approximately the same cost as spot repairs was a capital expenditure.[6] Expenditures to adapt a property to a different use are capital, even though the value or life of the property is not increased.[7]

Replacement of worn equipment with new equipment with a useful life of more than a year is capital. However, replacement of small worn parts of a larger machine or appliance is a repair. Thus, installation of new kitchen appliances is capital. However, replacing the electric burner elements of a stove is a repair.[8]

Often, if you recondition or make major improvements to your property, many of the tasks, if treated separately, would be deductible repairs. However, if they are integrated into the overall improvement plan, they must be capitalized. Thus, before reconditioning a property, analyze the overall job, and separate those expenses qualifying as repairs from those that must be capitalized. If possible, you should make the repairs in a different taxable year from the major improvements. A word of caution, however. If the facts show that the repairs are part of an overall improvement scheme, regardless of whether they are billed separately or performed in a different year, they are capitalized. Thus, there is a premium on careful planning to separate the different expenditures.[9]

Example: Thompson buys an unoccupied run-down townhouse. To make it rentable she must repair some broken windows, replace some leaking plumbing, and install a new burner in the furnace. The total cost is $3,000. If she makes these repairs, she can rent the house for $250 per month. However, if she makes more extensive improvements such as replacing all of the interior drywall, installing new kitchen appliances, and remodeling the bathrooms, she can get $700 per month rent. The cost of the total project (including the repairs) is $15,000. If she makes all of the improvements now, the cost of the repairs are capitalized along with the major improvements, and are deductible according to the depreciation rules, generally over 27.5 years (see below). However, if she makes the incidental repairs now, and waits until next year for the major improvements, she probably may deduct the $3,000 now. The tradeoff is the value of the increased rent as compared to the tax benefits from the current deduction.

## Insurance

You are permitted to deduct insurance premiums for protection against fire, storm, theft, accident or other similar losses.[10] If the policy extends into future years, you must prorate the premium to each future year even if you are a cash basis taxpayer.[11]

**Example:** Gorky, a cash basis taxpayer, purchases, for $600, a three year (36 month) fire insurance policy on a rental house. The policy covers the period from July 1, 19X1 to June 30, 19X4. The deduction for 19X1 is $100 (6/36 x $600). The deductions for 19X2 and 19X3 are $200 (12/36 x $600), for 19X4 the deduction is $100 (6/36 x $600).

## Casualty Losses

The rules for deducting casualty losses for property you hold for personal use (such as your residence) are discussed in Chapter 4. Generally, the rules for investment property casualty losses are similar. For instance the determination of what constitutes a casualty ("sudden", etc.) is the same for both types of property. However, there are a few differences. First, casualty loss deductions for investment property are taken from gross income in determining adjusted gross income rather than being itemized deductions (see Appendix A). Second, the $100 per casualty floor and 10% of adjusted gross income limitation for personal casualty losses do not apply for investment casualty losses. Third, the way you determine the amount of the loss may be different for investment property.

For both personal and investment casualty losses, the amount of the loss is the difference between the values of the property before and after the casualty. The deduction is limited to the adjusted basis of the property if the basis is less than the reduction in value. If property is completely destroyed, the reduction in value is the fair market value at the time of the casualty. Suppose the value at the time of the casualty is less than the basis. For personal casualties, the amount of the casualty is limited to the amount of the fair market value. However, for investment property you may deduct the entire basis.[12]

> **Example:** Newman owns a house with a market value of $50,000, and an adjusted basis of $65,000 (excluding land). The house is completely destroyed by fire. If the house is her principal residence, the amount of the casualty is $50,000. However, if it is a rental investment, she may deduct the entire basis of $65,000.

If investment property consists of more than one component, you must compute the casualty losses separately for each component. Thus, losses for land, buildings, and other components must each be calculated. For personal casualties, the losses are calculated as a single unit (see Chapter 4). The following example, adapted from the Regulations, illustrates how you calculate the losses.[13]

> **Example:** Pogash purchases an investment house in 19X3 for $90,000. The basis is allocated as follows: land, $18,000; building, $72,000. Later she plants shrubs and ornamental trees around the house at a cost of $1,200. In 19X7, when a hurricane damages them, the relevant facts about the components are as follows:

|  | Adjusted Basis | FMV Before | FMV After |
|---|---|---|---|
| Land | $18,000 | $18,000 | $18,000 |
| Building | $66,000 | $70,000 | $52,000 |
| Shrubs | $ 1,200 | $ 2,000 | $ 400 |

> Pogash receives insurance proceeds of $5,000 for the damage to the building. There is no loss for the land. The deduction allowable for the building is calculated as follows:

| | |
|---|---|
| Value of building before the casualty | $70,000 |
| Value of the building after casualty | 52,000 |
| Value of the property destroyed | $18,000 |

| | |
|---|---|
| Loss to be taken into account (lesser of decline in value, $18,000 or adjusted basis, $66,000) | $18,000 |
| Less: Insurance recovery | 5,000 |
| Casualty loss deduction allowable | $13,000 |

The deduction for the shrubs is calculated as follows:

| | |
|---|---|
| Value of shrubs before the casualty | $ 2,000 |
| Value of shrubs after the casualty | 400 |
| Value of the property destroyed | $ 1,600 |
| Loss to be taken into account (lesser of decline in value, $1,600 or adjusted basis, $1,200) | $ 1,200 |

Compare the computations in this example with the example in Chapter 4, that is based upon the same facts except that the property is used as a principal residence.

## Fees and Commissions

You may incur various fees and commissions in connection with your rental property. The deductibility of these expenses depends upon the reason why you incur them.

Expenses for acquiring property (whether business, investment, or personal use) are added to its basis (see Chapter 3). If the property is a rental investment or held for business use, the amount allocated to the building is recovered through depreciation deductions (see below). Expenses you incur for disposing of property reduce the amount realized for determining your gain or loss (see Chapter 3).

Fees and commissions you incur to obtain a tenant must be capitalized as a cost of the lease and amortized over the life of the lease, regardless of your tax accounting method. If the lease is prematurely cancelled, you may write-off the unamortized cost. If you sell the property before the lease expires, the unamortized cost is added to your basis, and reduces your gain from the sale.[14]

You may deduct fees and commissions incurred for services connected with operating the property. For example, commissions charged by a managing agent are deductible in the year when you pay them.[15]

Condominium and homeowner association fees for rental property are deductible. Sometimes utilities are included in such fees. You are allowed to deduct utilities you pay directly for rental property, so the portion of a condominium fee applicable to utilities is also deductible.

## Tax Aspects of Rental Agreements

Rental property investors usually focus their attention on deductions. Seldom are they aware that there are also tax implications for leases and other rental agreements. Most planning in this area involves large-scale commercial property, but there are several points worth noting for small-unit residential property.

You might receive a variety of payments from tenants, with various names such as rents, advance rents, security deposits, and rent bonuses. The important element for you is when, or if, you include these payments in your income. Sometimes, a payment that serves the same economic purpose has different tax consequences depending upon what you call it. For a discussion of recharacterization of leases into sales, see Chapter 11.

**Security Deposits.** Security deposits are payments by the tenant to insure performance under a lease. For instance, a lease usually stipulates that the deposit is forfeited if the tenant prematurely terminates the lease, or returns the property in damaged condition. If the tenant meets the lease's terms, you must return the security deposit at the end of the lease.

Because you must return the money if the tenant performs under the lease, the security deposit is treated as a loan.[16] At the time you receive the deposit, it is not taxable income, even if you have unrestricted use of the funds. If the tenant doesn't perform under the lease and forfeits the deposit, it is included in your income at that time. If the deposit is forfeited because the tenant prematurely terminates the lease, it is treated as a settlement of the unpaid rent for the remainder of the lease term. If it is forfeited for damages, you include it in income and you are permitted to deduct repairs to restore the property to its prior condition (see above).

**Advance Rent.** Even if you are a cash basis taxpayer, advance rent is taxed in the year you receive it regardless of the year to which it relates.[17] Thus, if you have a three year lease beginning June 1, 19X1, that requires the first and last month's rent to be paid in advance, the last month's rent is taxed in 19X1 even though it relates to May, 19X4. By characterizing the payment as advance rent you accelerate 19X4 income into 19X1. If you are paid a bonus to enter into a lease, it is treated as advance rent.

Sometimes it is difficult to determine if a deposit is for security or for advance rent. If the lease specifies that the payment is to guarantee performance under the lease, and is to be returned if the tenant performs, it probably is treated as a security deposit.[18] However, even if the payment guarantees performance under the lease, it is treated as advance rent if the lease specifies that it is to be applied against the last month's rent.[19] If the payment is advance rent but must be held in an escrow account until it is applied to the final rent payment, it is not taxable until it is so applied.

Many standard residential lease forms require a security deposit and stipulate that the first and last months' rent be paid in advance. Sometimes local law makes it beneficial to receive the last month's rent in advance. More often, however, the last month's rent is an additional security deposit. If this is the case, you are better off to call it a security deposit to avoid accelerating income from a future year.

### Improvement to Your Property Made by Your Tenant

If your tenant makes improvements to your property, you benefit if the property's value is increased. However, the increase in value is not taxable to you unless the improvements are *in lieu of rent*.[20] Your tax basis for the tenant's improvements is zero. Thus, you won't pay tax on your economic benefit until you sell the property.

There are both tax and financial advantages for having the tenant make improvements. You defer tax on the increase in your property's value, and you don't have the immediate cash outlay. Thus, if improvements are necessary, it is better that they be made by the tenant.

You are denied this happy tax result if the tenant makes the improvements in lieu of a higher rental payment. In many situations, it is in the tenant's interest to make the improvements. For example, if the tenant pays utilities, he might be motivated to insulate your rental house to lower his fuel bills. You should rent the property as-is and encourage him to install the insulation. Whether the tenant's improvements constitute additional rent depends upon the intent of the parties as indicated by the terms of the lease or by surrounding circumstances.[21]

There are some steps you can take to make it less likely that the tenant's improvements are in lieu of rent. The lease should allow the tenant to remove the improvements upon termination of the lease if such removal will not damage the property. Also, the lease should not require that costs of improvements be credited against the rent. And, of course, the lease should never provide that the improvements are in lieu of rent, or require a rent increase if the tenant doesn't make the improvements.

## DEPRECIATION

The value of some assets declines because of wear and tear or obsolescence. This decline is reflected in taxable income by the depreciation deduction. You are permitted to depreciate property used in your business or property you hold for investment. You are not permitted to depreciate personal-use property such as your principal residence.

Depreciation is allowed only for property with a limited economic life such as buildings, furniture, equipment, etc. You are not permitted to depreciate land. When you acquire land with a building, you must allocate the basis between the land and building. See Chapter 3 for a discussion of how to determine and allocate basis.

You may begin to depreciate an asset when you place it into service. This is usually when you acquire the asset or when you convert a personal-use asset to business or investment use (such as converting your principal residence into a rental investment). See Chapter 3 for determination of basis upon conversion from personal to investment use.

The tax rules for depreciation have undergone several revolutionary changes in the past several years. There are currently three different depreciation systems in operation. The first is for property placed into service before 1981, referred to here as "old-style" depreciation. The second is the Accelerated Cost Recovery System (ACRS) that operated between 1981 and 1987. For real estate, this system had several changes during this period. The third is the Modified Accelerated Cost Recovery System (MACRS) that has operated since 1986. In some situations, all three systems might apply at the same time for property you owned before 1981.

### Old-Style Depreciation -- Pre-1981

Before 1981, tax depreciation calculations closely resembled calculations for financial accounting. The basis was allocated over an estimated useful economic life. This was a rough attempt to match the period of the property's decline in value with the period that it would produce income.[22] After you determined the useful life, you could select various methods for calculating annual deductions. The simplest was to deduct the cost ratably over the useful life in equal amounts (straight-line depreciation).

In some circumstances you were permitted to take larger deductions in the initial years of the investment (accelerated depreciation). The amount of the annual deduction declined in each succeeding year, but the total depreciation over the entire useful life was the same regardless of the method you selected. The maximum rates depended upon whether the property was personal property or real estate, and whether it was new or used. There were different maximum rate rules for residential and non-residential real estate.

You were required to reduce the property's basis by its salvage value. This was the estimated scrap value of the property at the end of its useful life less the cost to remove it from its site. You were also allowed to fragment real estate into its component parts, and depreciate each separately. For instance you could separately depreciate a building's walls, roof, wiring, plumbing, heating system, etc.

### The Accelerated Cost Recovery System

The depreciation deduction, unlike the operating expense deductions described in this chapter, does not require an outlay of cash. If the property's value declines, the deduction reflects the economic loss, although the timing of the deduction and loss are not likely to coincide. However, if the property's value does not decline, the deduction is a tax gift from Uncle Sam. Thus, taxpayers always attempted to maximize the depreciation deduction to offset cash income without any corresponding economic outlay.

This taxpayer attempt was countered by an equally aggressive attempt by the IRS to curb the deduction. The most common dispute was the length of the property's economic life. The IRS often maintained that the economic life selected by a taxpayer was too short. The resulting squabble consumed considerable administrative and taxpayer time. Component depreciation was another subject of contention. Lengthly disputes involved the allocation of the cost of a building among its component parts.

Partly in response to the administrative problem and partly as an economic investment incentive, the Economic Recovery Tax Act of 1981 radically altered and attempted to simplify the old-style depreciation system. The new system, called the Accelerated Cost Recovery System (ACRS) replaced the old system, and you must use ACRS for any property placed into service after December 31, 1980. Old-style depreciation continues to apply for property placed into service before 1981, and for post-1980 property acquired in a transaction that violates an *anti-churning* rule (see below).

ACRS abandoned the concept of economic useful lives and adopted arbitrary recovery periods that generally are unrelated to, and shorter than, the old useful lives. The distinction between new and used property was eliminated, and the property's basis is not reduced by salvage value. Component depreciation is not allowed.

### Accelerated Cost Recovery System (ACRS) for Real Estate -- 1981-1986

The original ACRS recovery period for most investment or business real estate was fifteen years. The recovery period was extended to eighteen years for property placed into service after March 15, 1984, and before May 9, 1985. For property placed into service after May 8, 1985, and before December 31, 1986, the recovery period was nineteen years.[23] The purpose for lengthening the recovery periods was to raise revenue and to offset other tax changes beneficial for the real estate industry.

Cost is recovered according to a table (see Table 8-1 for the nineteen year recovery percentages) reflecting accelerated depreciation using the 175% declining balance method. The table has twelve columns, corresponding to the month during the year when you placed the property into service. Unlike old-style depreciation, ACRS does not require you to calculate manually the amount of each year's write-off. You merely multiply the basis of your property by the percentage for each year from the column corresponding to the month you place the property into service.

For property placed into service after June 22, 1984, (whether 18- or 19-year property) you use a *mid-month averaging convention*. This tax jargon merely means that property is treated as being placed into service in the middle of the month regardless of when during a month you actually place it into service. Thus, you are allowed one-half month's cost recovery in the first month even though you place the property into service on the last day of the month. The half-month averaging convention is built into the table, so you don't have to make a separate calculation.

> **Example:** Witner buys a rental house for $100,000 that he placed into service on September 23, 1986. $80,000 of the cost is allocated to the building, and $20,000 to the land. To determine his deduction for 1986, he uses the percentage in the ninth column of Table 8-1 (corresponding to September) for the first year, or 2.7%. Thus, his deduction is $2,160 (2.7% of $80,000). For 1987, he uses the second year's percentage in the ninth column, or 9%. His deduction for 1987 is $7,200 (9% of $80,000). If he continues to own the property for twenty years, each year he applies the appropriate percentage in the ninth column, that in the year 2005 is 3%. After that, no further cost recovery deductions are allowed.

Instead of using the accelerated table, you were permitted to elect to write off the property by using a straight-line method. However, you had a narrow choice for straight-line recovery periods. You could use the appropriate accelerated table period (15, 18, or 19 years). Alternatively, you could elect to write-off the property over 35 or 45 years. The election was on a property-by-property basis, but you could not change the recovery method for a property once you elected. The IRS issued tables for the straight-line elections that you use the same way as the accelerated table. These tables also reflect the mid-month averaging convention.

If you dispose of property before the end of its recovery period, you deduct one-half month's cost recovery for the month of disposition. You must prorate the table amount for the year of disposition to take into account the mid-month convention. The following example, adapted from an IRS illustration shows how this is done:[24]

> **Example:** Assume in the above example that Witner sold the property on August 1, 1987, for

$125,000. In this case, the Table 8-1 amount otherwise determined for the second year (9%) must be prorated by a fraction, the numerator of which is the number of months during the year the property is in service, and the denominator of which is 12. Witner is treated as if he disposed of the property in the middle of the month. Thus, he is treated as selling the property on August 15, and having used it for 7.5 months. The cost recovery allowance for 1987 is $4,500 (9% x $80,000 x 7.5/12).

There are several special recovery periods for real estate outside the United States and certain low income housing. Pre-1987 foreign real estate uses an accelerated table reflecting 150% declining balance depreciation over a thirty-five year recovery period. Pre-1987 low income housing uses an accelerated table reflecting 200% declining balance depreciation over a fifteen year recovery period. Both types of property are permitted to use specified alternative straight-line elections.

The ACRS system resulted in much larger deductions than old-style depreciation. There was concern that taxpayers might try to convert pre-1981 property into ACRS property by engaging in tax-free and other transactions (such as gifts and tax-deferred exchanges). To discourage this, a complex set of *anti-churning* rules were included to require that old-style depreciation continue to be used for property acquired in certain types of transactions.[25] Generally, the rules applied for property acquired from related persons (including related entities) who owned the property in 1980, property acquired in certain tax-deferred transactions in exchange for property you owned in 1980, and property you owned in 1980 and leased back after a post-1980 disposition.

### The Modified Accelerated Cost Recovery System (MACRS) for Real Estate — After 1986

The Tax Reform Act of 1986 (1986 TRA) overhauled the Accelerated Cost Recovery System into a revised system, called the Modified Accelerated Cost Recovery System (MACRS).[26] MACRS hits real estate particularly hard and permits much smaller deductions than ACRS. In addition to raising revenue to pay for tax rate cuts, the changes reflect an attempt to remove tax considerations from the investment decision process. MACRS generally applies for all property placed into service after 1986. There are transition rules permitting you to use ACRS for real estate constructed, reconstructed, or acquired under a binding written contract as of March 1, 1986, and placed into service by January 1, 1991.

MACRS requires you to use straight-line write-offs, and re-establishes the old-style depreciation's distinction between residential and non-residential property. However, as under ACRS, there is no salvage value, no distinction between new and used property, and no component depreciation.

The straight-line recovery period for residential property is 27.5 years. For non-residential property, the recovery period is 31.5 years. Property is classified as residential if at least 80% of the gross rental income is from the rental of dwelling units. A dwelling unit is defined as a house or apartment used to provide living accommodations, but does not include a unit in a hotel, motel, inn, or other establishment rented to transients.[27] Non-residential property is any property that is not residential property.

The mid-month averaging convention applies, and you calculate the annual deduction from tables using the same procedure as under ACRS. Tables 8-2 and 8-3 reflect the write-off percentages for residential and non-residential property, respectively. You must prorate the MACRS deduction for the year of disposition if you dispose of the property before the end of its recovery period to reflect the mid-month averaging convention.

**Example:** Continuing the above examples, assume that Witner places the $80,000 building into service on September 23, 1987. The applicable percentage from Table 8-2 for September is 1.061% (ninth column). Thus, the deduction for 1987 is $848 (1.061% x $80,000). In 1988, the deduction is $2,909 (3.636% x $80,000).

The deductions in this example, when compared to the deductions for the ACRS example above, illustrate the significant slow-down of depreciation for real estate under MACRS. The deductions for the first two years are summarized as follows:

|  | ACRS | MACRS |
|---|---|---|
| First year | $2,160 | $ 848 |
| Second year | $7,200 | $2,909 |

**Example**: Assume in the above example that Witner sells the property on August 1, 1992. The applicable percentage from Table 8-2 for 1992 is 3.636% (ninth column). The deduction must be prorated to reflect that Witner used the property in 1992 for 7.5 months. Thus, the depreciation deduction for 1992 is $1,818 ($80,000 x 3.636% x 7.5/12).

For multiple-use property, you must be careful to monitor the ratio of residential and non-residential rental income. In any year when residential rentals fall below 80%, you are restricted to the appropriate amount allowable under the non-residential table.

As an alternative to the regular recovery periods, you may elect to write-off real estate over a forty-year recovery period, using the mid-month convention.[28] The forty year period is applicable for both residential and non-residential property. Table 8-4 reflects the annual percentage deductions under the alternative election.

**Example**: Assume in the above examples that Witner elects the alternative forty-year recovery period for the property placed into service on September 23, 1987 (see Table 8-4). In 1987 his deduction is $583 ($80,000 x .0729%). If he sells the property on August 1, 1988, his deduction for 1988 is $1,250 ($80,000 x 2.5% x 7.5/12).

You are required to use the alternative recovery period for the Alternative Minimum Tax (see Chapter 9). You must also use it for property outside the U.S., property leased to a tax-exempt entity, and for several other purposes.

Improvements to real estate are treated as separate structures and are subject to the MACRS rules regardless of the depreciation or ACRS method for the underlying structure. The recovery period for the improvement begins at the date the improvement is placed into service, or the date the underlying structure is placed into service, whichever is later.[29]

**Example**: Betancourt owns a rental house he placed into service on June 15, 1985. He calculates depreciation by using the 19 year accelerated table (Table 8-1). In 1992, he adds a garage to the house. The garage is depreciated using the 27.5 year straight-line method (Table 8-2).

Leasehold improvements are depreciated using the 31.5 year recovery period (Table 8-2) regardless of the term of the lease. When the lease terminates, the undepreciated balance of the improvement is deducted in full.[30] Leasehold improvements may be depreciated only if you are a tenant who uses them for business. If the improvements are to enhance personal living accommodations, they are not depreciable. Regardless of what the tenant does with the improvements, they are not income to the landlord unless they are in lieu of rent (see above).

MACRS has no anti-churning rules for real estate because deductions under MACRS are less favorable than those under ACRS. However, the ACRS anti-churning rules (see above) continue to apply for certain transaction after 1986 where you receive old-style depreciation property.

### Accelerated Cost Recovery for Personal Property

Sometimes rental real estate contains items of personal property. For instance you may rent a furnished home, or rent property that contains appliances such as refrigerators, stoves, dishwashers, etc. Thus, you should be familiar with the ACRS rules for depreciating personal property.

As in the case of real estate, different rules apply for personal property placed into service between 1981 and 1987, and for personal property placed into service after 1986.

**Personal Property Placed Into Service 1981-1986.** ACRS assigned personal property to one of four recovery periods.[31] Most property was assigned to the three- and five-year recovery periods. The three year period applied for automobiles and light-duty trucks (with special rules for luxury automobiles). The five-year recovery period applied for other equipment, furniture or appliances associated with residential rental property. The ten and fifteen year recovery periods applied for specialized equipment and public utility property not relevant for residential real estate investors.

You determine the amount of the deductions from a table that reflects 150% declining balance depreciation (Table 8-5). The table uses a half-year averaging convention. This means that regardless of when during the year you placed the property into service, it is treated as if it were placed into service on the first day of the seventh month. Thus, unlike the real estate tables, there is only one column for each recovery period. You calculate the annual write-off by multiplying the basis of the property by the appropriate annual percentage. No deduction is allowed in the year you dispose of the property.

> **Example:** Marshak purchased furniture (5-year recovery property) for a condominium that he rented for the first time on December 30, 1985. The cost of the furniture was $5,000. The ACRS deduction for 1985 was $750 (15% x $5,000). The deduction for 1986 was $1,100 (22% x $5,000). Note that for 1985, the ACRS deduction reflects a six-month write-off even though the property is only in service for two days.

There were alternative straight-line ACRS recovery period elections for personal property as follows:

| Recovery Period | Straight-line Recovery Period |
|---|---|
| 3 year property | 3, 5, or 12 years |
| 5 year property | 5, 12, or 25 years |

**Personal Property Placed Into Service After 1986.** MACRS established two new recovery periods (7 and 20 years).[32] Automobiles and light-duty trucks formerly in the 3-year class were moved to the 5-year class. The old 5-year recovery property was moved to the 7-year class. Thus, most furniture and appliances associated with residential rental property are assigned to the new 7-year class. See Table 8-6 for the applicable percentages for the 5-and 7-year classes.

Although the recovery periods are longer, the write-off rate was increased. Deductions for the 5-year and 7-year classes were speeded up to 200% declining balance. As under ACRS, the half-year averaging convention is applicable. A special quarterly averaging convention applies if more than 40% of the personal property is placed in service during the last three months of the taxable year.[33]

Alternative straight-line recovery periods are also available for personal property under MACRS. The recovery periods are based on class lives under a pre-1981 elective depreciation system called the Class Life Asset Depreciation Range (CLADR). Personal property that was not assigned a class life under CLADR uses a twelve-year recovery period. Apparently, furniture and appliances used in rental property were not assigned a class life, so the twelve-year recovery period would apply. The alternative system must be used for the Alternative Minimum Tax (see Chapter 9).

**Table 8-1** ACRS COST RECOVERY TABLE
FOR 19-YEAR REAL PROPERTY

(For Property Placed into Service After
May 8, 1985, and Before December 31, 1986)

| Year | Month in Recovery Year | | | | | | | | | | | |
|------|------|------|------|------|------|------|------|------|------|------|------|------|
| | 1 | 2 | 3 | 4 | 5 | 6 | 7 | 8 | 9 | 10 | 11 | 12 |
| 1 | 8.8 | 8.1 | 7.3 | 6.5 | 5.8 | 5.0 | 4.2 | 3.5 | 2.7 | 1.9 | 1.1 | 0.4 |
| 2 | 8.4 | 8.5 | 8.5 | 8.6 | 8.7 | 8.8 | 8.8 | 8.9 | 9.0 | 9.0 | 9.1 | 9.2 |
| 3 | 7.6 | 7.7 | 7.7 | 7.8 | 7.9 | 7.9 | 8.0 | 8.1 | 8.1 | 8.2 | 8.3 | 8.3 |
| 4 | 6.9 | 7.0 | 7.0 | 7.1 | 7.1 | 7.2 | 7.3 | 7.3 | 7.4 | 7.4 | 7.5 | 7.6 |
| 5 | 6.3 | 6.3 | 6.4 | 6.4 | 6.5 | 6.5 | 6.6 | 6.6 | 6.7 | 6.8 | 6.8 | 6.9 |
| 6 | 5.7 | 5.7 | 5.8 | 5.9 | 5.9 | 5.9 | 6.0 | 6.0 | 6.1 | 6.1 | 6.2 | 6.2 |
| 7 | 5.2 | 5.2 | 5.3 | 5.3 | 5.3 | 5.4 | 5.4 | 5.5 | 5.5 | 5.6 | 5.6 | 5.6 |
| 8 | 4.7 | 4.7 | 4.8 | 4.8 | 4.8 | 4.9 | 4.9 | 5.0 | 5.0 | 5.1 | 5.1 | 5.1 |
| 9 | 4.2 | 4.3 | 4.3 | 4.4 | 4.4 | 4.5 | 4.5 | 4.5 | 4.5 | 4.6 | 4.6 | 4.7 |
| 10 | 4.2 | 4.2 | 4.2 | 4.2 | 4.2 | 4.2 | 4.2 | 4.2 | 4.2 | 4.2 | 4.2 | 4.2 |
| 11 | 4.2 | 4.2 | 4.2 | 4.2 | 4.2 | 4.2 | 4.2 | 4.2 | 4.2 | 4.2 | 4.2 | 4.2 |
| 12 | 4.2 | 4.2 | 4.2 | 4.2 | 4.2 | 4.2 | 4.2 | 4.2 | 4.2 | 4.2 | 4.2 | 4.2 |
| 13 | 4.2 | 4.2 | 4.2 | 4.2 | 4.2 | 4.2 | 4.2 | 4.2 | 4.2 | 4.2 | 4.2 | 4.2 |
| 14 | 4.2 | 4.2 | 4.2 | 4.2 | 4.2 | 4.2 | 4.2 | 4.2 | 4.2 | 4.2 | 4.2 | 4.2 |
| 15 | 4.2 | 4.2 | 4.2 | 4.2 | 4.2 | 4.2 | 4.2 | 4.2 | 4.2 | 4.2 | 4.2 | 4.2 |
| 16 | 4.2 | 4.2 | 4.2 | 4.2 | 4.2 | 4.2 | 4.2 | 4.2 | 4.2 | 4.2 | 4.2 | 4.2 |
| 17 | 4.2 | 4.2 | 4.2 | 4.2 | 4.2 | 4.2 | 4.2 | 4.2 | 4.2 | 4.2 | 4.2 | 4.2 |
| 18 | 4.2 | 4.2 | 4.2 | 4.2 | 4.2 | 4.2 | 4.2 | 4.2 | 4.2 | 4.2 | 4.2 | 4.2 |
| 19 | 4.2 | 4.2 | 4.2 | 4.2 | 4.2 | 4.2 | 4.2 | 4.2 | 4.2 | 4.2 | 4.2 | 4.2 |
| 20 | 0.2 | 0.5 | 0-9 | 1.2 | 1.6 | 1.9 | 2.3 | 2.6 | 3.0 | 3.3 | 3.7 | 4.0 |

# POST-1986 RECOVERY PERCENTAGES

**Table 8-2  POST-1986 RECOVERY PERCENTAGES FOR RESIDENTIAL RENTAL PROPERTY (27.5 YEAR)**

| Year | Month of Recovery Year | | | | | | | | | | | |
|---|---|---|---|---|---|---|---|---|---|---|---|---|
| | 1 | 2 | 3 | 4 | 5 | 6 | 7 | 8 | 9 | 10 | 11 | 12 |
| 1 | 3.485 | 3.182 | 2.879 | 2.576 | 2.273 | 1.970 | 1.667 | 1.364 | 1.061 | 0.758 | 0.455 | 0.152 |
| 2-18 | 3.636 | 3.636 | 3.636 | 3.636 | 3.636 | 3.636 | 3.636 | 3.636 | 3.636 | 3.636 | 3.636 | 3.636 |
| 19-27 | 3.637 | 3.637 | 3.637 | 3.637 | 3.637 | 3.637 | 3.637 | 3.637 | 3.637 | 3.637 | 3.637 | 3.637 |
| 28 | 1.970 | 2.273 | 2.576 | 2.879 | 3.182 | 3.485 | 3.636 | 3.636 | 3.636 | 3.636 | 3.636 | 3.636 |
| 29 | 0.000 | 0.000 | 0.000 | 0.000 | 0.000 | 0.000 | 0.152 | 0.455 | 0.758 | 1.061 | 1.364 | 1.667 |

**Table 8-3  POST-1986 RECOVERY PERCENTAGES FOR NON-RESIDENTIAL RENTAL PROPERTY (31.5 YEAR)**

| Year | Month of Recovery Year | | | | | | | | | | | |
|---|---|---|---|---|---|---|---|---|---|---|---|---|
| | 1 | 2 | 3 | 4 | 5 | 6 | 7 | 8 | 9 | 10 | 11 | 12 |
| 1 | 3.042 | 2.778 | 2.513 | 2.249 | 1.984 | 1.720 | 1.455 | 1.190 | 0.926 | 0.661 | 0.397 | 0.132 |
| 2-19 | 3.175 | 3.175 | 3.175 | 3.175 | 3.175 | 3.175 | 3.175 | 3.175 | 3.175 | 3.175 | 3.175 | 3.175 |
| 20-31 | 3.174 | 3.174 | 3.174 | 3.174 | 3.174 | 3.174 | 3.174 | 3.174 | 3.174 | 3.174 | 3.174 | 3.174 |
| 32 | 1.720 | 1.984 | 2.249 | 2.513 | 2.778 | 3.042 | 3.175 | 3.175 | 3.175 | 3.175 | 3.175 | 3.175 |
| 33 | 0.000 | 0.000 | 0.000 | 0.000 | 0.000 | 0.000 | 0.132 | 0.397 | 0.661 | 0.926 | 1.190 | 1.455 |

**Table 8-4  POST-1986 ALTERNATIVE RECOVERY PERCENTAGES FOR ALL RENTAL PROPERTY (40 YEAR)**

| Year | Month of Recovery Year | | | | | | | | | | | |
|---|---|---|---|---|---|---|---|---|---|---|---|---|
| | 1 | 2 | 3 | 4 | 5 | 6 | 7 | 8 | 9 | 10 | 11 | 12 |
| 1 | 2.396 | 2.188 | 1.979 | 1.771 | 1.563 | 1.354 | 1.146 | 0.938 | 0.729 | 0.521 | 0.313 | 0.104 |
| 2-40 | 2.500 | 2.500 | 2.500 | 2.500 | 2.500 | 2.500 | 2.500 | 2.500 | 2.500 | 2.500 | 2.500 | 2.500 |
| 41 | 0.104 | 0.312 | 0.521 | 0.729 | 0.937 | 1.146 | 1.354 | 1.562 | 1.771 | 1.979 | 2.187 | 2.396 |

**Table 8-5** RECOVERY PERIODS FOR PERSONAL PROPERTY

1981-1986

| Recovery Year | 3-Year | 5-Year |
|---------------|--------|--------|
| 1 | 25% | 15% |
| 2 | 38% | 22% |
| 3 | 37% | 21% |
| 4 | | 21% |
| 5 | | 21% |

**Table 8-6** RECOVERY PERIODS FOR PERSONAL PROPERTY

AFTER 1986

| Recovery Year | 5-Year | 7-Year |
|---------------|--------|--------|
| 1 | 20.00% | 14.29% |
| 2 | 32.00% | 24.49% |
| 3 | 19.20% | 17.49% |
| 4 | 11.52% | 12.49% |
| 5 | 11.52% | 8.93% |
| 6 | 5.76% | 8.92% |
| 7 | | 8.93% |
| 8 | | 4.46% |

# FOOTNOTES

1. Reg. §1.212-1(b).

2. *Gertrude C. Gorod*, ¶81,632 P-H MemoTC (1981), permitting deductions; ¶85,023 P-H MemoTC, 787 F2d 578 (CA 2, 1986), denying deductions.

3. Reg. §1.162-4.

4. *Illinois Merchants Trust Co.*, *Ex.*, 4 BTA 103 (1926), Acq.

5. *Robert M. Craig*, ¶48,143 P-H MemoTC (1948).

6. *Southwest Ornamental Iron Co.*, ¶53,171 P-H MemoTC (1953).

7. *Popular Dry Goods Co.*, 6 BTA 78 (1927); *Yost & Herrell*, 2 BTA 745 (1925); *Edwin Dumble Co., Inc.*, 9 BTA 591 (1927).

8. *Joseph J. Otis*, 73 TC 671 (1981).

9. *I. M. Cowell*, 18 BTA 997; *Joseph Merrick Jones*, 24 TC 563, aff'd 242 F2d 616 (CA 5, 1957); *Cobleigh*, ¶56,261 P-H MemoTC (1956).

10. Reg. §1.162-1(a).

11. Rev. Rul. 70-413, 1970-2 C.B. 103; *Comm'r. v. Boylston Market Ass'n*, 131 F.2d 966 (CA 1, 1942).

12. Reg. §1.165-7(b)(1).

13. Reg. §1.165-7(b)(3), Example 2.

14. Reg. §1.162-11(a); *Manhattan Life Insurance Co.*, 28 BTA 129 (1933); *Post v. Comm'r.*, 199 F.2d 135.

15. IRC §212; Reg. §1.212-1.

16. *Clinton Hotel Realty Corp. v. Comm'r.*, 128 F.2d 968 (CA 5, 1942; *Warren Service Corp. v. Comm'r.*, 110 F.2d 161 (CA 2, 1940).

17. Reg. §1.61-8(b).

18. *George E. Barker Est.*, 13 BTA 562 (1928).

19. *Hirsch Improvement Co. v. Comm'r.*, 143 F.2d 912 (CA 7, 1944).

20. IRC §109.

21. Reg. §§1.109-1(a); 1.61-8(c).

22. Generally, see IRC §167.

23. The ACRS rules are contained in IRC §168. However, there are two versions of §168. The original version applicable to property placed into service before 1987 is hereinafter referred to as "old §168." The version as amended by the 1986 TRA applicable to property placed into service after 1986 is hereinafter referred to as "new §168."

24. Treasury Department News Release R 2890.

25. Old IRC §168(e)(4); Prop. Reg. §1.168-4(d).

26. Generally, see New IRC §168.

27. New IRC §168(e)(2)(A); IRC §167(j)(2)(B).

28. New IRC §168(g).

29. New IRC §168(i)(6).

30. New IRC §168(i)(8).

31. Old IRC §168(b)(1).

32. New IRC §168(e)(3).

33. New IRC §168(d)(3).

# Chapter

# NINE

# THE ALTERNATIVE MINIMUM TAX
# FOR INDIVIDUAL TAXPAYERS

The roots of the Alternative Minimum Tax (AMT) go back to 1969, and its purpose remains much the same as when it was introduced. It is designed to insure that you must pay a substantial amount of tax if you have economic income. It also precludes you from avoiding tax by taking undue advantage of "loopholes" in the regular income tax.

Originally, the minimum tax was a back-up tax added to the regular income tax. In 1978, the AMT took on its present form as an alternative to the income tax. You must make two tax calculations: one to determine your income tax (regular tax), and the second to determine your AMT. You pay the higher of the two taxes.[1] This means that in some years you may be subject to the regular tax, and in others you may be subject to the AMT.

Until the Tax Reform Act of 1986 (1986 TRA), the AMT didn't affect many taxpayers. This was because the old AMT tax rate (20%) was much lower than the old maximum regular tax rate (50%). Additionally, the tax base for the AMT was not significantly different from that for the regular tax. The result was that the AMT liability rarely exceeded the regular tax liability.

This has all changed for two reasons. First, the new AMT rate (now 24%) is much closer to the maximum regular tax rate (28% or 31%). Second, the base for the AMT was redefined, and is now considerably broader than the base for the regular tax. Although this discussion is limited to the AMT for individual taxpayers, you should be aware that the AMT also applies for corporations.

All rental property investors must cope with the redesigned AMT. Its new structure completely distinguishes it from the regular income tax. Its status has been elevated to that of a parallel tax as important as the regular tax. Many investors are now required to make separate AMT calculations every year. At the least, this requires more burdensome documentation and record-keeping.

## HOW TO CALCULATE THE ALTERNATIVE MINIMUM TAX

One consequence of the AMT is to delay certain regular tax deductions, and to accelerate certain types of income that the regular tax defers (called AMT timing adjustments). In addition, some items that are not subject to the regular tax are taxed by the AMT (called AMT preferences). Finally, there are fewer itemized deductions for the AMT than for the regular tax.

To calculate the AMT, you begin with regular taxable income and then make a series of adjustments.[2] The AMT formula is summarized in Figure 9-1.

The only tax credit available to reduce the AMT is the foreign tax credit (as specially calculated for the AMT). Other business tax credits (such as the rehabilitation and low income housing credits) don't reduce the AMT.

Many aspects of the AMT involve specialized activities that are usually not relevant for rental property investors. This discussion focuses on those elements of the AMT that you are most likely to encounter. The other aspects are briefly summarized in Figures 9-3 and 9-4.

## ALTERNATIVE MINIMUM TAX TIMING ADJUSTMENTS

The purpose for AMT timing adjustments is to delay certain regular tax deductions and to accelerate certain regular tax income. This creates timing differences between the regular tax and the AMT. To avoid the danger of double taxation because of timing differences,

a special AMT tax credit offsets the regular tax in subsequent years
(see below).

---

### Figure 9-1

### ALTERNATIVE MINIMUM TAX FORMULA

Regular taxable income

**Add or deduct:** Timing adjustments

**Add:** AMT preferences (items not included in regular
taxable income)

**Add:** Adjustments for itemized deductions (deductions
allowed for regular taxable income but not for the
AMT.

**Equals:** Alternative minimum taxable income (AMTI)

**Deduct:** AMT exemption

**Equals:** Alternative minimum tax base

**Multiply by:** AMT rate - 24%

**Equals:** Alternative minimum tax (AMT)

**Less:** Regular income tax liability

**Equals:** Alternative minimum tax
(if amount is positive)

---

### Depreciation of Real Estate

Real estate placed into service after 1986 must use the
alternative depreciation system discussed in Chapter 8.[3] This means
that the deduction is limited to the amount for straight-line depreci-

ation over a forty-year recovery period (see Table 8-4 in Chapter 8). This produces a smaller deduction for the AMT than that for the regular tax when you use the normal straight-line 27.5 or 31.5 year recovery periods.

> **Example:** Norris placed a rental house with a basis of $100,000 into service on January 24, 19X1 (after 1986). The regular 19X1 tax deduction is $3,480 (3.48% x $100,000 -- Table 8-2). The 19X1 AMT deduction is $2,400 (2.4% x $100,000 -- Table 8-4).

Before 1987, there were AMT consequences only if you used accelerated depreciation. AMT treatment for real estate placed into service before 1987 continues as it was under prior law. Essentially, you are permitted to deduct only the straight-line amount using the appropriate recovery period from the accelerated table (15, 18, or 19 years - See Chapter 8).[4]

### Depreciation of Personal Property

You must use the alternative recovery method for personal property placed into service after 1986. As discussed in Chapter 8, the deduction is calculated by using the 150% declining balance method. The recovery period is the midpoint or class life under the old-style depreciation system's Class Life Asset Depreciation Range (CLADR). If property doesn't have a class life, the write-off period is twelve years. Apparently, there is no class life for furniture or appliances in a residential rental unit. Therefore, the twelve year recovery period would apply (see Chapter 8). The new AMT rules apply for all personal property used in business or held for investment.[5]

Before 1987, only *leased* personal property used for investment (such as furniture and appliances in a rental house) required AMT adjustment. The regular tax depreciation method applied for personal property used in your business. AMT treatment for pre-1987 property is the same as it was under prior law. The amount deductible for the AMT is the straight-line amount calculated by using extended recovery periods. The extended straight-line period for three year recovery property was five years, and the extended period for five year recovery property was eight years.[6]

### Adjusted Basis for the Alternative Minimum Tax

Because depreciation is calculated differently for the AMT and the regular tax, the property's adjusted basis for each tax is different. The AMT basis is calculated by deducting depreciation under the alternative system. The basis for the regular tax is calculated by deducting the normal depreciation. You make the two basis adjustments regardless of which tax you are subject to in any given year.[7]

Thus, it is possible that when you sell the property, you will have a gain for one tax and a loss for the other. Which gain (or loss) you use depends upon which tax you are subject to in the year of sale.

**Example:** Assume in the above example that Norris sells the property for $90,000 on December 31, 19X3. The basis of the property and gain or loss for the two taxes are calculated as follows:

|                      | Regular Tax<br>Table 8-2 | AMT<br>Table 8-4 |
|----------------------|------------------|-------------------|
| Cost basis           | $100,000         | $100,000          |
| 19X1 Depreciation    | (3,480)          | (2,400)           |
| 19X2 Depreciation    | (3,640)          | (2,500)           |
| 19X3 Depreciation    | (3,640)          | (2,500)           |
| Adjusted basis       | $ 89,240         | $ 92,600          |
| Amount realized      | $ 90,000         | $ 90,000          |
| Adjusted basis (above) | 89,240         | 92,600            |
| Gain (Loss)          | $      760       | $(2,600)          |

If Norris is subject to the regular tax in 19X3, he reports the $760 gain. If he is subject to the AMT, he reports the $2,600 loss. The loss for the AMT compensates for the smaller depreciation deductions taken for the AMT during ownership of the property.

### Installment Sales

For both the regular tax and the AMT, the installment method is not permitted for reporting gains from sales of dealer property. The entire gain is included in AMT income in the year of sale regardless of when the installment payments are received.[8] See Chapter 10 for discussion of the installment method of reporting, and see Appendix B for a discussion of dealer property.

### Other Timing Adjustments

There are several other AMT timing adjustments for activities that are not usually encountered by residential real estate investors. These are summarized in Figure 9-3.

## ALTERNATIVE MINIMUM TAX PREFERENCES

Tax preferences are items of income that are not taxed under the regular income tax. You must add these items to AMT income. There are several preference items that could have adverse AMT impact for some rental property investors.

### Tax-Exempt Interest

The tax law has invaded the sanctity of the exclusion for state and local bond interest. You must add interest on private-activity tax-exempt bonds issued after August 7, 1986 to AMT income, though such interest is excluded from regular taxable income.[9] This includes interest from industrial development bonds where the proceeds are used by private businesses, and bonds to finance qualified multifamily residential projects, mortgage interest subsidies, mass commuting facilities, etc. Interest on general obligation bonds to finance basic government services (e.g., police, schools, and general government administration) is not subject to this rule, and is not included in AMT income.

### Charitable Contributions of Appreciated Property

If you contribute appreciated capital gain property to a charity, you must add the amount of the increase in value to your AMT income.[10] Like the regular tax, the AMT permits you to take an itemized deduction for the full market value of the contributed property. However, for the regular income tax, the amount of the appreciation is not included in income.

**Example:** Perry has land with a basis of $5,000 and a fair market value of $12,000. He donates the land to his local church. His other income for the regular tax and the AMT is $50,000. His taxable income for the two taxes are calculated as follows:

|  | Income Tax | AMT |
|---|---|---|
| Other taxable income | $50,000 | $50,000 |
| Add: Appreciation of contributed property |  | 7,000 |
|  | $50,000 | $57,000 |
| Less: Contribution ded. | 12,000 | 12,000 |
| Taxable income | $38,000 | $45,000 |

### Other Alternative Minimum Tax Preferences

Other AMT preferences associated with specialized activities not normally encountered by residential property investors are summarized in Figure 9-4.

## PASSIVE ACTIVITY LOSSES UNDER THE ALTERNATIVE MINIMUM TAX

Losses from passive activities generally are treated the same for the AMT and for the regular tax.[11] Thus, the definitions of passive activities, the special allowance for up to $25,000 of passive losses for rental real estate, etc., also apply for the AMT. See Chapter 7 for a discussion of the passive loss rules.

## ALTERNATIVE MINIMUM TAX ITEMIZED DEDUCTIONS

Some itemized deductions are treated alike for both taxes, but others are considerably more restricted for the AMT than for the regular tax. These deductions are either disallowed, or subject to more severe limitations by the AMT.

### Itemized Deductions Treated Alike by Both Taxes

The following expenditures are handled the same way for both the regular tax and the AMT:

**Charitable Contributions**. You are allowed the same charitable contribution deduction for both the regular tax and the AMT. However, if you contribute appreciated property, you must add the amount of the appreciation to AMT income (see above).

**Casualty Losses**. The deduction for personal casualty losses is the same for the AMT and the regular tax. The losses are measured the same way for both taxes, and the excess over 10% of regular tax adjusted gross income is deductible (see Chapter 4).

**Consumer Interest**. The AMT, like the regular tax, prohibits deduction of personal or consumer interest (see Chapter 4).

**Investment Interest**. For both the regular tax and the AMT, the deduction for interest on loans to finance portfolio investments (including unimproved land) is limited to your investment income (see Chapter 7).

**Other AMT Deductions**. Gambling losses (to the extent of gambling winnings), and estate taxes on income in respect of a decedent are deducted the same way for the regular tax and the AMT. The AMT net operating loss deduction is generally similar to that for the regular tax. However, the calculation of the amount of the loss is subject to special AMT rules.[12]

### Regular Income Tax Itemized Deductions Not Permitted for the AMT

The AMT does not permit deductions for personal and dependency exemptions, itemized employee and miscellaneous expenses (see Appendix A), state and local taxes, or the standard deduction.[13] These items must be added back to regular taxable income to calculate the AMT. However, there is a special AMT exemption (discussed below).

### Itemized Deductions Modified for the AMT

There are several regular tax itemized deductions that are modified to reduce AMTI.

**Medical Expenses**. The AMT permits you to deduct medical expenses in excess of 10% of your regular tax adjusted gross income.

The regular tax allows a deduction for the excess over 7.5% of adjusted gross income.[14]

**Home Mortgage Interest**. The AMT deduction for home mortgage interest differs from the deduction for the regular tax. For both taxes, you are allowed a deduction for interest on loans secured by your principal residence and one second home (see Chapter 4). However, the amount deductible for the AMT may be less than that for the regular tax.[15]

For both taxes, you are permitted to deduct the interest on a purchase-money loan, and on any loan used to finance capital improvements (acquisition indebtedness). In addition, for the regular tax, you are permitted to deduct the interest on up to $100,000 of home equity indebtedness, regardless of how you use the loan proceeds. This additional interest deduction is not permitted for calculating the AMT. Your AMT deduction is limited to the interest on the acquisition indebtedness. Thus, your interest deduction for a refinanced home mortgage, a second mortgage, or a home equity line of credit could be considerably less in years when you are subject to the AMT.

> **Example:** Kennedy purchased his principal residence in 19X0 for $100,000, with an original mortgage loan of $80,000. In 19X7 the market value of the home is $215,000, and the outstanding balance of the original loan is $50,000. He refinances the property for $175,000. For the regular tax, he may deduct the interest on $150,000 of the refinanced loan ($50,000 acquisition indebtedness + $100,000 home equity indebtedness). However, for the AMT, he is only permitted to deduct the interest on the $50,000 acquisition indebtedness.

## ALTERNATIVE MINIMUM TAX EXEMPTION

The AMT has a threshold exemption so that most middle-income taxpayers avoid the tax. The amount of the exemption phases out at higher income levels.

The amount of the exemption depends upon your filing status (see Appendix A) as follows:[16]

| | |
|---|---|
| Unmarried; Head of Household | $30,000 |
| Married Filing Jointly; Surviving Spouse | $40,000 |
| Married Filing Separately | $20,000 |

The exemption is reduced by 25% of your AMTI above specified levels. The levels are also determined by your filing status. The phase-out begins at the following amounts of AMTI:[17]

| | |
|---|---|
| Unmarried; Head of Household | $112,500 |
| Married Filing Jointly; Surviving Spouse | $150,000 |
| Married Filing Separately | $ 75,000 |

**Example**: Metzenbaum, a married taxpayer, has $195,000 of alternative minimum taxable income. His $40,000 exemption is reduced by $11,250 ($195,000 less $150,000 x 25%). Thus, his AMT exemption is $28,750 ($40,000 less $11,250).

## THE AMT CREDIT AGAINST THE REGULAR TAX

The timing adjustments of the AMT have the effect of postponing regular tax deductions, or accelerating recognition of regular tax income. For example, AMT depreciation is slower than regular tax depreciation.

If you are subject to the regular tax in some years, and to the AMT in others, there is a danger that you might be taxed twice on the same income. To alleviate this problem, the AMT provides a credit that is carried forward indefinitely (but not back) to reduce regular tax liability in any year when you are subject to the regular tax. The amount of the credit is the excess of your AMT tax liability over your regular income tax liability for any year when you are subject to the AMT. However, the credit may not reduce the regular tax liability below the AMT tax liability.[18]

**Example**: In 19X1, Danforth's AMT tax liability is $5,000, and his regular tax liability is $4,500. His AMT credit carryforward is $500 ($5,000 less $4,500). In 19X2, his regular tax liability is $6,000, and his AMT tax liability is $4,000. He is therefore subject to the regular tax for 19X2, but he

> reduces it by the amount of the AMT credit carryforward and pays $5,500 ($6,000 less the credit of $500).
>
> **Example**: Assume in the above example that Danforth's AMT tax liability for 19X2 is $5,700. He may only use $300 of the credit because he may not reduce his regular tax below the AMT tax. The remaining $200 of AMT credit continues to be carried forward.

The AMT credit only cancels double taxation created by timing differences between the AMT and the regular tax. You never recoup AMT tax liability resulting from preferences added to the AMT tax base. Examples are adjustments for tax-exempt interest, percentage depletion, and charitable contributions of appreciated property. Further, you will not recoup itemized deductions allowed for the regular tax but not allowed for the AMT.

## ILLUSTRATION OF ALTERNATIVE MINIMUM TAX CALCULATION

Figure 9-2 illustrates how to calculate the regular tax and the AMT. The differences in the treatment of specific items for the two taxes are explained in the notes following the calculations.

In 19X1, Mona Mogal, an unmarried taxpayer, has a salary of $30,000 from her job as a public school teacher. Her other relevant financial transactions during the year are as follows:

o She sells 60 residential lots in a subdivision she developed on land she inherited from her grandfather. The total sales price for the lots is $200,000, and her adjusted basis is $50,000. She agrees to help the buyers finance their purchases by providing part of the financing. She receives a total of $50,000 cash down payments, and carries back $150,000 in installment notes. The interest she receives on the notes for 19X1 is $13,500. Assume that her subdividing activities qualify her as a dealer (see Appendix B).

o In January, 19X1, she refinances her home. Its cost in 1975 was $90,000, and the market value in January is $180,000. The outstanding balance on the original loan is $40,000. The amount of the new loan is $150,000. It is an amortizing loan for 30 years with an interest rate of 9.5%. She uses $20,000 of the loan proceeds to pay college expenses for four of her grandchildren, and $30,000 for a trip around the world.

o In appreciation for her success with her real estate development, she donates some land worth $90,000 to her local church. Her basis for the land is $10,000.

o She has $6,000 of state income tax and real estate taxes on her home. She is entitled to one personal exemption for the regular tax (see Appendix A).

o She receives interest of $1,000 on private purpose industrial development bonds issued by the state of Idaho.

The calculations for the regular income tax and for the alternative minimum tax are as follows (the bracketed letters refer to the notes following the calculations):

---

## Figure 9-2

## CALCULATION OF REGULAR INCOME TAX

| | | |
|---|---|---|
| Salary | | $ 30,000 |
| Interest on installment notes | | 13,500 |
| Installment sale income (a) | | $150,000 |
| Adjusted gross income | | $193,500 |

Less: Itemized deductions

| | | |
|---|---|---|
| Charitable contribution | $ 90,000 | |
| State and local taxes | 6,000 | |
| Mortgage interest (b) | 13,263 | |
| Total itemized ded. | $109,263 | |
| Reduction (c) | 2,648 | 106,615 |

| | |
|---|---|
| Income before exemption | $ 86,885 |
| Exemption (d) | 644 |
| Taxable income | $ 86,241 |
| Income tax | $ 22,389 |

## CALCULATION OF ALTERNATIVE MINIMUM TAX

| | | |
|---|---|---|
| Regular taxable income | | $ 86,241 |
| Less: Itemized deduction reduction (c) | | 2,648 |
| | | $ 83,593 |
| Add: Preferences | | |
| Appreciation (e) | $80,000 | |
| Tax exempt interest | 1,000 | 81,000 |
| | | $164,593 |
| Add: Adjustments | | |
| State and local taxes | $ 6,000 | |
| Mortgage interest (b) | 9,473 | |
| Exemption (d) | 644 | 16,117 |
| AMTI | | $180,710 |
| Less: AMTI Exemption (f) | | 12,947 |
| AMT tax base | | $167,763 |
| Times AMT tax rate | | 24% |
| Tentative AMT | | $ 40,263 |
| Regular income tax | | 22,389 |
| AMT | | $ 17,874 |

Notes to Figure 9-2:

(a) Because dealer property is sold, the installment method of reporting is not available either for the regular income tax of the alternative minimum tax. See Chapter 10.

(b) The amount of the refinanced home mortgage loan qualifying for the interest deduction is $140,000 -- $40,000 acquisition indebtedness plus $100,000 home equity indebtedness (see Chapter 4). The interest on this amount at 9.5% is $13,263. For the AMT, only $3,790, the interest on the $40,000 refinanced acquisition indebtedness, is deductible (see above). There is no deduction for interest on the $100,000 home equity indebtedness. The difference of $9,473 ($13,263 less $3,790) is a positive AMT itemized deduction adjustment.

(c) Adjusted gross income exceeds the itemized deduction reduction threshold. The itemized deductions are reduced as follows (see Appendix A):

(1) 80% x $109,263 = $87,410
(2) 3% x ($193,500 less $105,250) = $2,648

Lesser of (1) or (2) = $2,648

This reduction of itemized deductions does not apply for the AMT. Thus, for calculating the AMT, the reduction must be subtracted from regular taxable income.

(d) Adjusted gross income exceeds the exemption reduction threshold. The reduction in the exemption is calculated as follows (see Appendix A):

| | |
|---|---:|
| Adjusted gross income | $193,500 |
| Reduction threshold | 105,250 |
| Excess | $ 88,250 |

$$\frac{\$88,250}{\$2,500} = 35.3 \ (36)$$

36 x 2% = 72%
72% x $2,300 (exemption amount) = $1,656
$2,300 - $1,656 = $644

(e)
| | |
|---|---:|
| Fair market value - Land | $ 90,000 |
| Adjusted basis - Land | 10,000 |
| Appreciation | $ 80,000 |

(f)
| | |
|---|---:|
| AMTI | $180,710 |
| AMT exemption base | 112,500 |
| Excess | $ 68,210 |
| Reduction Percentage | 25% |
| Reduction amount | $ 17,053 |

| | |
|---|---:|
| Exemption | $ 30,000 |
| Reduction | 17,053 |
| Exemption amount | $ 12,947 |

The amount of the AMT credit carryover is $17,874 ($40,263 tentative AMT less $22,389 regular tax). The credit may reduce the regular tax in a future year (but not below the AMT for that year - see above).

## TAX PLANNING FOR THE ALTERNATIVE MINIMUM TAX

The illustration in the preceding section shows several telltale signs of vulnerability to the AMT, and suggests ways that planning can help you avoid its traps. Because Mona engaged in transactions with different AMT and regular tax consequences in same year, she was subject to the AMT. Further, her AMT taxable income was so large that she lost most of her AMT exemption.

### Refinancing Your Home

Because you permanently lose the interest deduction on the amount of the refinanced loan in excess of the balance when you refinance, you should never refinance in a year when you are subject to the AMT. You should either rearrange the mix of your transactions to avoid the AMT, or delay refinancing, a second mortgage or a home equity line of credit to a year when you are subject to the regular tax.

Further, the limitation on the interest deduction (and the consequent loss for the AMT of the deduction allowed under the regular tax) applies not only for the year you refinance, but also for any subsequent year when you are subject to the AMT. Thus, if you refinance in excess of the existing loan balance, you should avoid the AMT for the duration of the new loan.

### Charitable Contributions of Appreciated Property

This problem is easy to avoid. Don't contribute appreciated property to charity in a year when you are subject to the AMT.

Also, be careful that the appreciation of contributed property, when added as an AMT preference, will not by itself subject you to the AMT.

### Itemized Regular Tax Deductions Not Available for the AMT

To the extent possible, you should avoid these expenses in a year when you are subject to the AMT. Sometimes, this is difficult because the expenditures are not discretionary. For example, it is difficult to alter the amount of real estate taxes or state income taxes. However, you may have flexibility for timing unreimbursed employee expenses and miscellaneous itemized deductions.

### Other AMT Danger Signals

Besides the commonly encountered transactions discussed above, you must be wary of the more specialized preferences and timing adjustments described in Figures 9-3 and 9-4. Although these items may have little impact when considered separately, taken in combination with other items, they may tip the scale to make you subject to the AMT.

---

### Figure 9-3

### OTHER TIMING ADJUSTMENTS

o **Amortization of Pollution Control Facilities.** Post-1986 property is treated like any other personal property, so the AMT adjustment is made in the manner described above for personal property.[19]

o **Mining and Exploration and Development Costs.** Expenses must be amortized over ten years rather than written off in the year they are incurred.[20]

o **Research and Development Expenses.** Costs must be amortized over ten years rather than written off in the year they are incurred.[21]

o  **Circulation Expenditures**. Costs must be amortized over three years rather than written off in the year they are incurred.[22]

o  **Completed-Contract Method of Accounting**. For long-term contracts after March 1, 1986, you must use the *percentage-of-completion* method for reporting. This accelerates income for the AMT. Thus, if you have a four-year, $100,000 contract, and if the work is done ratably over the four-year period, you are required to include $25,000 per year in AMT income. For the regular tax, the completed-contract method defers taxation of the entire $100,000 until the fourth year, when the contract is completed.[23]

o  **Tax Shelter Farm Losses**. These are losses (after 1986) generated by farming syndicates (as defined under prior law) and passive farming activities (a farming business where you don't materially participate - see Chapter 7). For the AMT, you make the appropriate AMT depreciation adjustments (see above), and the resulting loss cannot reduce AMT taxable income. You carry the disallowed loss forward indefinitely, until the activity produces income to absorb the loss, or until you dispose of the activity.[24]

---

**Figure 9-4**

**OTHER ALTERNATIVE MINIMUM
TAX PREFERENCES**

o  **Intangible Drilling Costs (IDCs)**. You first determine your "excess" IDCs, which is the difference between the amount incurred and the amount you would be allowed if you amortize the IDCs over 120 months. The preference added to the AMT tax base is the excess of "excess" IDCs over 65% of your net income from all oil, gas and geothermal properties.[25]

o **Percentage Depletion**. The amount added to the AMT tax base is the excess of the percentage depletion deduction over the adjusted basis of the property at the end of the year. The preference applies for percentage depletion of *all* minerals, not just oil and gas as under prior law.[26]

---

## FOOTNOTES

1. The rules for the AMT are contained in Internal Revenue Code (IRC) §§53, 55, 56, 57 and 58. Technically, the AMT as the excess of 24% of the AMT tax base (AMTI less the AMT exclusion) over the regular tax liability. This amount is paid in addition to the regular tax. Since the total of these two amounts is the same as 24% of the AMT tax base, the economic result is that you pay the higher of the two taxes. IRC §55(a) and (b).

2. IRC §56(a).

3. IRC §56(a)(1).

4. Pre-1986 law defined the depreciation adjustment as a preference equal to the excess of accelerated over straight-line depreciation using the appropriate accelerated recovery period. This had the effect of limiting the amount of depreciation to the straight-line amount.

5. IRC §56(a)(1)(A)(ii). See Chapter 8 for a discussion of the alternative depreciation system recovery periods.

6. IRC §57(a)(12)(A) as it read before 1986.

7. IRC §56(a)(7).

8. IRC §§56(a)(6), and 453(b)(2)(A).

9. IRC §57(a)(5).

10. IRC §57(a)(6).

11. IRC §56(b). The rule is different for passive losses that otherwise create AMT preferences.

12. IRC §56(d).

13. IRC §§56(b)(1)(A) and (b)(1)(E).

14. IRC §56(b)(1)(B).

15. IRC §56(e).

16. IRC §55(d)(1).

17. IRC §55(d)(3).

18. IRC §53.

19. IRC §56(a)(5).

20. IRC §56(a)(2).

21. IRC §56(b)(2).

22. IRC §56(b)(2).

23. IRC §56(a)(3).

24. IRC §§58(a) and (c)(2).

25. IRC §§57(a)(2) and (b).

26. IRC §57(a)(1).

# NOTES

# CREATIVE FINANCING
# AND TAX-DEFERRED TRANSACTIONS

## CHAPTER 10

*Tax Consequences of Seller Financing*

## CHAPTER 11

*Other Creative Financing Techniques: Shared Equity, Lease-Options, Like-Kind Exchanges*

## CHAPTER 12

*Involuntary Conversions*

*part*

# Chapter

# TEN

# TAX CONSEQUENCES OF
# SELLER FINANCING

What if you aren't able to buy real estate for cash, and your financial position isn't strong enough to support a bank loan? Then the seller must provide the financing to complete the sale. This can be done by the seller taking a note secured by the property, often called "carryback financing."

Until recently, seller financing was unusual for single family home sales, but it became more common when soaring interest rates made it difficult for buyers to qualify for loans. Carryback financing in the residential real estate market has become known as "creative financing." Actually, there is nothing particularly creative about it. For years, seller financing has been extensively used for many types of real estate transactions, particularly for sales of land.

Although you might resist seller financing, its desirability (or undesirability) depends upon the circumstances. If you defer or exclude the gain when you sell your principal residence (see Chapter 5), the absence of up-front cash may be a disadvantage. You might need the cash to buy another home. However, if you sell property and your gain is taxable, seller financing gives you an opportunity to postpone payment of tax if you don't need the cash immediately. Though bank financing may be available, carryback financing gives you a valuable tax benefit. From the buyer's viewpoint, it is always good to keep a bank out of a transaction. Seller financing makes this possible.

## STRUCTURING A SELLER FINANCED TRANSACTION

You can arrange carryback financing in various ways to achieve non-tax legal and financial objectives. You should consider the timing of principal and interest payments, when title to the property passes, and how the note is structured. The overriding objective is that both you and the buyer are comfortable with the payment terms. When you are unrealistic about the buyer's ability to make timely payments, a foreclosure is likely to result. You also must be careful not to be too optimistic about the future availability of institutional financing to pay off the carryback loan.

Regardless of how you structure carryback financing, the tax consequences are the same. As long as there is a payment of principal in a future year, you may use the installment method of reporting gain. Although the installment method is favorable for you, it is laden with tax traps that you must recognize to avoid tax disaster.

### Timing of Principal and Interest Payments

The time-honored method for structuring a real estate loan is an amortizing mortgage. Each payment includes both principal and interest on the unpaid balance. Payments remain constant throughout the life of the loan, so that in the early years, most of each payment is interest. As the loan gets older, the amount applied to principal increases.

Although time honored, amortizing loans are not sacred. The payment terms might be too inflexible. Even institutional lenders are uncomfortable with long-term fixed interest loans in periods of fluctuating interest rates. You might be willing to finance the sale for a certain period, but don't want to wait twenty or thirty years to be paid off. Fixed payments might be burdensome for a buyer during the early years of the loan, but become more comfortable in later years when income increases. In response to these concerns, several techniques are popular for institutional and carryback loans. Two of these are discussed below. The discussion is by no means exhaustive, but illustrates how creative buyers and sellers can tailor transactions to meet their mutual needs.

**Balloon Payments.** A "balloon" is a lump-sum payment of the outstanding balance of a loan. Balloon payments are useful when you are willing to finance the buyer, but you want total payment within a relatively short period. You must use balloon payments carefully. If the term for the balloon is too short, the buyer might not be able to come up with the cash to pay the loan. Then you must either renegotiate or foreclose. Often short-term balloons (three to five years) are used during tight money markets in the hope that institutional financing will become available to pay the balloon. Watch out. Many buyers have found to their dismay that when the time comes to pay, the money market is worse than when they purchased the property. A balloon note should always contain an escape valve for such a contingency. For instance, you could have a provision to extend the loan under specified circumstances.

There are many variations for balloon payment terms. The simplest is where all payments during the term of the loan are interest-only, and the entire principal is paid at the end.

> **Example:** Kahn sells his home to Nadell for $100,000. Nadell has $10,000 for a down payment, but can only obtain a bank loan for $70,000. Kahn agrees to carry back a note for the remaining $20,000, at 10% interest, but wants the entire balance paid within five years. The note is structured so that Nadell pays $166.67 interest per month with the entire $20,000 loan payable in a balloon in five years.

Sometimes you might want some principal reduction with each payment, but you are unwilling to hold the note for a long period. In such a case, the note may be amortized using a long-term payment schedule, with the unpaid principal payable in a balloon within a shorter period.

> **Example:** Assume the facts of the above example, except that the $20,000 loan is payable monthly using a 20-year amortization schedule, with the balance of the loan payable at the end of five years. The monthly payment is $193.00, and the balloon payment of principal at the end of five years is $17,960.80.

You may have a series of balloons, using either interest-only payments or an amortizing loan schedule.

> **Example:** Assume the facts of the above example except that $10,000 is paid at the end of the third year, and the remaining $10,000 is paid at the end of the fifth year. The monthly payments of interest-

only for the first three years are $166.67, when, after payment of the first $10,000 balloon, the payments drop to $83.33.

**Adjustable Rate Loans**. If you are willing to finance a transaction for a long period, but you are unwilling to bear the risk of interest rate increases, an adjustable rate loan may be the solution. These are popular with institutional lenders, and there is no reason you can't use them for carryback financing. The interest rate for adjustable rate loans changes periodically according to an index such as the prime rate, a Federal funds rate or the consumer price index. Often there is a cap on how much the rate may be increased within a specified period.

There are many other combinations of interest and principal payment terms that you may design to meet your needs. However, the choice among alternatives always requires realistic analysis of the cash flow position for yourself and the buyer.

### Passing Title to the Property

Usually, title to property passes at the time of closing. However, when you carry back a note, you might delay passing title until the note is paid in full. The document transferring beneficial ownership to the buyer is called a land sale contract, land contract, contract for deed, or conditional sale contract. The contract is recorded to establish that the buyer has beneficial ownership even though he does not possess legal title.

**Buyers Beware.** Delayed passage of title has long been common for sales of land. Now, in an attempt to avoid "due-on-sale" clauses in non-assumable mortgages, the device is also being used for home sales. This is based on the assumption that a "sale" occurs only when title passes, and that if title doesn't pass, the lender cannot call the loan. Several state courts have ruled that lenders may exercise due-on-sale clauses when the borrower transfers the beneficial ownership of the property. In these states, this ploy doesn't work. Further, more recent due-on-sale clauses list other events that trigger acceleration of a loan, such as transfer of beneficial ownership, granting of options, and long-term leases.

In some states, the rights of a seller's creditors against the property are unclear when you delay passage of title. There are cases where a seller's creditors successfully levied against property even though the buyer's beneficial interest was recorded. If this happens, you must establish the superiority of your rights. The problem has been particularly troublesome when the seller files under the Federal bankruptcy laws. Accordingly, you should be wary of delayed title passage in states where it is not a long-standing procedure.

For tax purposes, it doesn't matter who holds legal title.[1] You are the tax owner if you have beneficial ownership of the property. You are the beneficial owner if you have the benefits and burdens of ownership, or if you bear the risk of loss if the property is destroyed.

The amount of the borrower's personal liability for payment of the loan depends upon whether the note is *recourse* or *nonrecourse*. If it is a recourse loan, the lender can levy against both the loan's collateral and the other assets of the borrower. Conversely, if the loan is nonrecourse, the lender can only levy against the collateral. The other assets of the borrower are shielded from a nonrecourse loan. Usually, the tax law does not distinguish between recourse and nonrecourse loans. Since most loans for homes and investment rental property are recourse, the discussions in this book assume that the borrower has personal liability.

### Structuring the Note

If the seller finances the entire price in excess of the down payment, structuring the transaction is easy. He simply takes a note secured by a first mortgage (or deed of trust) on the property. Suppose you have an existing mortgage that the buyer assumes. There are several ways to structure a carryback note. The easiest is for the seller to take a note for the carryback financing secured by a second mortgage on the property.

> **Example:** Berman sells his home to McGinnies for $100,000. McGinnies pays Berman $10,000 cash and assumes an existing 30-year, 8% FHA $30,000 mortgage. The monthly payments on this mortgage are $220.13. Berman takes back a 10-year $60,000 note secured by a second mortgage bearing interest at 10%, with monthly payments of principal and interest of $792.91. McGinnies makes the two payments separately to the bank and to Berman.

As an alternative, you could use a "wraparound" note for $90,000, secured by a second mortgage on the property. The amount of the note is the entire amount of financing, both existing and carryback. It acknowledges and includes existing superior liens in the total of the new note. The buyer makes payments to you, and you then make the payments on the underlying note. Wraparound mortgages are sometimes called "all inclusive deeds of trust." If the interest rate on the wraparound note is higher than that on the underlying note, your overall yield on the wraparound note is higher that its stated interest rate.

> **Example:** Assume in the above example, Berman creates a wraparound note for $90,000 bearing interest of 10%, acknowledging and including the existing $30,000 loan. The wraparound note is secured by a second mortgage and provides that all payments are made to Berman, and that Berman makes the payments on the underlying note. The monthly payment of principal and interest on the wraparound note is $1,189.36. From this payment, Berman makes the monthly payment of $220.13 on the underlying note.

**Buyer Beware:** You may transfer title to the property at the time of closing, or delay transfer until the wraparound loan is fully paid. Buyers of property under a wraparound note must be careful that the payments are made on the underlying mortgage. In the above example, if Berman fails to make the payments on the underlying debt, the lender will foreclose. Since that lender's lien is superior to McGinnies' ownership rights, there is a danger that McGinnies might lose the property. One solution is to establish an escrow arrangement where an independent agent collects McGinnies' payments, makes the payment on the underlying note, and then remits the excess to Berman.

## THE INSTALLMENT METHOD OF TAX REPORTING

Generally, gains are taxed in the year of the sale. This can be a severe hardship if you receive little or no up-front cash and collect the bulk of the sale price in future years. If you have a large gain, you could be placed into the position of not having enough cash from the transaction to pay your tax. You may be forced to sell other assets, or take out a loan.

To alleviate these problems, the installment method of reporting gives you relief when you receive payments in years after the sale year. Gain is taxed only when you receive payments of principal, either in the sale year, or in subsequent years.[2]

Installment reporting provides three economic benefits:

o Tax is not payable until there is cash available to pay it,

o Tax is spread over the years of the installment payments, which may result in a lower overall tax burden than if the entire gain is taxed at one time (see Chapter 2), and

o Tax is only paid on gain that materializes, and insulates you (at least tax-wise) from the buyer's cash flow and financial problems.

**How to Qualify for Installment Reporting**

The installment method of reporting is available for gains resulting from deferred payment sales of property held for any purpose other than for sale as a *dealer*.[3] Thus, it is applicable for nondealer property used in trade or business, property held for investment, or property used for personal purposes (such as a principal residence or a second home). The alternative minimum tax (AMT) also permits installment reporting for all real estate sales other than sales of dealer property (see Appendix B for a discussion of *dealer* property and Chapter 9 for a discussion of the AMT).[4] However, the installment method is available only for reporting gains. You must report losses in the year of sale.[5]

Installment reporting is automatic for any transaction where there is a payment of principal in any year after the sale. No down payment or any other installment payments in the sale year are required. To qualify, you only need one future payment.

Example: Leventhal sells his home for $80,000. He is in the top tax bracket and currently needs no cash. However, in five years he plans to take the entire year off and travel for pleasure. During that year he will have no income. He takes no down payment and carries back a note for $80,000 to be paid in a balloon in the fifth year when he needs the money for his travels. Though there is only one payment of principal, Leventhal qualifies for installment reporting. Thus, he reports the entire gain in the fifth year, and he pays the tax then. Probably, since Leventhal will have no other income in that year, he will be in a lower tax bracket so that the tax on the gain will be less than if it were reported during the intervening years.

There is no limit on the amount you may receive in the year of sale. The Installment Sale Revision Act of 1980 (ISRA) eliminated the old limitation that disallowed installment reporting if you received more than 30% of the selling price as *initial payments*. This rule caused the infamous folk custom of "29% down" transactions, leading many taxpayers down the primrose path to tax disaster because they did not understand what initial payments were.

If you don't want your tax to be deferred you must elect not to use installment reporting. You do this by reporting the gain and paying tax in the year of sale.[6] Considerations for making the decision whether to use the installment method are discussed in the Tax Planning Ideas below.

You don't have to use installment reporting for all transactions in the same year, even if the transactions are similar. However, once you report a transaction by using the installment method, you must continue to use it for that transaction, and may not change without prior permission of the Internal Revenue Service (IRS).[7]

**What are "Initial Payments," and Why do They Matter?**

Initial payments determine how much gain is taxed in the year of sale. Initial payments are not necessarily limited to the down payment. Although ISRA eliminated the old 30% trap, it did not change the definition of initial payments. They can result from economic benefits other than cash. Thus, you might be required to pay tax in the year of sale without cash from the transaction to pay the tax. This danger requires that you always heed the following:

*WARNING: ALWAYS MAKE SURE THAT THE SALE GENERATES ENOUGH CASH TO PAY TAX TRIGGERED BY NON-CASH BENEFITS IN THE YEAR OF SALE.*

Much has been written about the joys of buying property for "nothing down." Nobody, however, seems to write about the tax terrors of selling property for nothing down. The following discussion should help correct that oversight by highlighting situations where installment sales may put you into a cash bind.

The buyer's installment notes generally are not initial payments. This rule has exceptions, however. For instance, if the notes are payable on demand, they are initial payments.

**Down Payment and Payments of Principal in the Year of Sale.** Initial payments include the amount of any cash down payment (including earnest money or other deposits applied to the down payment), and any installment payments of principal in the year of sale.[8] Initial payments also include the value of other property (securities, jewelry, boats, automobiles, etc.) received as part of the down payment. Initial payments do not include the value of *like-kind* real estate received. Usually, like-kind property is investment or business real estate received as a down payment for investment or business property (see Chapter 11).[9] When you receive like-kind property, you have a partial tax-free exchange and a partial installment sale (See Chapter 11).

Money you receive as consideration for a purchase option and that you apply to the purchase price is an initial payment. At the time you receive payment for the option, the transaction is considered open until the option is exercised, at which time it is treated as part of the down payment (see Chapter 3).[10]

**Debts Assumed by the Buyer That are Related to the Property.** Often, a buyer assumes or pays your debts as part of the consideration for the property. The most common situation is where the buyer assumes your outstanding mortgage. However, he also may pay other debts related to the property such as real estate taxes and mortgage interest in arrears. Sometimes, he might pay your debts unrelated to the property. It is important to examine whether such assumptions or payments are initial payments.

When the buyer assumes a debt directly related to the property, there is no initial payment. The types of indebtedness qualifying under this rule include:[11]

o  An existing mortgage loan outstanding on the property,

o  Other liens encumbering the property such as real estate taxes or mortgage interest in arrears, and

o  Debts not secured by the property, but incurred or assumed by the buyer in connection with the property's acquisition, holding or operation in the ordinary course of business or investment.

There is one very important exception to this rule, however. If the mortgage and other directly-related indebtedness assumed by the buyer exceed your basis for the property, the amount of the excess is an initial payment.

> **Example:** Chambless sells her home to Parker for $90,000. Parker pays no cash down, but assumes the existing $45,000 mortgage, pays real estate taxes in arrears of $8,000, and mortgage interest in arrears of $2,000. Chambless' basis for the property is $50,000, so her gain is $40,000 ($90,000 less $50,000). Although there is no cash payment, the indebtedness assumed or paid by Parker of $55,000 ($45,000 + $8,000 + $2,000) exceeds Chambless' basis by $5,000. The $5,000 excess is an initial payment.

The excess indebtedness assumed by the buyer triggers tax without a corresponding receipt of cash. The hazards of this trap in nothing down transactions are fully discussed in the Tax Planning Ideas below.

**Other Liabilities of Seller Paid by Buyer.** Initial payments include payments by the buyer of your debts unrelated to the transaction, such as your medical expenses or car insurance premiums. They also include payment of your transaction-related costs such as legal fees and real estate commissions. Such payments to third parties are treated as payment of cash to you followed by payment by you to the third party. Accordingly, they trigger tax the same way as a direct cash payment to you. However, because the payments are made to third parties, you get no cash to pay the tax.

**Cancellation of a Debt You Owe the Buyer.** If you are indebted to the buyer, and as part of the consideration for the sale the buyer agrees to cancel your debt, the amount of the cancellation is an initial payment.[12] This is another example of an initial payment that triggers tax without generating cash.

The following examples illustrate the calculation of initial payments:

> **Example:** Silverberg sells a lot to Weiss for $12,000 on June 30, 19X1. $1,000 is received as a down payment, and Weiss executes notes of $9,000 payable in monthly principal installments of $200 beginning on September 1, 19X1. The notes bear interest at the rate of 10%. In addition, Weiss gives Silverberg XYZ Corporation stock with a value of $500 to be applied against the purchase price, and Weiss agrees to cancel a $1,500 debt owed to him by Silverberg incurred when Silverberg bought a

car from Weiss. The initial payments are $3,800 (the down payment of $1,000, four installment payments totaling $800, the $500 value of the stock, and the $1,500 debt cancelled).

**Example:** In 19X0 Slotnick gave Yates $500 for an option to purchase a rental house. On June 30, 19X1, Slotnick exercises the option and purchases the house for $100,000, giving Yates a down payment of $5,000, assuming an existing first mortgage of $25,000, and giving installment notes for a total of $70,000, payable in $1,000 monthly installments of principal beginning October 1, 19X1. Yates' adjusted basis for the house is $20,000. Slotnick also pays the $6,000 commission on the transaction to Yates' real estate broker. The notes bear interest at the rate of 10%. The initial payments are calculated as follows:

| | |
|---|---:|
| Option price applied to purchase price | $    500 |
| Excess of mortgage over basis | 5,000 |
| Down payment | 5,000 |
| Three installment payments (Oct.-Dec.) | 3,000 |
| Yates' commission paid by Slotnick | 6,000 |
| Total initial payments | $19,500 |

## How Gain is Reported

The installment method treats part of each principal payment as taxable gain, and part as a nontaxable return of capital. You determine the amount of gain by applying the *gross profit ratio* to the payment. This ratio is the *gross profit* divided by the *contract price*. The following formula determines how much of each principal payment is taxable:

$$\frac{\text{Gross Profit}}{\text{Contract Price}} \quad X \quad \text{Principal Payment} = \text{Gain Taxed}$$

There is a special method for calculating the gross profit ratio when you use a wraparound mortgage.[13]

**Gross Profit.** Gross profit is the selling price of the property less its basis. The calculation for purposes of installment reporting differs from the usual method for determining gain (see Chapter 3). When you use the installment method, you don't reduce the selling price by selling expenses and other transaction costs. Instead, you add these costs to your basis for the property.[14] Although shifting the selling expenses doesn't reduce the amount of gain, it affects the gross profit ratio in some situations.

**Contract Price.** The contract price is the selling price less the amount of existing mortgage loans and related debt (as described above) that the buyer assumes. However, if the mortgage loans and related debt assumed by the buyer exceed the basis for the property, the amount of the excess is added to the contract price. Remember, under the installment sale rules, you increase your basis by your transaction costs.[15]

**Example:** Frailey sells his home to Geiser for $95,000. Geiser gives a $10,000 down payment out of which Frailey pays his $5,700 real estate commission. Geiser agrees to assume Frailey's outstanding $50,000 mortgage, and to pay Frailey's $2,000 real estate taxes in arrears. For the balance of the price, Geiser gives Frailey installment notes for $33,000. Frailey's basis for the house is $30,000. For installment sale purposes, Frailey's basis is $35,700 (the $30,000 basis plus the $5,700 real estate commission). The debt assumed by Geiser is $52,000 (the $50,000 mortgage plus Frailey's real estate taxes of $2,000). The total debt assumed by Geiser in excess of Frailey's basis is $16,300 ($52,000 less $35,700). The contract price is calculated as follows:

| | |
|---|---|
| Selling price | $95,000 |
| Less: Debt assumed by Geiser | (52,000) |
| Add: Debt assumed in excess of basis | 16,300 |
| Contract price | $59,300 |

**Example:** Continuing the above example, the gross profit ratio is 100%. The gross profit is $59,300 ($95,000 less $35,700). The ratio is calculated as follows:

$$\frac{\text{Gross profit}}{\text{Contract price (above)}} \quad \frac{\$59,300}{\$59,300} = 100\%$$

At this point it is important to summarize that when a buyer assumes debt in excess of your basis, you have *two* tax consequences for installment sale reporting:

o The excess debt assumed by the buyer is an initial payment triggering taxation of gain in the year of sale, and

o The excess debt assumed by the buyer is added to the contract price to determine the gross profit ratio, and the gross profit ratio is always 100%.

### Illustrations of Installment Sale Calculations

The following examples are adapted from the Income Tax Regulations.[16] First, an illustration of the computation where the buyer does not assume a mortgage:

> **Example:** Hawke sells his home to Karch for $100,000. Karch pays $10,000 down and the remainder is payable in equal annual installments of $10,000 over the next nine years, together with adequate stated interest. Hawke's basis for his home is $38,000, and he pays selling expenses of $2,000. For installment sale reporting purposes, his basis is $40,000 ($38,000 plus $2,000). His gross profit is $60,000 ($100,000 less $40,000). Since Karch doesn't assume any debts, the contract price is the same as the selling price: $100,000. The gross profit ratio is determined as follows:
>
> $$\frac{\text{Gross profit}}{\text{Contract price}} \quad \frac{\$60,000}{\$100,000} = 60\%$$
>
> Accordingly, $6,000 (60% of $10,000) of each $10,000 installment payment is gain attributable to the sale and $4,000 ($10,000 less $6,000) is a tax-free recovery of capital. The interest Hawke receives in addition to the principal payments is ordinary income.

The next two examples show how you make the calculations when the buyer assumes a mortgage. The first example illustrates how you reduce the contract price by the debt assumed by the buyer when the debt is less than your basis. The second example illustrates how you compute the contract price when the debt assumed by the buyer exceeds your basis.

> **Example:** Burr, age 35, sells his home to Gross for $160,000, and doesn't reinvest the proceeds. The home is encumbered by a long standing mortgage with a balance of $60,000. Gross assumes the $60,000 mortgage and pays the remaining $100,000 in ten equal annual $10,000 installments together with adequate stated interest. Burr's basis for the home is $90,000. There are no selling expenses. The contract price is $100,000 ($160,000 selling price less the $60,000 mortgage assumed by Gross). The gross profit is $70,000 (selling price of $160,000 less the basis of $90,000). The gross profit ratio is determined as follows:
>
> $$\frac{\text{Gross profit}}{\text{Contract price}} \quad \frac{\$70,000}{\$100,000} = 70\%$$

Thus, $7,000 (70% of $10,000) of each $10,000 annual payment is gain attributable to the sale, and $3,000 ($10,000 less $7,000) is a recovery of capital.

**Example:** Assume the facts of the above example, except that Burr's basis for the house is $40,000. Therefore, the debt Gross assumes exceeds Burr's basis by $20,000. As discussed above, this has two tax consequences for Burr: (1) the excess debt assumed is an initial payment, and (2) the excess debt assumed is added to the contract price. The gross profit is $120,000 ($160,000 selling price less $40,000 basis). The contract price is determined as follows:

| | |
|---|---:|
| Selling price | $160,000 |
| Less: Debt assumed by Gross | (60,000) |
| Add: Debt assumed in excess of basis | 20,000 |
| Contract price | $120,000 |

The gross profit ratio is 100%, determined as follows:

$$\frac{\text{Gross profit}}{\text{Contract price}} \quad \frac{\$120,000}{\$120,000} = 100\%$$

Thus, Burr reports the entire initial payment of $20,000 (mortgage assumed in excess of Burr's basis) in the year of sale, and 100% of each subsequent $10,000 payment as gain attributable to the sale. Although $20,000 of taxable income is generated in the year of sale, Burr receives no cash from the transaction to pay the tax.

Now let's take the example one step further by assuming that Burr incurs and pays selling expenses.

**Example:** Assume the facts of the above example except that Burr pays a $10,000 real estate commission. For installment reporting purposes, his basis is $50,000 ($40,000 plus the selling expenses). Burr's gain is $110,000 ($160,000 less $50,000). The debt assumed by Gross in excess of Burr's basis is $10,000 ($60,000 debt assumed less basis of $50,000). The contract price is determined as follows:

| | |
|---|---:|
| Sale price | $160,000 |
| Less: Debt assumed by Gross | (60,000) |
| Add: Debt in excess of basis | 10,000 |
| Contract price | $110,000 |

The gross profit ratio is 100%, as follows:

$$\frac{\text{Gross profit}}{\text{Contract price}} \quad \frac{\$110,000}{\$110,000} = 100\%$$

Thus, the entire $10,000 initial payment (excess debt assumed by Gross) is taxable gain, and the entire amount of each subsequent $10,000 installment payment is taxable gain.

### Installment Sale of a Home Where You Defer or Exclude Gain

Suppose you sell your home and reinvest less than the adjusted sale price in another home. Part of the gain is deferred under the home-sale rollover (see Chapter 5). As part of the sale price you carry back installment notes. You calculate your gross profit ratio by considering only the amount of gain not deferred.[17]

**Example:** Elektra sells her home for $100,000. Kitkat pays $20,000 down, and gives Elektra notes for $80,000, payable $5,000 per year for the following sixteen years. The notes bear adequate interest. Elektra's basis for the home is $40,000, and her gain is $60,000 ($100,000 less $40,000). One year later, Elektra buys a replacement home for $80,000. Therefore, $20,000 of her $60,000 gain is taxed because she under-reinvests ($100,000 adjusted sales price less $80,000 reinvestment). Elektra's contract price is $100,000. The gross profit is $20,000, the amount of gain *not* deferred under the home-sale rollover rules. The gross profit ratio is 20%, determined as follows:

$$\frac{\text{Gross profit}}{\text{Contract price}} \quad \frac{\$20,000}{\$100,000} = 20\%$$

Therefore, $4,000 (20% of $20,000) of the down payment is taxable gain and the remaining $16,000 is a tax-free return of capital. Similarly, $1,000 (20% x $5,000) of each $5,000 payment is taxable gain, and the remaining $4,000 is a tax-free return of capital.

A similar rule applies for installment home sales where you exclude gain by electing the over-55 exclusion (see Chapter 5). Here, you determine your gross profit ratio by using only the gain in excess of the gain excluded.[18]

**Example:** Sparky sells his home to Wana for $200,000. His basis is $50,000, so his gain is $150,000. He qualifies for the over-55 exclusion, and elects to exclude $125,000 of the gain. Wana gives Sparky a $50,000 down payment, and notes for $150,000, payable in annual installments of $15,000 for ten years. The notes bear adequate interest. After the exclusion, only $25,000 of

Sparky's gain is taxable, and for installment reporting, this is the gross profit. His contract price is $200,000. His gross profit ratio is 12 1/2% as follows:

$$\frac{\text{Gross profit} \quad \$25,000}{\text{Contract price} \quad \$200,000} = 12\ 1/2\%$$

Thus, $6,250 (12 1/2% of $50,000) of the down payment is taxable gain, and the remaining $43,750 is a tax-free return of capital. Similarly, $1,875 (12 1/2% of $15,000) of each $15,000 installment is taxable gain, and the remaining $13,125 is a tax-free return of capital.

### Disposing of Installment Notes

What can you do with the installment notes you receive when you finance a sale? One possibility is to hold the notes and collect the payments. Here, gain is reported as you collect the principal payments.

If you decide to dispose of the notes, however, there could be tax trouble. The notes are ticking tax time bombs waiting to explode. This is because any disposition of installment notes triggers the untaxed gain from the underlying sale.[19] If you sell or discount the notes, this result makes sense. It is in line with the general idea of installment reporting that when notes are cashed-in (either by collecting payments or selling them) tax liability should result. However, the reason for the result is not so obvious when you give the notes away. No cash is received, but you have a taxable event. Two types of transfers don't trigger taxation of gain:

o Transfer of the notes at death, and

o Transfer between spouses or incident to a divorce (see Chapter 6)

In these situations, the person receiving the notes steps into your shoes. He continues to report income the same way as you would have.

Here is how you report gain when you dispose of installment notes. Generally, you calculate gain the same way as for any other sale or exchange: the amount realized less the basis of the notes (see Chapter 3). If you sell or discount the notes, the amount realized is the amount of cash you receive. For a gift, the amount realized is the fair market value of the notes at the time of the gift. Your basis for the notes is the face value less the gain you would report if you collected payment on the notes in full. Put another way, the basis of the notes is the face value less the gross profit ratio.

**Example:** Allen sells a rental house for $250,000. His basis for the house is $150,000, so that his gross profit is $100,000. He receives a $10,000 cash down payment, and takes back twelve annual notes of $20,000 each. The notes bear adequate interest. The contract price is $250,000 and the gross profit ratio is 40% as follows:

$$\frac{\text{Gross profit}}{\text{Contract price}} \quad \frac{\$100,000}{\$250,000} = 40\%$$

Six months later, Allen sells two of the notes for $36,000. The basis for the notes is $24,000 (face value of $40,000 less the gross profit ratio of 40%). The gain from the sale of the notes is $12,000 ($36,000 less $24,000).

**Example:** Assume in the above example that Allen gives the notes to his son, Michael. The fair market value of the notes is 80% of their face value, or $32,000. Taxable gain resulting from the gift is $8,000 ($32,000 less the basis determined above of $24,000).

**Example:** Assume in the above example that Allen transfers the notes to his wife, Agnes, as part of their divorce settlement. A gift to a spouse or a transfer incident to a divorce is not a taxable event (see Chapter 6), and Agnes' basis for the notes is the same as Allen's basis, or $24,000. As Agnes collects the payments, she reports income the same way Allen did before he transferred the notes to her.

## Pledging Installment Notes for a Loan

The net proceeds of any loan secured by pledging installment notes arising from the sale of nondealer real estate are treated as a payment received on those notes.[20] This rule applies only if the sale price of the property giving rise to the notes exceeds $150,000. All sales that are part of the same transaction are treated as one sale for purposes of this threshold. The rule does not apply for pledges of installment notes arising from sales of personal use property (such as a principal residence) or property used in the business of farming.

The amount of the deemed payment is limited to the amount of untaxed gain attributable to the pledged notes. The amount of gain taxed is determined by multiplying the deemed payment by the gross profit ratio applicable to the installment notes.

The gain is taxed at the time the loan becomes secured by the note, or the time you receive the loan proceeds, whichever is later. Thus, if you secure a line of credit with an installment note, it is not treated as a disposition until you draw on the funds. To avoid double taxation, subsequent installment payments are treated as tax-paid amounts to the extent of the gain previously taxed because of the deemed payment.

### The Impact of Installment Sales on Suspended Passive Losses

Normally, when you have suspended passive losses from an investment (see Chapter 7), you may deduct the losses in full in the year you dispose of the property. The rule is modified, however, when you report gain under the installment method.

If you don't elect out of installment reporting, you are allowed to deduct only a portion of the accumulated suspended losses in the year of the sale. The remainder of the accumulated loss continues to be suspended until future years when the gain is taxed.

You determine the portion of the suspended losses you may deduct each year by using the ratio that the installment gain recognized each year bears to the gross profit from the installment sale.[21] In the year of sale, this is the gain triggered by initial payments.

> **Example:** Morrison sells a rental house for $100,000, taking a down payment of $20,000, and eight annual installment notes of $10,000, the first being payable in the following year. His basis for the property is $40,000, and he has accumulated suspended losses of $8,000 related to the property. His gain is calculated as follows:
>
> | | |
> |---|---:|
> | Down payment | $ 20,000 |
> | Installment notes (8 x $10,000) | 80,000 |
> | Amount realized | $100,000 |
> | Less: Adjusted basis | 40,000 |
> | Gain realized | $ 60,000 |
>
> The gross profit ratio is 60% ($60,000/$100,000). In the year of sale, he recognizes gain of $12,000 (60% of the $20,000 down payment). This represents 20% of the total gross profit ($12,000/$60,000). Thus, he may deduct $1,600 of the suspended passive losses (20% of $8,000).

In each of the subsequent eight years he recognizes income of $6,000 (60% of $10,000), that represents 10% of the total gross profit ($6,000/$60,000). In each year he may deduct $800 of the suspended passive losses (10% of $8,000).

### Imputed Interest

The tax law assumes that any sale of property where you receive principal payments in future years includes interest. If you don't provide for any (or for insufficient) interest, it is imputed by the tax law. Interest is imputed whether or not you report the sale under the installment method. Without such a requirement, you might be encouraged to "disguise" interest as part of the selling price, thereby converting ordinary income (interest) to long-term capital gain.

If you carry back a note for less than $2.8 million, the stated rate must be the lesser of 9% or the applicable Federal Rate.[22] Federal Rates are published monthly by the Treasury Department for short-term (1-3 years), mid-term (3-9 years), and long-term (over 9 years) Federal notes. The applicable Federal Rate is the one corresponding to the duration of the carryback note. If the applicable Federal Rate exceeds 9%, the "safe-harbor" stated interest rate of 9% satisfies the imputed interest requirement. There are exceptions to the this rule for certain carryback sales such as sales of raw land to family members, and sale-leaseback transactions. Also, the imputed interest rules do not apply where the sale price is less than $3,000.

If you finance more than $2.8 million, different rules apply. Since most carryback financing for homes and residential investment property is less than $2.8 million, these rules are not discussed here.

If the interest rate stated in the carryback notes is inadequate, formulas in the Income Tax Regulations recharacterize part of the selling price as interest. This, in turn, reduces the amount realized from the sale, the gross profit, and the contract price. Thus, tax consequences resulting from payments or dispositions of the notes are altered. You can easily avoid these problems simply by stating an adequate interest rate. You should be careful to do so.

### Foreclosure and Repossession of Seller
### Financed Property

Unfortunately, buyers sometimes fail to meet their payment obligations. If you can't renegotiate the contract or payment terms, you might be forced to foreclose and repossess the property. The repossession could be a taxable event for you, even though you receive no cash, and really don't want to take back the property.

If you are in this predicament, Congress has provided tax relief which accomplishes the following:[23]

o Postpones tax on the property's increase in value between the original sale and the time of repossession,

o Limits the amount of taxable gain from the original sale to the amount of cash payments you received before the repossession that you reported as tax-free returns of capital, and

o Reduces the amount of your taxable gain by the costs of repossession.

The relief provision treats gain from repossession of real estate in a uniform manner, despite the nature of the property sold. You may not report a loss from repossession. The gain you report is the lesser of:

o The total payments (initial and installment) you received before repossession less the gain you reported, or

o Your original gain from the sale less (a) gain you reported before repossession and (b) your repossession costs.

**Example:** McGinley sells property for $90,000 that has a basis of $60,000. He receives $15,000 cash at the time of sale, the balance being payable in ten annual installments of $7,500 plus adequate interest. After three installments are paid, the buyer defaults and McGinley repossesses the property. The gain is $30,000 ($90,000 less $60,000). Repossession costs are $500. The contract price is $90,000, and the gross profit ratio is 33 1/3% as follows:

$$\frac{\text{Gross profit}}{\text{Contract price}} \quad \frac{\$30,000}{\$90,000} = 33 \ 1/3\%$$

The total amount received before repossession is $37,500 ($15,000 down payment plus three installment payments of $7,500 each). The gain reported before repossession is $12,500 ($37,500 x 33 1/3%). Gain from repossession is calculated as follows:

*A*

| | |
|---|---|
| Money received before repossession | $37,500 |
| Less: Gain taxed before repossession | 12,500 |
| Trial amount of gain | $25,000 |

*B*

| | |
|---|---|
| Gain from original sale | $30,000 |
| Less: Gain taxed before repossession | (12,500) |
| Less: Repossession costs | (500) |
| Trial amount of gain | $17,000 |

The gain taxed because of repossession is the lesser of the above trial amounts, or $17,000

The basis for repossessed real estate is the sum of (1) the basis of the installment notes outstanding at the time of repossession, (2) the gain taxed because of the repossession, and (3) the repossession costs.

**Example:** In the above example, the basis of the outstanding notes at the time of repossession is $35,000 (7 notes x $7,500 less the gross profit ratio of 33 1/3%). The basis of the repossessed property in the above example is $52,500 calculated as follows:

| | |
|---|---|
| Basis of the outstanding notes | $35,000 |
| Add: Gain taxed on repossession | 17,000 |
| Add: Repossession costs | 500 |
| Basis of repossessed property | $52,500 |

If you sell personal property (such as furniture or equipment) on the installment basis and later repossess it, gain or loss is recognized. Here, your gain or loss is the difference between the fair market value of the property when you repossess it, and your basis for the installment notes (as defined above). Your basis for repossessed personal property is its fair market value at the date of repossession.

## Repossession of a Principal Residence

A special rule applies when you repossess your principal residence, and you have deferred or excluded part or all the gain.[24]

If you don't resell the property within one year after repossession, the general rules discussed in the preceding paragraph apply. However, if you resell the home within one year after repossession, the original sale and the resale are treated as one transaction, and the repossession is ignored. Your new adjusted sales price is the resale price plus any cash or property you retained from the original sale. The amount of deferred or excluded gain is recomputed, and if the recomputed taxable gain is more or less than what you originally reported, the difference is added or deducted in your return for the year of resale.

### Sales With a Contingent Selling Price

Sometimes you base the price for property on future events, such as a percentage of the income from the property. This might happen when you sell a business (such as a farm), and base the price on a percentage of future gross receipts, or when you sell mineral property, basing the price on a percentage of the receipts from minerals extracted. In such cases, it is impossible to determine your amount realized and gain in the year of sale. The Income Tax Regulations establish an extensive set of rules for reporting gain for these types of sales.[25]

### Deferred Payment Sales

The deferred payment method is an alternative to installment reporting. This method was important under the law before ISRA, because of the 30% limitation on the amount of initial payments. It was particularly important for real estate developers and others who could not use installment reporting because their loan commitments required down payments exceeding 30%.

Under the deferred payment method, you use the market value of the carry-back notes (rather than the face value) to determine your amount realized and gain. Since the market value of the notes is usually less than their face value, the gain is less. The difference between the market and face values is taxed when the notes are paid. Unlike installment reporting, the deferred payment method transforms capital gain into ordinary income when the notes are paid.

### Depreciation Recapture in Installment Sales

Installment reporting is not available for the part of a gain taxed as ordinary income because of depreciation recapture (see Appendix B for a discussion of depreciation recapture).[26] Thus, even if you don't have initial payments to trigger tax in the year of sale, you must report any amount of ordinary income caused by depreciation recapture. This is one of the most dangerous aspects of installment reporting for investment property. If you used accelerated depreciation (or ACRS), large amounts of income can be taxable without cash to pay the tax. After 1986, accelerated depreciation is no longer available, and depreciation recapture rules for property placed into service after 1986 are repealed. However, if you contemplate an installment sale of investment property where you used accelerated depreciation under prior law, you must be wary.

### Sales Among Related Persons

There is a special rule designed to thwart a device once used to obtain full cash payment in the year of sale without paying tax on the gain.[27] This was done by making an installment sale to a closely related party, followed by an immediate cash sale by the related party to the ultimate buyer. The installment notes received from the related party were not payable until a future time. Here is how the device worked under prior law:

> **Example:** Papa received a cash offer of $100,000 for his rental property. His basis was $40,000, so his gain was $60,000. If he took the cash, the gain was immediately taxed. To avoid this, Papa sold the house to his daughter for $100,000, the entire price being represented by the daughter's installment notes, with payments to begin after ten years. The daughter immediately sold the property for cash to the buyer. Since the daughter's basis for the property was $100,000 (the amount of the notes she gave Papa), she had no taxable gain. Papa wouldn't have taxable income until the daughter began to pay the notes ten years later. However, the $100,000 was within the family group, tax-free.

To prevent this, the law now provides that if the second sale by the related party (the daughter) occurs within two years after the first sale (by Papa to the daughter), the gain is taxed to the first seller (Papa) at the time of the second sale.

> **Example:** In the above example, if the daughter sells the property within two years after she buys it from Papa, Papa's $60,000 gain is taxed to him at the time the daughter sells the property.

Related family members are your spouse, children, grandchildren, and parents. Certain trusts, estates, corporations, and partnerships in which you have an interest are also related parties. Special rules adjust the taxable gain for the first seller if gain was taxed because of installment payments received before the second sale by the related party. There are also special rules for installment sales of marketable securities, and for other specialized dispositions.

## TAX PLANNING IDEAS FOR INSTALLMENT SALES

### Deciding Whether to Use Installment Reporting

If you defer principal payments, installment reporting is required unless you elect not to use it. When should you make such an election? Since the election is irrevocable, this up-front decision is important. Sometimes the decision is dictated by your present tax situation. Often, however, it rests to a large extent on crystal ball gazing and predictions of future economic events.

If you have losses or potential losses to offset the gain, it may be wise to elect out of installment reporting. This may be a way, for instance, to bail out of securities investments that have gone sour. Offsetting these losses by gain from the real estate sale avoids the restriction on the deduction for capital losses (see Appendix B).

You should consider electing out of installment reporting when you have suspended passive losses in excess of the gain. This way you may use the losses immediately. If your suspended losses are less than the total gain, your decision whether to elect out is more difficult. You must assess the desirability of paying tax on the gain in excess of the suspended losses.

If you expect future inflation rates to be high, you may want to receive as much cash as possible in the year of sale. The disadvantage of accelerating taxation of the gain is offset because dollars you receive in future years are worth less. You might be able to invest the after-tax up-front dollars to yield a higher overall return after taking into consideration the purchasing power erosion caused by inflation. Such an analysis can become very complex, since it also must take into account your anticipated future tax brackets, anticipated future interest rates, and, most unpredictable of all, future changes in the tax law. These problems are most serious for long-term carrybacks. If you are uncomfortable with these potential problems, you might consider a shorter term balloon payment.

### Sale Year Tax Savings By Shifting Your Transaction Costs

In most sales, you incur transaction costs such as real estate commissions, legal fees, etc., that you must pay in cash. To provide funds, the down payment should at least cover these costs. The down payment, however, triggers taxation of gain. If your costs are shifted to the buyer, and the sale price and down payment are decreased by the amount of the costs, you reduce your sale year gain.

> **Example:** Hodinko sells a rental home to Leedy for $100,000. His real estate commission is $10,000, and he takes a down payment for that amount. For the balance, he takes notes of $90,000 payable in ten equal installments. His basis for the property is $60,000, so his gain is $30,000 ($100,000 sale price less $60,000 basis and $10,000 selling costs). The gross profit ratio is 30% ($30,000/$100,000). In the year of sale he has taxable income of $3,000 (30% of $10,000 down payment). Leedy agrees to be legally liable for the commission by signing the listing agreement with the real estate broker, and pays the commission directly to the broker. Accordingly, the sale price is reduced to $90,000, and there is no down payment. Hodinko's gain is $30,000 ($90,000 sale price less $60,000 basis), and his gross profit ratio is 33 1/3% ($60,000 divided by $90,000). However, he has no taxable gain in the year of sale because he receives no initial payments.

The example shows that the buyer's economic results are the same under the two alternatives: he must pay $10,000 in the sale year, his overall purchase price for the property is $100,000, and his basis for the property is $100,000. It is important that the documentation shows that the buyer has legal liability for the transaction costs. If the buyer pays your legal liability, a tax trap is created.

### Dealing With Tax Traps in "Nothing Down" Sales

The key to dealing with tax traps in sales with little or no up-front cash is to be aware of the traps. The object is to avoid creating taxable income without cash from the sale to pay the tax. The danger areas are discussed above. This section summarizes the red flags that should wave when you carry back financing. Specifically, taxable income is created without cash when:

o The buyer assumes mortgage loans and other related debts in excess of your basis,

o The buyer pays your legal obligations,

o The buyer cancels a debt you owe him,

o You apply option consideration you received in prior years to the down payment, and

o Ordinary income is generated by depreciation recapture.

**Assumption of Mortgages in Excess of Your Basis.** There are two reasons why an existing mortgage loan may exceed your basis for the property:

o The property has increased in value, and you refinanced in an amount exceeding your basis, or

o The depreciation on investment property (that reduces its basis) has been faster than your loan amortization payments.

If you refinance the property, you obviously should be careful about this problem, although there isn't much you can do other than be sure that adequate cash is generated in the transaction.

**Buyer Pays Your Legal Obligations.** Initial payments include the buyer's payment or assumption of your liabilities other than those directly related to the property. The related liabilities include real estate taxes or mortgage interest payments in arrears. Payment of related liabilities is treated the same as an assumption of your mortgage (see the preceding paragraph).

Sometimes the buyer pays your transaction costs such as real estate commissions or legal fees. These payments by the buyer are initial payments. If your understanding with the buyer is that he will pay the commission, you can solve the problem easily by having the buyer sign the listing agreement with the real estate broker, and reducing the selling price by the amount of the commission. This makes the commission the buyer's legal liability.

You may do the same thing with your other transaction costs such as legal fees. The above section discusses how shifting transaction costs to the buyer creates a positive tax break for you.

Less often, the buyer may pay your liabilities unrelated to the transaction, such as your personal living expenses. To avoid the resulting initial payment, you should avoid such payments.

**Cancellation of Your Debt to Buyer**. If you owe money to the buyer, your debt may be cancelled as part of the consideration for the sale. This is an initial payment. If this causes a problem, you should continue the debt according to its original terms, and add its amount to the selling price and the amount you carry back. This technique also creates a tax advantage for the buyer. The amount of his prior loan to you, that was unrelated to his acquisition of the property, now increases his basis for the property.

**Option Payments**. The problem with option payments is one of timing. At sometime before the sale, you received cash for the option. Tax consequences are postponed until the buyer exercises the option or lets it lapse (see Chapter 3). If he exercises the option the option consideration becomes an initial payment to you. If he lets it lapse, you have ordinary income. In either situation, if you granted the option very far in advance of its exercise or expiration, you may have spent the cash you received, and may not have cash available to pay the tax. If this is a potential problem, you should keep the option consideration in a liquid investment until it is determined when, and whether, the buyer will exercise the option.

## FOOTNOTES

1. *Roy, et al v. Comm'r.* 69 F2d 786 (CA 5, 1934).

2. Generally, see Internal Revenue Code (IRC) §453.

3. IRC §§453(b)(2)(A) and 453(l)(1)(B).

4. IRC §56(a)(6).

5. Rev. Rul. 70-430, 1970-2 CB 51.

7. IRC §453(d)(3).

8. Rev. Rul. 73-369, 1973-2 CB 155.

9. IRC §453(f)(6)(C).

10. *Comm'r. v. Stuart,* 300 F2d 872 (CA 3, 1962).

11. Temp Reg. §15A.453 1(b)(2)(iv).

12. Rev. Rul. 76-398, 1976-2 CB 130; Rev. Rul. 71-515, 1971-2 CB 222.

13. Temp. Reg. §15A.453-1(b)(5), Examples 5 and 6; but see *Professional Equities, Inc. v. Comm'r,* 89 TC 165 (1989) Acq. By implication, the case not only invalidates Temp. Reg. §15A.-1(b)(3)(ii), but also invalidates the examples in Temp. Reg. § 15A-1(b)(5), cited above.

14. Temp. Reg. §15A.453-1(b)(2)(v).

15. Temp. Reg. §15A.453-1(b)(2)(iii).

16. Temp. Reg. §15A.453-1(b)(5), Examples 1 through 3.

17. Rev. Rul. 75, 1953-1 CB 83.

18. Rev. Rul. 80-249, 1980-2 CB 166.

19. IRC §453B; Reg. §1.453-9.

20. IRC §§453A(a)(2) and 453A(d).

21. IRC §469(g)(3).

22. IRC §§483 and 1274A.

23. IRC §1038.

24. IRC §1038(e); Reg. §1.1038-2.

25. Temp. Reg. §15A.453-1(c).

26. IRC §453(i).

27. IRC §453(e).

# Chapter

# ELEVEN

## OTHER CREATIVE TECHNIQUES: SHARED EQUITY, LEASE-OPTIONS, AND LIKE-KIND EXCHANGES

Most so-called "creative financing" techniques are variations of seller carryback loans. However, in the wake of high interest rates and tight institutional lending policies, two other truly creative techniques have emerged to help you fulfill your dream of home ownership. Shared equity financing is a technique for matching prospective homeowners who can't qualify for a loan with investors who can. Lease-options adapt a long-standing commercial real estate technique to help you buy a home. Another technique, used by commercial real estate investors for decades, is the tax-free exchange. Although the tax advantages of like-kind real estate exchanges have been available since 1921, small-unit residential investors have only recently begun to recognize the potential. You should be familiar with the tax and financial benefits of these techniques. The purpose of this chapter is to provide an introduction.

### SHARED EQUITY FINANCING

What do you do when your income is sufficient to qualify for a home mortgage loan, but you don't have enough cash for the down payment? Or what if you have enough for the down payment, but you won't be comfortable with the mortgage payments until your income increases? What if your parents want to help you buy your first home, but they need cash return and investment appreciation greater than that generated by lending you the down payment?

You can solve these and other problems by using shared equity financing arrangements. You team up with one or more investors who provide part or all of the cash for the down payment and/or help you with the mortgage payments. In return, you give the investor an equity interest in the property. You and the investor take title to the property as co-owners, usually as tenants in common (see Chapter 3). You usually agree that you will be permitted to buy the investor's interest at a specified time in the future.

> **Example:** Investor and Homeowner each provide one-half of the down payment for a home costing $80,000, and each will pay one-half of the mortgage. They take title to the property as equal tenants in common. Homeowner has an option to acquire Investor's one-half interest after five years for its fair market value as determined by appraisal at that time. If the option is not exercised and the property is sold, they will divide the proceeds equally.

> **Example:** Assume the facts of the above example except that Investor provides the 20% down payment of $16,000, and agrees to pay one-half of each mortgage payment. He takes a 60% interest as a tenant in common (20% down plus one-half of the 80% of the property that is financed), and Homeowner takes a 40% interest. Homeowner has an option to acquire Investor's 60% interest after five years. If the option is not exercised and the property is sold, Investor will receive 60% of the proceeds and Homeowner will receive 40%.

Shared equity arrangements are truly "win-win" situations for all parties. You can buy a home you couldn't otherwise afford. In addition, you build equity and reduce your tax bill because you get tax deductions for interest and real estate taxes that are not available if you rent your home. Further, your share of the gain from the home's sale qualifies for the home-sale rollover and the over-55 exclusion (see Chapter 5). The investor has the usual tax benefits of rental property ownership, but at little or no risk. Who could be a better tenant than a co-owner who wants to build a nest egg with his home?

Although you have considerable flexibility for structuring the terms of shared equity arrangements, the tax law allows the good tax things to happen only if you satisfy certain requirements:[1]

> o The arrangement must be pursuant to a *shared equity financing agreement* that must be in writing,

o At least one party to the agreement must occupy the property as a principal residence as defined for the home-sale rollover (see Chapter 5) for a period of at least twelve months,

o The occupant must pay fair rental to the investor for the portion of the property owned by the investor, and

o The parties must acquire the property with undivided ownership interests for more than fifty years.

### How To Write a Shared Equity Financing Agreement

A shared equity financing arrangement is something like a partnership. The tax benefits, however, are not as flexible as those allowed by the partnership tax rules.

Your written agreement should specifically address all the requirements of the tax law. Thus, it should state that you intend the arrangement to be a qualifying shared equity financing agreement, require that you will occupy the property as a principal residence, confirm that you and the investor each have an undivided interest in the property lasting more than fifty years, and show that the rent you pay to the investor is fair rental.

In addition, it should explain how you and the investor share mortgage payments and other expenses, and how you will divide the proceeds and gain from the property's sale. If you and the investor agree that you will have the right to buy his interest (or vice-versa), you should clearly outline the terms of the buyout. For example, you should specify how you will determine the buyout price, the time frame, the terms of payment, etc.

### What is Fair Rent?

You are deemed to pay fair rent if you pay an amount equal to the fair rent for the entire property multiplied by the investor's fractional ownership interest.[2]

> **Example:** Assume in the above example that the fair rent for the house is $900 per month and the investor's ownership interest is 60%. Thus, $540 per month (60% of $900) is fair rent.

You determine fair rent by examining comparable rents in the neighborhood at the time you enter into the agreement. The law is silent about what happens in subsequent years. However, it is probably advisable to increase the rent to keep pace with comparable rents in the area. If you are related to the investor, you should be careful about gifts from the investor to you. Such gifts might be construed as rent rebates, and destroy the arrangement because it lacks fair rent. You should sign a standard residential lease to document the amount of the rent and other terms of the rental arrangement. In addition, you should give the investor a normal security deposit.

### Fifty-Year Undivided Interest

Undivided fee simple ownership (tenancy in common or joint tenancy) satisfies this requirement. The ownership requirement has nothing to do with the length of your lease. Thus, it is not necessary that you have a lease of more than fifty years. A standard two or three year residential lease is sufficient.

There may be a potential problem if the agreement *requires* you to buy the investor's interest (or vice-versa), or *requires* a future sale of the property to a third party. Although the law is not entirely clear, this may be interpreted as a violation of the fifty-year requirement. A safer route is to use an option for your right to buy the interest of the investor (or vice-versa). Since you have discretion whether or not to exercise the option, the fifty-year requirement is satisfied, even if you do exercise the option.

### Allocating Deductions

You allocate tax deductions according to the ratio of the ownership interests in the property. Depreciation is probably the most important deduction for the investor. He determines the amount of his deduction by multiplying the property's basis by his percentage of ownership, and then applying the appropriate depreciation rates to this amount. As the homeowner, you get no depreciation deduction because you don't own the property for investment.

You and the investor deduct the mortgage interest and real estate taxes that you each actually pay. The payments and deductions need not be in the ratio of your ownership interests. You may deduct all the interest if you make the mortgage payments. Shifting the payments to you is advantageous for the investor if the payment of his share creates negative cash flow. At the same time, you get the tax deductions because you are a homeowner (see Chapter 4).

Other expenses (insurance, repairs, condominium fees, etc.) should be paid by you and the investor in the ratio of your ownership interests. If the investor pays an amount greater than his proportionate share, the excess could be construed as a rent rebate, and jeopardize the entire arrangement. However, there is no problem if the investor pays *less* than his proportionate share of the other expenses.

The investor's deduction for his tax losses resulting from a shared equity investment, like losses from any other rental property investment, is subject to the passive loss limitations (see Chapter 7).

### Examples of Shared Equity Financing Arrangements

The following examples illustrate the flexibility of shared equity arrangements to accomplish your tax and financial objectives. All three examples assume that Homeowner and Investor enter into a shared equity agreement to buy a $100,000 home that Homeowner uses as her principal residence. The fair rental for the home is $600 per month ($7,200 per year). The annual real estate taxes are $1,000, and other expenses (insurance, repairs, etc.) are $500. The cost allocated to the building is $80,000.

Homeowner has taxable income of $43,000, and her combined Federal and state marginal tax rate is 28%. See Chapter 1 for a discussion of the financial impact of tax rates. Investor has taxable income of $125,000 with a combined Federal and state marginal tax rate of 33%.

**Example:** Investor provides $20,000 for the down payment, and the parties obtain a mortgage loan for $80,000 at 10% interest. The mortgage payments total $8,424 annually, of which $7,880 is interest in the first year. Each party pays one-half the mortgage payments and real estate taxes. The other expenses are allocated according their percentages of ownership. Investor gets a 60% interest in the property reflecting his 20% down payment and one-half of the 80% financed. The cash flow and tax consequences for Homeowner and Investor are calculated as follows:

|  | Homeowner 40% | Investor 60% |
|---|---|---|
| **Cash Flow:** | | |
| Rent (60% of $7,200) | $(4,320) | $ 4,320 |
| Mortgage (50%-50%) | (4,212) | (4,212) |
| Taxes (50%-50%) | ( 500) | ( 500) |
| Other (40%-60%) | ( 200) | ( 300) |
| Cash flow | $(9,232) | $( 692) |

|  | | |
|---|---|---|
| **Tax Consequences:** | | |
| Rent | | $ 4,320 |
| Interest | $(3,940) | (3,940) |
| Real estate taxes | ( 500) | ( 500) |
| Other expenses | | ( 300) |
| Depreciation on $48,000 | | (1,670) |
| Tax loss | $(4,440) | $(2,090) |
| | | |
| Tax Savings | $ 1,243 | $ 690 |

Homeowner's net monthly after-tax cash outflow of $666 is not significantly more than the $600 fair rent she would pay to an outside landlord. The net monthly cash outflow is calculated as follows:

| | |
|---|---|
| Cash out (1/12 of $9,232) | $769 |
| Cash in (1/12 of tax savings of $1,243) | 103 |
| After-tax cash out | $666 |

Assuming that Investor may deduct his tax loss from other income under the passive loss rules (see Chapter 7), he is effectively in a break-even position with cash-out of $692, and cash-in from tax savings of $690.

The following two examples illustrate shared equity arrangements resulting in passive income for Investor. The large down payment may be appropriate when parents help their children buy a home. The examples assume the facts of the above example, except that Investor provides a down payment of $50,000, and the parties borrow the other $50,000 at 10% interest. The annual mortgage payments are $5,265, of which $4,987 is interest in the first year.

**Example:** Investor provides the down payment, and Homeowner makes all payments for the mortgage and real estate taxes. Other expenses are allocated according to their ownership interests. Investor gets a 50% interest in the property, representing his down payment.

| | Homeowner 50% | Investor 50% |
|---|---|---|
| **Cash Flow:** | | |
| Rent (50% of $7,200) | $( 3,600) | $ 3,600 |
| Mortgage payments | ( 5,265) | |
| Real estate taxes | ( 1,000) | |
| Other (50%-50%) | ( 250) | ( 250) |
| Cash flow | $(10,115) | $ 3,350 |
| | | |
| **Tax Consequences:** | | |
| Rent | | $ 3,600 |
| Interest | $(4,987) | |
| Real estate taxes | (1,000) | |
| Other expenses | | ( 250) |
| Depreciation on $40,000 | | (1,392) |
| Taxable income (loss) | $(5,987) | $ 1,958 |
| | | |
| Tax liability (savings) | $(1,676) | $ 646 |

Homeowner's net monthly after-tax cash outflow of $703 is somewhat more than that in the prior example, but it is still only $103 more than the $600 fair rental she would pay to an outside landlord. The net monthly cash outflow is calculated as follows:

| | |
|---|---|
| Cash out (1/12 of $10,115) | $843 |
| Cash in (1/12 of tax savings of $1,676) | 140 |
| After-tax cash out | $703 |

Investor's after tax cash-on-cash return depends upon whether he has passive losses (current or suspended) to absorb the $1,958 of passive income generated by the investment (see Chapter 7).

**Example:** Investor provides the down payment, and he and Homeowner each make one-half of the mortgage, real estate tax, and other expense payments. Investor gets a 75% interest in the property, reflecting his 50% down payment and half of the 50% financed.

| | Homeowner 25% | Investor 75% |
|---|---|---|
| **Cash Flow:** | | |
| Rent (75% of $7,200) | $(5,400) | $ 5,400 |
| Mortgage payments | (2,632) | (2,633) |
| Real estate taxes | ( 500) | ( 500) |
| Other (50% - 50%) | ( 250) | ( 250) |
| Cash flow | $(8,782) | $ 2,017 |

*Tax Consequences*:

| | | |
|---|---:|---:|
| Rent | | $ 5,400 |
| Interest | $(2,493) | (2,494) |
| Real estate taxes | ( 500) | ( 500) |
| Other expenses | | ( 250) |
| Depreciation on $60,000 | | (2,088) |
| Taxable income (loss) | $(2,993) | $ 68 |
| | | |
| Tax liability (savings) | $( 838) | $ 22 |

As in the first example, Homeowner's net monthly after-tax cash outflow of $662 is not significantly more than the $600 fair rental she would pay to an outside landlord. The net monthly cash outflow is calculated as follows:

| | |
|---|---:|
| Cash out (1/12 of $8,782) | $732 |
| Cash in (1/12 of tax savings of $838) | 70 |
| After-tax cash out | $662 |

Again, Investor's after tax cash-on-cash return depends upon whether he has passive losses to absorb the $68 passive income generated by the investment. However, the taxable income is so small that it won't make much difference.

## LEASE-OPTIONS

A lease-option is useful when you can't qualify for a mortgage loan, but expect your income to increase so that you will be able to qualify within a relatively short period. It is also useful when you want to wait for high interest rates to decline. A lease-option enables you to occupy the property and to tie down a fixed price until you can buy it. Because you lease and occupy the property, the seller/landlord has a low-risk tenant. In addition, he gets the usual tax breaks available for residential rental property.

In the normal lease-option, you lease the property for a relatively short period (two or three years) and the seller gives you an option to buy the property at a specified price any time during the lease period, or at a defined time in the future. You usually pay something for the option, and you forfeit the payment if you don't exercise the option. If you exercise the option, the payment for the option is usually deducted from the purchase price. Sometimes, part or all of the rental payments during the option period are also deducted from the purchase price.

If this "win-win" situation seems too good to be true, sometimes it is. Although you and the seller win, the silent party, Uncle Sam, may feel that he loses. Sometimes the terms of a lease-option look like an installment sale. Uncle Sam may invoke the judicial principle of *substance over form* (see Chapter 2) to recharacterize the "lease" and to tax it as an installment sale. Treating a lease-option as a sale has two tax consequences:

o It changes the timing of the property's transfer. In a true lease-option, ownership doesn't transfer until the option is exercised. However, if it is treated as an installment sale, ownership transfers when the parties enter into the lease. Thus, in situations where timing is crucial, the tax consequences are altered.

o It changes the tax characterization for the payment to acquire the option, and for the rent payments during the lease period.[3]

### Timing Problems of Lease-Options for Homeowners

Because recharacterization as a sale changes the timing of ownership transfer, you must be careful not to violate the reinvestment period requirements of the home-sale rollover (see Chapter 5). This is particularly dangerous when you deliberately use a lease-option to avoid the reinvestment timing restrictions.

**Example:** Mazis is relocated by his employer on June 30, 19X1, and has a buyer who is willing to buy his home on that date. Because of the real estate market, he fears that he will be unable to buy a new home by July 1, 19X3, the end of the reinvestment period for the home-sale rollover. To delay the sale of the old home, he and buyer enter into a lease-option, giving the buyer the right to purchase the home at the end of a two-year lease. The consideration for the option is the amount the buyer would have paid as a down payment and the rent is equal to the mortgage payments if the buyer purchased the home outright. When the option is exercised, the option consideration and the rent are to be deducted from the purchase price. Buyer exercises the option on July 1, 19X3, and Mazis buys and occupies his new home on January 1, 19X4, six months after the sale of the old home. If the transaction stands as a lease-option, Mazis' reinvestment qualifies because it occurs within two years after the sale of the old home. If the transaction is recharacterized as a sale, however, the transfer of the old home's ownership is deemed to be on June 30, 19X1, the date the lease began. Since this is more than two years before the reinvestment in the new home, the rollover is not available.

Timing of property acquisition is also crucial for involuntary conversions (see Chapter 12).

### Tax Consequences of Lease-Options

In a true lease-option, the tax consequences of the lease and those of the option are treated separately.

**Taxation of the Buyer and the Seller During the Lease.** If the property is a rental investment, the seller treats the property as if the option didn't exist. The rent he receives is ordinary income, and he deducts depreciation and other operating expenses until the option is exercised and ownership passes.

If the property is the seller's principal residence however, he must be careful not to disqualify it for the home-sale rollover and over-55 exclusion. Although the rent he receives is ordinary income, if he deducts depreciation and other rental expenses, the government may assert that he has converted the property from a qualifying principal residence to a non-qualifying investment. See Chapter 5 for a discussion of the perils of renting a principal residence before its sale.

Your tax consequences (as the buyer) depend on how you use the property. If it is your principal residence or vacation home, the rent is a nondeductible personal expense. However, if you sublet the property or otherwise use it for investment or business (such as using part as a home office) you may deduct the rent and other operating expenses applicable to such use. Because you don't own the property, you can't deduct depreciation.

**Taxation of Payments for the Option.** Usually, you pay something to the seller as consideration for granting an option, and you forfeit the payment if you don't exercise the option. The tax consequences of this payment are held in limbo until you exercise the option or you let it expire. If you exercise the option, the payment becomes part of the seller's amount realized from the sale, thereby increasing his gain. As the buyer, the payment increases your basis for the property. If you fail to exercise the option, the payment is ordinary income for the seller when the option expires.[4] For you, the loss from forfeiture is treated as a loss from the sale of the underlying property.[5] Thus, the tax consequences depend on how you would use the property if you exercise the option. If you intend to rent the property, the loss is a capital loss. The holding period of the option determines whether it is long- or short-term. If you intend to use the property as your principal residence or a second home, you get no tax benefit from the loss, since losses from sales of such property have no tax consequences.

See Chapter 3 for a discussion and examples of the tax treatment of option payments.

### Tax Consequences if a Lease-Option is Treated as a Sale

If the government successfully recasts the transaction as an installment sale, ownership is deemed to transfer at the time you give the seller payment for the option and the lease begins. The tax results are altered considerably for both you and the seller.

The payment for the option is treated as a down payment, and the "rent" payments are treated as installment payments of principal and interest. Reporting the gain by using the installment method is discussed in Chapter 10. These rules cause taxable income for the seller in the year he receives the option payment. As an initial payment, it triggers taxation of gain to the extent of his gross profit ratio. Similarly, part of each installment payment ("rent") is taxable gain. Since no interest is stated in the "rent" payments, it is imputed (see Chapter 10). Because he is deemed to have disposed of the property, the seller is denied deductions for depreciation and other rental expenses.

The part of your "rent" payments treated as payments of principal add to your basis for the property. You may deduct the part of the "rent" payments treated as interest under the imputed interest rules (see Chapter 10). If you use the property for investment or business, you may not deduct the rent payments as such, but you may deduct depreciation and other expenses associated with the property. If, however, you occupy it as a home or otherwise use the property for personal purposes, you may not deduct anything except the imputed interest and your real estate taxes.

### When is a Lease-Option Treated as a Sale?

Economic circumstances surrounding a transaction determine whether it is a lease-option or a sale. Usually, no single factor controls. However, if all the economic factors at the outset indicate a very strong likelihood that you will exercise the option, the Internal Revenue Service (IRS) probably will treat the transaction as a sale. If you acquire equity in the property during the lease period, it is more likely that you will exercise the option. This is the only way you can protect your investment.

A signal that you are acquiring equity is when rental payments exceed market rent for comparable property, and the total of the rent payments and option price approximate the market value of the property.[6]

**Example:** Losey agrees to lease Cao's house for two years for an annual rental of $12,000. At the same time, Losey pays Cao $2,000 for an option to purchase the property at the end of the two years for $24,000. At the time the lease begins, the value of the property is $50,000, and an annual fair rental is $5,000. The facts indicate that Losey acquires equity of $7,000 during each of the two lease years ($12,000 rent paid less $5,000 fair rent), and that the total payments ($2,000 option consideration + two $12,000 rent payments + $24,000 option price) by Losey equal the value of the house. The economic circumstances at the outset indicate that this is a sale, and that the $2,000 payment for the option is the down payment.

The government may come to the same economic conclusion if the property's purchase price is its market value, but the rent payments and option payment are deducted from the purchase price.

**Example:** Assume the facts of the above example except that the option price is $50,000 and the $2,000 option payment and the two $12,000 rent payments are deducted from the price. The result is that when Losey exercises the option, he pays Cao $24,000 ($50,000 less $2,000 option payment and $24,000 rent).

If seller charges fair rent, the analysis becomes more complex. Here, you are paying no more than you would pay without the option, so that you are not acquiring equity during the lease period. However, if the rent is deducted from the option price, the transaction looks like an installment sale with a balloon payment, particularly when the rent approximates the amount of installment payments if you use an amortizing loan schedule with a market interest rate (see Chapter 10).

In this situation, however, there is no certainty that you will exercise the option. Therefore, if you can demonstrate that the reason for the lease-option is the impossibility of a cash sale because of economic conditions, the form of the transaction probably will stand.[7] This would be the case, for instance, where your purpose is to tie down the property during a tight money market, with the expectation that within the option period you can get institutional financing.

Other factors may indicate that a lease-option should be treated as a sale. For instance, the lease may require you to make improvements to the property. Your investment in the improvements may be substantial enough that you must exercise the option to recoup the investment.

## LIKE-KIND REAL ESTATE EXCHANGES

Normally, you are taxed on gain from the sale or exchange of property in the year of the transaction. Section 1031 of the Internal Revenue Code alters this rule for a qualifying exchange, and allows you to defer or postpone tax until you subsequently dispose of the property you receive. See Chapter 2 for discussion of the economic advantages of tax deferral. In addition, exchanges give you other tax benefits, such as avoiding depreciation recapture, increasing your future depreciation deductions, and increasing your tax basis for property. You can accomplish all this without any immediate tax cost.

The primary non-tax purpose for exchanging is to relocate or diversify your investment properties. For example, you may have a tax-free exchange of a ranch in Texas for a motel in Florida, a rental house in Cleveland for a more suitable rental house in the same city, or unimproved rural farmland for suburban residential rental property.

### Requirements of Section 1031

Section 1031 provides that no gain *or loss* is taxed if you exchange investment or business property solely for like-kind investment or business property. Thus, to qualify for tax deferral the property you give and the property you receive must meet two separate tests: (1) it must be business or investment property, and (2) it must be like-kind.

Although these requirements seem straightforward, the key terms need further clarification. For instance, what is an exchange? What property qualifies as business or investment property? Does *solely* mean that the entire transaction is disqualified if you include some non-qualifying property? And most important (and most misunderstood), what is the meaning of "like-kind?"

Unlike its close deferral cousins, the home-sale rollover (see Chapter 5) and the involuntary conversion rollover (see Chapter 12), Section 1031 does not permit you to defer tax if you sell the property and reinvest the proceeds in qualifying replacement property. It requires a direct exchange of properties. This means that you and the other party must be very careful to adhere strictly to the nitty-gritty mechanics.

If a transaction meets the requirements of Section 1031, tax deferral is mandatory. Further, Section 1031 requires you to defer losses as well as gains. Thus, Section 1031 can work both ways. You are permitted to use it as a shield against taxation of gains, but also the government may use it as a sword to disallow your losses.

### What is the Meaning of "Like-Kind?"

The definition of like-kind is very broad. Any business or investment real estate is like-kind with any other business or investment real estate. The Income Tax Regulations provide that *like-kind* refers to the nature or character of the property and not to its grade or quality.[8] The property's function doesn't matter. Thus, improved property is like-kind with unimproved property, since the improvements relate solely to the grade or quality of the property and not to its nature or character.

The Regulations further provide that a leasehold with thirty or more years to run (including renewal options) is like-kind with a fee simple interest in real estate. One point is clear, however. Real estate is *not* like-kind with personal property, even though you own both for business or investment. Thus, you don't qualify if you exchange a rental house for investment diamonds.

The Regulations give guidance about when exchanges of personal property qualify under Section 1031.[9] These guidelines also discuss exchanges of businesses. Among many other rules regarding the like-kind status of personal property, the Regulations provide that the goodwill or going concern value of one business can never be of like-kind to that of another business.

Section 1031 specifically excludes certain types of property from the like-kind classification. If you receive these items in a real estate exchange, some or all of the tax may be triggered. The statutory non-like-kind items are inventory or property held primarily for sale, accounts receivable (that the law calls *choses in action*), stocks, bonds, notes, certificates of trust or beneficial interest, and partnership interests.

### The Requirement for Business or Investment Property

Most Section 1031 exchanges involve investment property rather than business property (see Chapter 2 for a discussion of the distinction between business and investment). The business classification permits tax deferral for trade-ins of business equipment or automobiles. It also permits tax deferred exchanges of business real estate. For instance, a manufacturing firm may exchange an inadequate factory building for a more favorably located building site or factory.

All property except inventory, business property, or property you use for personal purposes is investment property. If you are not a dealer (see Appendix B), investment property includes unimproved real estate you hold for future use or for appreciation in value. Property owned by a dealer is inventory, so it doesn't qualify.

You must hold both the property you give and the property you receive for a period of time for it to qualify as investment property. The length of time depends on the facts and circumstances. Thus, if you hold property for immediate resale, it doesn't qualify, even though you are not a dealer.[10]

It is not necessary for you to exchange business property only for business property, or investment property only for investment property. You may exchange investment property for business property, and vice-versa, as long as the properties you give and receive are like-kind.

The business or investment status of the property is important only for the party who wants tax deferral under Section 1031. The status of the property for the other party is irrelevant. Thus, a transaction may be tax deferred on one side only.

> **Example:** Striner owns a condominium apartment as an investment. He exchanges it for Glazer's principal residence, and rents the house to tenants after the exchange. The transaction qualifies under Section 1031 for Striner, because the properties he gives and receives are held for investment. The transaction does not qualify under Section 1031 for Glazer because he does not own the house for investment or business. Because the house is Glazer's principal residence, however, he may defer tax under the home-sale rollover (see Chapter 5) if he uses the condominium he receives as a principal residence.

### How to Structure a Real Estate Exchange

Structuring an exchange involves two separate and distinct steps. The first step is to balance the equities of the properties involved. The second step is to determine the tax consequences of the transaction.

You analyze the economics of a transaction by balancing the equities. For this analysis, equity is defined as the difference between the property's fair market value and the outstanding debt assumed by the other party (mortgages, taxes and interest in arrears, etc.). This is different from the financial accountant's definition of equity. He defines equity as the difference between the property's *historical cost* and the debts assumed. The different definitions might cause confusion when you or your real estate advisor try to communicate with an accountant.

After you have structured the economics of the transaction, you determine the tax consequences. To do this, you use the technical definitions of the tax law. These may or may not correspond to economic concepts.

It is dangerous to use pre-printed forms to analyze the economic and tax consequences of an exchange. Such forms are available from associations of realtors, tax publications, specialized real estate broker exchange groups, etc. The vast number of variables available for real estate exchanges makes it impossible to design a form that always gives you correct answers simply by plugging in numbers. Most forms confuse the economic analysis of the exchange (balancing the equities) with the tax consequences. This often leads to the wrong tax answers.

The IRS has a form for reporting Section 1031 exchanges (IRS Form 8824), but this is a supporting statement for the exchanges reported on other forms. It is intended primarily to provide information about deferred and related person exchanges. However, in summary form, it also is used to compute the realized and recognized gain and the basis of the property received. The Form 8824 is not designed for structuring the basic exchange transaction or balancing the equities. Therefore, instead of using this or other forms, the examples in this chapter use a two-step analysis process: first, we balance the equities, and then we calculate the tax consequences.

### The Effect of "Boot"

The equities of the properties you and other parties include in an exchange will rarely be equal. Someone usually adds cash or other property to balance the equities. If the equalizing property is like-kind, there is no problem. What, however, if someone adds cash or non-qualifying property? Such property is called "boot." Does boot disqualify the entire transaction? Total disqualification would frustrate the basic purpose of Section 1031. Consequently, Section 1031 provides for partial taxation if you receive boot. The boot you receive is a yardstick measuring how much of your gain is taxed. The boot itself is not taxed. The rule is that gain is taxed to the extent of the fair market value of the boot received.[11] Thus, if the gain is less than the value of boot received, income includes only the amount of the gain.

> **Example:** Bulmash has a rental house with a fair market value (FMV) of $90,000 and a basis of $40,000 that he exchanges for Shen's rental duplex with a fair market value of $80,000, and a basis to Shen of $50,000. To equalize the equities, Shen gives Bulmash $10,000 cash in addition to the duplex. The equities are balanced as follows:

|  | Bulmash | Shen |
|---|---|---|
| FMV - property given | $90,000 | $80,000 |
| Cash given |  | 10,000 |
| Equities | $90,000 | $90,000 |

The tax consequences for the parties are as follows:

|  | Bulmash | Shen |
|---|---|---|
| FMV - property received | $ 80,000 | $ 90,000 |
| Cash received | 10,000 |  |
| Total amount realized | $ 90,000 | $ 90,000 |
| Less: Cash given |  | (10,000) |
| Basis | (40,000) | (50,000) |
| Realized gain | $ 50,000 | $ 30,000 |

$10,000 of Bulmash's $50,000 gain is taxed because he receives boot of that amount. None of Shen's $30,000 gain is taxed because he receives no boot. If, instead of cash, Shen gives Bulmash like-kind property worth $10,000 (such as an investment lot), Bulmash has no taxable income.

**Example:** Assume in the above example that Bulmash's basis for his rental house is $85,000. His gain is $5,000 ($90,000 less $85,000). The taxable gain is limited to the total gain of $5,000, even though the boot received is $10,000

If you receive boot, you have taxable gain. What happens if you give boot to the other party? The above examples show that when you give cash, no gain is triggered. If, however, the boot you give is property, you recognize any of the boot property's potential gain or loss. Section 1031 only defers gain or loss from qualifying like-kind property. If you give non-cash boot, it is treated as a sale of the boot property.

### Treatment of Mortgages and Other Debts

Under Section 1031, if the other party assumes or pays your debts (mortgage, real estate taxes and interest in arrears, etc.) you are treated as if he paid you cash. Thus, your gain is taxed to the extent of the debt assumed or paid by the other party.[12]

For tax calculations, the two elements of the equity you receive are treated separately. The property's fair market value is included in full as part of your amount realized. The debt is treated as part of the basis of the property you give up. This is an example of how the tax calculation differs from economic balancing of the equities. The mechanics are illustrated in the following examples, that are also used later in this chapter to illustrate how you calculate the basis of the property you receive.

**Example A:** Newton owns a rental house with a fair market value (FMV) of $100,000, a basis of $60,000 and subject to a mortgage of $30,000. She exchanges the house for a rental duplex owned by Davis having a FMV of $70,000 with a basis to Davis of $10,000. Davis agrees to assume Newton's $30,000 mortgage. The equities are balanced as follows:

|  | Newton | Davis |
|---|---|---|
| FMV - property given | $100,000 | $70,000 |
| Less: Mortgage assumed | (30,000) |  |
| Equity | $ 70,000 | $70,000 |

The tax consequences for the parties are as follows:

|  | Newton | Davis |
|---|---|---|
| FMV - property received | $ 70,000 | $100,000 |
| Plus: Mortgage relief | 30,000 |  |
| Amount realized | $100,000 | $100,000 |
| Less: Basis | (60,000) | (10,000) |
| Mtg. assumed |  | (30,000) |
| Gain realized | $ 40,000 | $ 60,000 |

$30,000 of Newton's $40,000 gain is taxed because she has debt relief in that amount. None of Davis' gain is taxed since he has no debt relief, and receives no other boot.

Often, both you and your exchange partner assume or pay debts related to the other's property. In this case you offset the amount of your debt relief against that of the exchange partner. The party getting the larger amount of debt relief is treated as receiving cash for the excess.

**Example B:** Assume the facts of Example A, except that Davis' duplex has a FMV of $110,000, a basis of $10,000, and is subject to a mortgage of $40,000. The equities are balanced as follows:

|  | Newton | Davis |
|---|---|---|
| FMV - property given | $100,000 | $110,000 |
| Less: Mtg. assumed | ( 30,000) | (40,000) |
| Equity | $ 70,000 | $ 70,000 |

The tax consequences for the parties are as follows:

|  | *Newton* | *Davis* |
|---|---|---|
| FMV - property received | $110,000 | $100,000 |
| Plus:Mortgage relief | 30,000 | 40,000 |
| Amount realized | $140,000 | $140,000 |
| Less: Basis | (60,000) | (10,000) |
| Mtg. assumed | (40,000) | (30,000) |
| Gain realized | $ 40,000 | $100,000 |

The debt relief of Newton and Davis are $30,000 and $40,000 respectively. These amounts are offset, and this results in Davis being relieved of $10,000 more debt than Newton. Accordingly, $10,000 of Davis' $100,000 gain is taxed. None of Newton's $40,000 gain is taxed because she has no excess debt relief, and does not otherwise receive boot.

**Treatment of Transaction Costs**

Transaction costs such as real estate commissions, legal fees, etc., have three effects in a Section 1031 exchange:[13]

o Reduce the amount realized, thus reducing the amount of gain (the normal result in any sale - see Chapter 3).

o Increase the basis of the property received as discussed below, and

o Reduce the amount of cash boot received. Thus, gain is taxed only to the extent of the excess of cash received over the transaction costs.

**Basis of Property Received in a Section 1031 Exchange**

The tax mechanism for deferring gain in a Section 1031 exchange is the *substituted basis*. This means that the basis of the property you receive is the same as the basis of the property you give up. Thus, when you subsequently sell the property you receive in the exchange, you pay tax on the deferred gain from the property you gave up.

**Example:** Flaherty exchanges property with a FMV of $60,000 and a basis of $20,000 for like-kind property with a FMV of $60,000. His realized gain of $40,000 is deferred, and his basis for the property he receives is the same as that of the property he gave up: $20,000. Five years later, he sells the property he received for $90,000. His taxable gain is $70,000 ($90,000 less his basis of $20,000). $40,000 of this gain is the gain deferred from the property he gave in the exchange. The remaining $30,000 is the increase in the value of the new property after the exchange ($90,000 less $60,000, the value of the property at the time of the exchange).

The basis calculation becomes more complex when debt is involved, when boot is transferred, and when gain is taxed. Figure 11-1 summarizes the formula to determine the basis of property you receive in an exchange.[14]

---

### Figure 11-1

### BASIS OF PROPERTY RECEIVED IN A SECTION 1031 EXCHANGE

Basis of like-kind property given

**Add**:  Cash given

Basis of non-cash boot property given

Gain taxed in the transaction

Mortgages and other debt assumed or paid

Transaction costs paid in the exchange

**Deduct**:  Cash received

Mortgages and other debt relief

**Equals**:  Basis of all property received

---

If you receive non-cash boot property (such as securities or other personal property) in the exchange, you assign it a basis equal to its fair market value. Any basis left over is assigned to the like-kind property you receive. If you get more than one like-kind property, you allocate the basis to the properties in the ratio of their relative market values.[15]

The mechanics of the basis rules are illustrated by continuing Example A and Example B in the preceding section.

**Example:** Assume the facts of Example A where Newton had taxable gain because Davis assumed her $30,000 mortgage. No other boot was involved. The basis of the property received by the parties is calculated as follows:

|  | Newton | Davis |
|---|---|---|
| Basis - Property given | $60,000 | $10,000 |
| Add: Gain taxed | 30,000 | |
| Mtg. assumed | | 30,000 |
| | $90,000 | $40,000 |
| Less: Mortgage relief | (30,000) | |
| Basis - Property received | $60,000 | $40,000 |

This example illustrates two important points about exchanges. First, when you increase the amount of your debt as a result of an exchange, your basis is increased accordingly. This permits you to take larger future depreciation deductions, but you incur no tax to get this advantage. Thus, in the example, Davis increases his basis by $30,000 because he assumes additional debt.

Second, when you have taxable income in a transaction, your basis usually is increased by the amount of such income. Note in the above example, however, that Newton has taxable income of $30,000, but her basis for the property she receives is the same as that for the property she gives up. In effect, what has happened is that Davis gets the basis increase benefit of Newton's taxable income.

**Example:** Assume the facts of Example B where Davis had taxable gain of $10,000 because of excess debt relief. No other boot was involved. The basis of the property received by the parties is calculated as follows:

|  | Newton | Davis |
|---|---|---|
| Basis - Property given | $ 60,000 | $10,000 |
| Add: Gain taxed | | 10,000 |
| Mtg. assumed | 40,000 | 30,000 |
| | $100,000 | $50,000 |
| Less: Mortgage relief | (30,000) | (40,000) |
| Basis - Property received | $ 70,000 | $10,000 |

In this example Newton gets a basis increase of $10,000, the excess of the debt she assumed over her debt relief. Davis, on the other hand, has no basis increase even though he had to pay tax on a $10,000 gain.

### Combination Installment Sale and Exchange

Sometimes you receive like-kind property as part or all of the down payment in an installment sale, and you carry back installment notes for the remainder of the selling price. Under Section 1031, the notes are boot, so normally you would report and pay tax on gain to the extent of the fair market value of the notes you receive. However, if the sale otherwise qualifies as an installment sale, you are permitted to report the gain under the installment method as you collect the notes (see Chapter 10).

For installment reporting, the like-kind property is not an initial payment, and is not included in the contract price for determining the gross profit ratio.[16] The gain you report is the total gain less the amount of gain deferred under Section 1031.

> **Example:** Westbrook exchanges a duplex with a market value of $100,000 for an unimproved lot with a market value of $20,000, $10,000 cash, and notes of $70,000 payable $10,000 per year with adequate stated interest. Her basis for the duplex is $10,000. The gain from this transaction is calculated as follows:
>
> | | |
> |---|---:|
> | FMV - Like-kind property received | $ 20,000 |
> | Cash received (boot - §1031) | 10,000 |
> | Notes received (boot - §1031) | 70,000 |
> | Amount realized | $100,000 |
> | Less: Basis of duplex | 10,000 |
> | Gain realized | $ 90,000 |

Under Section 1031, $80,000 of this gain is taxed (the amount of cash and notes received). The boot represented by the notes may be reported as the notes are collected. The initial payment is the cash of $10,000 received in the year of sale. The like-kind property is not an initial payment. The contract price is the total of the down payment and the installment notes. The like-kind property is not included in the contract price. The gross profit ratio is 100% as follows:

$$\frac{\text{Gross profit (after applying Section 1031) \$80,000}}{\text{Contract price (not including like-kind) \quad \$80,000}} = 100\%$$

Thus, in the year of the sale/exchange taxable gain is $10,000 (the down payment x 100%). In each subsequent year, the entire $10,000 collected from each installment payment is taxed.

### Nature of Gain Taxed — Impact of Depreciation Recapture

Only capital assets qualify as like-kind under Section 1031. See Appendix B for discussion of what assets qualify as capital assets. Accordingly, if gain is taxed because you receive boot or because you have debt relief, it is capital gain. Although the rate differential between long-term capital gain and ordinary income is now minimal, the rules discussed below remain important because without planning, you can trigger taxation of gain in the year of an exchange without otherwise receiving boot.

If the property you give in an exchange is subject to depreciation recapture, there is no recapture if the property you receive is depreciable. See Appendix B for discussion of depreciation recapture. The recapture potential attaches to the property you receive. Later, when you dispose of that property in a taxable transaction, gain is ordinary income for the recapture potential of both properties. This opportunity to circumvent depreciation recapture is one of the valuable tax benefits of Section 1031 exchanges.

If the property you receive is non-depreciable (such as land), the recapture potential is taxed immediately whether or not you would otherwise have taxable gain because you receive boot or have debt relief.[17]

**Example:** Gruber exchanges a free-and-clear rental house with a market value of $80,000 and a basis of $30,000 for a lot worth $80,000. He has used accelerated depreciation, and the recapture potential is $7,000. Under normal circumstances, no gain would be taxable since no boot is received and there is no debt relief. However, because the land received in the exchange is non-depreciable, the $7,000 recapture potential is taxed as ordinary income in the year of the exchange.

You can avoid taxation of recapture if you receive depreciable like-kind property with a market value at least equal to the amount of the recapture potential.

> **Example:** In the above example if Gruber receives depreciable like-kind property with a value of at least $7,000 in addition to the lot, the recapture from the rental house is not taxed. The recapture potential attaches to the depreciable property received, and is taxed when that property is sold.

### Simultaneous Multiple Party Exchanges

What if the owner of the property you want doesn't want your property? Or what if you find a buyer for your property, but the buyer doesn't own suitable property for an exchange?

To solve these problems, most exchanges involve three parties: the taxpayer (you), who wants a tax deferred exchange, a buyer for your property, and a seller who owns the property you want to receive in the exchange. Once you locate the buyer for your property and the seller of the property you want, you arrange two interdependent transactions, a sale and an exchange. The sale and the exchange are closed simultaneously. The sequencing of the transactions depends upon where in the process the buyer for your property comes into the picture. Regardless of the sequencing, however, the result is the same. You acquire the property you want, the seller of the exchange property has his sale, and the buyer gets your property. You determine your tax consequences the same way regardless of the sequencing of the transactions.

**You Have a Buyer for Your Property**. The most common pattern is where you have a buyer for your property, but you have not found suitable exchange property. Here, you and the buyer (B) enter into an exchange agreement that obligates the buyer to purchase property that you will designate and then exchange it for your property. The sequence of documentation is as follows:[18]

   o Contract between you and B - You agree to exchange your property to B for property that you will designate and B will acquire. This contract is contingent upon B being able to acquire the exchange property.

o You locate suitable property owned by seller (C). B contracts with C to buy C's property. This contract is contingent upon the exchange between you and B.

**Example:** Taxpayer owns a duplex with a fair market value of $400,000 and a basis of $50,000. Buyer wants to buy the duplex for cash. Taxpayer and Buyer enter into a contract where Taxpayer agrees to exchange the duplex for property that Buyer will acquire at the direction of Taxpayer. This contract is contingent upon Buyer being able to acquire the designated exchange property. Later, Taxpayer locates an apartment house owned by Seller with a FMV of $1,000,000, subject to a mortgage of $600,000, and directs Buyer to buy the apartment house for the exchange. Buyer contracts with Seller to buy the apartment house, and this purchase/sale contract is contingent upon closing the exchange with Taxpayer. The two contracts are closed simultaneously.

Suppose that the buyer is willing to go along with this program for awhile, but wants to be guaranteed that ultimately he can buy your property if the exchange doesn't work out. Here, you can include a clause in the exchange contract providing that if you don't designate suitable exchange property by a specified date, you agree to sell your property to the buyer for cash. Of course, if you sell the property under the cash-out alternative, you must pay tax on the gain.

If the buyer is unwilling to enter into a three-way exchange, but is willing to wait to purchase your property, you may bring a fourth party into the transaction. This party acts as a principal to facilitate the exchange. The fourth party purchases the exchange property from the seller with cash provided by the buyer, exchanges your property for the exchange property, then transfers your property to the buyer.[19]

**The Owner of the Exchange Property Wants a Sale**. Suppose that you have located the property you want to receive in exchange, but the owner of the property wants a sale, and doesn't want your property. In this case, you and the owner of the exchange property (C) enter into an agreement to exchange your properties provided that a buyer (B) is located to purchase your property simultaneously with the exchange. B purchases your property from C, not from you. The sequence of documentation is as follows:[20]

o Contract between you and C - You agree to transfer your property to C in exchange for property owned by C.

This exchange is contingent upon an immediate (or simultaneous) sale by C of the property he receives from you.

o After you locate a buyer for your property, C contracts with B to sell the property acquired from you in the exchange. This purchase/sale contract is contingent upon C acquiring the property in the exchange with you.

**Example:** Assume in the above example that Taxpayer has located the apartment house he wants to receive in the exchange. Seller, however, does not want to exchange, but wants an outright sale of the apartment house. Taxpayer and Seller contract for an exchange of the duplex for the apartment house, contingent upon a sale of the duplex by Seller concurrently with the exchange. A buyer is located, who contracts with Seller to buy the duplex from Seller. This contract is contingent upon Seller acquiring the duplex from Taxpayer in the exchange. The two contracts are closed simultaneously.

**Determination of Tax Consequences for the Taxpayer.** Regardless of how you sequence the transactions, your tax consequences are determined by treating the transaction as a direct exchange between you and the seller of the exchange property. The intermediate purchase/sale transaction between the buyer and the seller is ignored. Thus, your amount realized is determined by the property you receive in the exchange.

**Example:** The equities in the two above examples are balanced as follows:

|  | Taxpayer Gives Duplex | Taxpayer Gets Apartments |
|---|---|---|
| Fair market value | $400,000 | $1,000,000 |
| Less: Debt assumed |  | 600,000 |
| Equity | $400,000 | $ 400,000 |

Taxpayer's realized gain is calculated according to the rules discussed above, as follows:

| Amt. realized (FMV - apartment house) | $1,000,000 |
|---|---|

| Less: Basis of duplex | $ 50,000 |  |
|---|---|---|
| Debt assumed | 600,000 | 650,000 |
| Gain realized |  | $ 350,000 |

Since Taxpayer receives no boot and has no debt relief, the entire gain is deferred. His basis for the apartment house is determined as follows:

| Basis of duplex | $ 50,000 |
|---|---|
| Add: Debt assumed | 600,000 |
| Basis of apartment house | $650,000 |

Note that because Taxpayer assumed additional debt, his basis for depreciation is increased, at no tax cost to him.

### Deferred ("Starker") Multiple Party Exchanges

The discussion so far has assumed that you transfer the properties in the exchange simultaneously, even when, at the time of the exchange *contract*, the property you will receive in the exchange is not identified. What if the other party wants your property immediately, but is willing to promise to transfer acceptable like-kind property designated by you and acquired later?

In the famous *Starker* decision, the court held that such a delayed transfer of the exchange property qualified under Section 1031. However, in 1984, Congress placed severe restrictions on this technique. Now, a delayed exchange does not qualify unless:[21]

o You designate the exchange property within forty-five days after the date you transfer your property, and

o The exchange property is transferred to you no later than the earlier of (a) 180 days after you transfer your property, or (b) the due date (with extensions) for your tax return for the year when you transfer your property.

The short fuse time for finding suitable exchange property makes the delayed exchange device dangerous when you have no idea what property you want to receive. If you don't locate suitable property within forty-five days, the transaction becomes taxable. In addition, even when you locate suitable property, it may be difficult to arrange financing, appraisals, and other steps necessary to close the transaction within the 180 day time limit.

These problems are mitigated somewhat by the deferred exchange Income Tax Regulations issued by the IRS to provide answers to many questions involving the mechanics for identifying replacement property, and for structuring the transaction to avoid the constructive receipt problem.[22] The Regulations are lengthly and intricate, but fortunately they contain examples explaining the rules.

Anyone contemplating a deferred exchange should become thoroughly familiar with the structuring mechanics set forth in these Regulations.

### Impact of the Passive Loss Limitations on Exchanges

Although deferral of taxable gain is usually desirable, the story might be different if you have suspended passive losses (see Chapter 7). During your ownership of the passive investment, such losses may only be deducted from passive income. However, when you dispose of the investment in a *taxable* transaction, you may deduct, in full, all suspended losses from that activity.[23]

A Section 1031 exchange is not a taxable disposition that permits you to deduct all your suspended passive losses. If you have gain taxed because you receive boot or have debt relief, you are permitted offset it with suspended losses. Any excess of the suspended losses over the taxed gain attaches to the property you receive in the exchange (in a manner similar to depreciation recapture potential), and may be deducted when you dispose of that property in a taxable transaction.[24] Therefore, if you have substantial suspended passive losses from an investment, you might want to avoid a Section 1031 exchange deliberately, and to opt for a taxable sale.

### Using Exchanges to "Unlock" a "Land Poor" Property Owner

In addition to tax deferral, you can use exchanges to get the tax benefit of increased depreciation without paying tax. As discussed above, one way to do this is to "leverage up" or assume more debt on the property you receive in the exchange than that on the property you give up. The additional debt is added to determine your depreciable basis of the new property.

Another way to increase depreciation is to give up non-depreciable property and get back depreciable property. Suppose you own appreciated land that will produce a large tax bill if you sell it. You might need cash income, but you feel "locked in" to the land. If you are elderly, you might be reluctant to sell the property because the gain is avoided entirely if you hold the property until your death. At that time, your beneficiary gets a "stepped-up" basis equal to the property's fair market value, so that there is no gain on its subsequent sale (see Chapter 3). An exchange is perfect for "unlocking" you. You can exchange the land, that produces no cash income, for rental property. This gives you cash flow two ways: from the rent, and from your tax savings from your newly found depreciation deductions.

### Exchanges of Multiple-use Properties

What if you exchange property that you use for more than one purpose? For instance, you may live in half of a duplex as a principal residence and rent the other half to tenants. Similarly, a farmhouse may be your principal residence, and the remainder of the property is operated as a business.[25] For purposes of Section 1031, these are treated as separate properties: one held for investment or business, and one held for personal use. Only the investment or business portion qualifies under Section 1031. You should structure exchanges of such properties as two transactions. First, a sale of the portion used as a home, and second, an exchange of the business or investment portion for qualifying like-kind property. You may defer gain from the residential portion if you make a qualifying reinvestment in another residence or exclude it under the over-55 exclusion (see Chapter 5).

## FOOTNOTES

1. Internal Revenue Code (IRC) §280A(d)(3)(B); Prop. Reg. §1.280A-1(e)(3).

2. Prop. Reg. §1.280A-1(g).

3. For a list of the changes in tax consequences because a lease-option is recast as a sale, see Rev. Rul. 72-408, 1972-2 CB 86.

4. Reg. §1.1234-1(b).

5. IRC §1234(a)(1).

6. Rev. Rul. 55-540, 1955-2 CB 39; *Haggard v. Comm'r*, 241 F.2d 288, aff'g 24 TC 1124, (CA 9, 1956).

7. *Clarence B. Eaton, Est.*, 10 TC 869 (1948) Acq.

8. Reg. §1.1031(a)-1(b) and (c).

9. Reg. §1.1031(a)-2.

10. *Regals Realty Co. v Comm'r*, 127 F.2d 931, (CA 2, 1942).

11. IRC §1031(b); Reg. §1-1031(b)-1.

12. Reg. §1.1031(d)-2.

13. Rev. Rul. 72-456, 1972-2 CB 468.

14. IRC §1031(d); Reg. §1.1031(d)-1.

15. Rev. Rul. 68-36, 1968-1 CB 357.

16. IRC §453(f)(6).

17. IRC §1250(d)(4); Reg. §1.1250-3(d)(1) and (5).

18. *Alderson v. Comm'r.*, 317 F.2d 790, (CA 9, 1963); *Coastal Terminals, Inc. v. US*, 320 F.2d 333, (CA 4, 1963).

19. *Leslie Q. Coupe*, 52 TC 394 (1969).

20. *W.D. Haden Co. v Comm'r.*, 165 F.2d 588, (CA 5, 1948); Rev. Rul. 57-244, 1957-1 CB 247.

21. IRC §1031(a)(3); *Starker v. US*, 602 F.2d 1341, (CA 9, 1979).

22. Reg. §1.1031(k)-1.

23. IRC §469(g).

24. Sen. Rept. 99-313, 99th Cong., 2d Sess., p. 726.

25. *Sayre v. US*, 163 F.Supp. 495, (DCWVa, 1958).

Chapter

# TWELVE

# INVOLUNTARY CONVERSIONS

Sometimes you are forced to dispose of property whether you want to or not. This happens when the property is destroyed, or when a government agency takes it for public use. The tax law calls these forced dispositions involuntary conversions. Tax consequences of involuntary conversions usually get little attention until it is too late for effective planning. You should be familiar with the tax rules. You never know when disaster will strike a well-insured property. Also, with increasing urbanization, government agencies frequently take property for public use.

### TAX CONSEQUENCES OF
### INVOLUNTARY CONVERSIONS

Congress decided that it is unfair to force you to pay tax on gains when you have no control over the property's disposition. Consequently, sometimes you may roll over, or defer, gains from the involuntary sale or destruction of property.[1] However, you may not postpone losses from involuntary conversions. Such losses are deductible (if otherwise permitted by the tax law) only in the year of conversion.

An involuntary conversion occurs when you receive money or other property because of your property's destruction, theft, or government condemnation or threat of condemnation. When property is destroyed or stolen, the cash comes from insurance. Thus, the rollover applies when you have, in effect, sold property to your insurance company. For a condemnation, the government agency must pay you fair value for the property taken. The tax law treats this as a sale.

The rollover is available for any property regardless of its use, and regardless of whether it is real estate or personal property. You are permitted to elect to postpone tax on gains from involuntary conversions of real or personal property held for sale to customers, used in business, held for investment, or held solely for personal use.

### What is Destruction of Property?

The definition of destruction is the same as the definition for the casualty loss deduction, except that there is no requirement for the destruction to be "sudden" (see Chapter 4 for a discussion of the casualty loss deduction).[2]

Sometimes a voluntary sale of property damaged by a casualty qualifies, though the property is not destroyed. For instance, a sale of timber damaged by high winds or earthquake qualifies if you reinvest the proceeds in qualifying property.[3] However, adverse business or sociological conditions are not casualties. Sale of rental housing because of extensive and recurring vandalism doesn't qualify for the rollover.[4]

### What is Condemnation or Threat of Condemnation?

Condemnation is the taking of property by a public authority under the Constitutional power of eminent domain. The taking must be for public use. If property is condemned because it is unfit for occupancy and is sold later, it is not taken for public use, and the gain doesn't qualify for the rollover.

Most problems arise when the government takes only part of your property. Sometimes, you can't continue to use the remaining property for its prior purpose. Here, a sale of the remaining property to a third party sometimes qualifies as an involuntary conversion. You must prove that the two pieces of property sold (one to the government and the other to a third party) constitute an economic unit, and that suitable nearby replacement property for the condemned portion is not available.[5] You often get severance damages when there is a partial taking. These damages are to compensate for the decline in the value of the remaining property because of the partial condemnation. The tax consequences of severance damages are discussed below.

When part of your property is taken, it might not be feasible to reinvest the proceeds in qualifying property. For instance, a city may take a few feet from the front of your property to construct a sidewalk, widen a street, or install a sewer. In such cases, the remaining property probably retains its economic utility, so you don't sell it. Unfortunately, you must bite the bullet and pay tax on the gain from sale of the strip. You may minimize this problem by classifying part of the award as severance damages as discussed in the Tax Planning Ideas below.

Involuntary conversions include sales to third parties under threat of or imminence of condemnation. The threat must be real. You must be notified by the authorities orally or in writing of a decision to acquire your property for public use, *and* you must have reasonable grounds to believe that the property will actually be taken.[6] Notification by the media that condemnation is under consideration is not sufficient unless you have confirmation that a decision has been made. For example, there was not a sufficient threat where complaints of the offensiveness of a fertilizer plant resulted in a visit by public officials to see how the problem could be solved.[7] If you sell property at the request of a local chamber of commerce to protect your business goodwill, there is not a sufficient threat.[8]

### What is the Gain From the Conversion?

Gains from involuntary conversions are calculated the same way as for any other sale or exchange. Gain is the excess of the amount realized over the adjusted basis of the property (see Chapter 3). The amount realized is insurance proceeds or damages you receive because of the property's destruction, or the amount of a condemnation award. If there is a partial condemnation, the amount realized does not include severance damages. If the government assumes or pays an outstanding mortgage in a condemnation, the amount of the mortgage is added to the amount realized.[9]. Legal fees, appraiser fees, and other expenses you incur to obtain the condemnation award reduce the award, thereby reducing the amount realized.

The property's basis is determined under the normal rules (see Chapter 3). If only part of the property is taken, you must allocate the basis of the entire property between the part taken and the part retained. You usually do this in the ratio of the number square feet taken and retained. If parts of the property vary in value, you may allocate according to the relative values of the property. You determine relative values by appraisal, or by other evidence such as the allocation between land and improvements in the property tax assessment.

### How Do You Defer the Gain?

The mechanics for the involuntary conversion rollover are similar to those for the home-sale rollover discussed in Chapter 5. However, unlike the home-sale rollover, the involuntary conversion rollover is elective. You may cause the gain to be taxed simply by not electing to defer it.

Gain is taxed for the amount of the proceeds from the conversion not reinvested in qualifying replacement property within the specified period.[10] If you reinvest the total proceeds, the entire gain is deferred. If you don't reinvest anything, all the gain is taxed. In no event, however, can your taxable gain be larger than the realized gain.

> **Example:** Smith's investment house is destroyed by a hurricane. The insurance recovery is $75,000, and his basis for the house is $40,000. His realized gain is $35,000 ($75,000 less $40,000). He reinvests $70,000 in qualifying property within the reinvestment period. Thus, $5,000 ($75,000 proceeds less $70,000) is taxed.

You determine the basis of the replacement property the same way you determine the basis of a replacement home in a home-sale rollover. It is the cost of the replacement property less the untaxed gain from the conversion.[11]

> **Example:** In the above example, the untaxed gain from the conversion is $30,000 (gain realized, $35,000 less the $5,000 gain taxed). The basis of the replacement property is $40,000 (its cost, $70,000 less the untaxed gain of $30,000).

If you replace a converted property with more than one property, you allocate the basis to the various replacement properties in the ratio of their respective costs.

## What is the Replacement Period?

For stolen or destroyed property, the replacement period begins on the date of theft or destruction, and ends two years after the close of the year of theft or destruction.[12]

> **Example:** Seay's rental house is destroyed by fire on May 1, 19X6. The replacement period begins on that date, and ends on December 31, 19X8.

The replacement period for condemned property depends on whether it is personal property or real estate. In both cases, the period begins on the earlier of the date of condemnation or the date of the threat of condemnation. For real estate, the period ends at the close of the third year after year of condemnation or threat of condemnation.[13] For personal property, the period ends at the close of the second year.

Usually, the year of condemnation is the year when title to the property passes and you acquire the right to compensation. If you have a threat of condemnation, you may acquire replacement property before the actual condemnation takes place. For such property to qualify for replacement, however, you must still own it at the actual date of condemnation.[14]

> **Example:** Jenkins receives formal notice that her real property will be condemned for a highway sometime in the following year. She receives this notice on March 1, 19X5. The actual condemnation takes place on May 31, 19X6. The replacement period begins March 1, 19X5 and ends December 31, 19X9. Replacement property acquired between the date of notice and the date of condemnation (May 31, 19X6) qualifies if Jenkins still owns it on May 31, 19X6.

If you construct property for replacement, you must complete construction within the replacement period. Advance payments to the contractor do not qualify as replacement unless you complete the construction within the period.

If it is impossible for you to replace converted property within the required time, you can apply to the Internal Revenue Service (IRS) for an extension of the replacement period. The extension will normally be granted if you can show that you have reasonable cause for the inability to replace within the specified time.[15] In this respect, the involuntary conversion rollover differs from the home-sale rollover. There are no extensions permitted for the home-sale rollover (Chapter 5).

### What Kind of Property Qualifies for Replacement?

The general rule is that the replacement property must be *similar or related in service or use* to the property taken or destroyed. As an alternative, you may acquire an 80% controlling interest in a corporation that owns qualifying replacement property. You must acquire the replacement property in a transaction that gives you a cost basis. Thus, if you lease the replacement property or receive it by gift or inheritance it doesn't qualify (see Chapter 3 for a discussion of basis).[16]

If you are an *owner-user*, the replacement property must serve the same function or end use as the property converted. A mere difference in capacity or size of the replacement property does not disqualify it. The properties must have similar end uses and closely related physical characteristics. For instance, replacing a manufacturing plant with a wholesale grocery warehouse won't qualify.

If you are an *owner-investor*, the replacement rule is less restrictive. In general, if you use the property for rental, any type of rental property qualifies for replacement. In the above example where a manufacturing plant is replaced by a wholesale grocery warehouse, the replacement qualifies if you rent both properties to tenants, though it would not qualify if you use the converted and replacement properties. Even under the more liberal test, however, the IRS examines the nature of the business risks connected with the properties, the management required, and the services and relationship to the tenants. If these factors are significantly different for the converted and replacement properties, the replacement doesn't qualify even when both properties have the same end use of rental.[17]

A different replacement test applies for business or investment *real estate* converted by *condemnation* or *threat of condemnation*. Here, the replacement property qualifies if it is *like-kind*.[18] The definition of like-kind is the same as that for tax-free exchanges (see Chapter 11), and is considerably more liberal than the similar or related in service or use test. Generally, like-kind real estate is any business or investment real estate despite its end use. The like-kind test only applies if you acquire the replacement property directly. If you acquire stock in a corporation owning the replacement property, the more restrictive similar or related in service or use test continues to apply. Also, the more restrictive test applies when the real estate is converted by destruction or theft rather than by condemnation.

## Severance Damages

When only part of your property is condemned, you often are paid severance damages to compensate you for the decrease in the value of the remaining property caused by the partial taking. The decline may be due to various causes such as erosion or flooding. You may be required to make expenditures to restore the remaining property for economic use. Examples are amounts paid for fences, shrubbery, grading, drainage facilities, etc.

If clearly specified in the award or by stipulation, severance damages are not part of the proceeds from the condemnation. They are not part of your amount realized for determining the gain, or for determining how much you must reinvest to defer the gain. Severance damages reduce the basis of the remaining property.[19] If the severance damages are more than the basis of the remaining property, the excess is taxable gain. You reduce severance damages by the costs of obtaining them. Such costs include legal, appraising, engineering or expert witness fees.

> **Example:** Part of Booker's property is condemned. The total award is $12,000, of which $10,000 is for the property and $2,000 is stipulated as severance damages. The total expenses of obtaining the award (legal, appraising, etc.) are $1,200 of which $400 specifically relates to obtaining the severance award. The basis of the remaining property is reduced by $1,600 ($2,000 severance award less $400 expenses of obtaining it). The proceeds of the condemnation are $9,200 ($10,000 condemnation award less the $800 expenses relating to it).

Sometimes you can't trace the expenses directly to the severance award. Here, you allocate the total expenses of obtaining a combined condemnation and severance award in the ratio that each part of the award bears to the total award.

> **Example:** Assume the facts of the above example except that the expenses cannot be directly traced to the specific parts of the total award. The expenses are allocated in the ratio of each part of

the award to the total award. Thus, $200 (2/12 of $1,200) is allocated to the severance award, and $1,000 (10/12 of $1,200 to the award for the property taken. You reduce the basis of the remaining property by the net severance damages of $1,800 ($2,000 less $200). The proceeds from the condemnation are $9,000 ($10,000 less $1,000).

Often, the government takes property to make an improvement that benefits the remaining property. For instance, the condemned property may be used to build a sidewalk or install a sewer. As compensation for the improvement, the government may make a special assessment against the remaining property benefited. Here, you reduce the net severance damages by the amount of the special assessment. If the special assessment exceeds the net severance damages, you reduce the condemnation award by the excess. If the assessment exceeds the entire award, you add the excess to the basis of the remaining property.

**Example:** Assume in the above example that $1,100 is assessed against the remaining property. The net severance damages of $1,800 as calculated above are reduced by the assessment. The basis of the remaining property is reduced by $700 ($1,800 less $1,100).

**Example:** Assume in the above example that the special assessment is $2,200. The assessment first offsets the net severance damages of $1,800, and the excess of $400 reduces the award for the property taken. The proceeds for the condemnation are $8,600 ($9,000 less $400).

**Example:** Assume in the above example that the special assessment is $14,000. Since the assessment exceeds the entire award ($12,000), the excess of the assessment over the award ($2,000) is added to the basis of the remaining property.

To qualify as severance damages, the amount must be specifically stated in the award or stipulated by the parties at the time of the award.[20] The IRS will accept an itemized statement or closing sheet furnished by the condemning authority specifying the portion of the total condemnation award paid for severance damages. Without such a stipulation or statement, the entire proceeds are compensation for the property taken. The IRS will not accept your unilateral attempt to establish severance damages after the award.

### How to Elect to Defer Gain

You report all details of an involuntary conversion in the tax return for the year of conversion. If any gain is taxed because you plan not to make an adequate reinvestment, you report and pay tax on it in the year of conversion. You report all details relating to the replacement of converted property, the failure to replace, or the expiration of the replacement period in the appropriate year when such events occur.[21]

Failure to include gain or information in the return for the year of conversion is deemed to be an election to defer gain. Subsequently, if gain is taxed because you fail to replace the property or your reinvestment is inadequate, you amend the return for the year of conversion to include the taxable gain. If you don't want to defer the gain, you report the gain and pay the tax in the year of conversion. If you later change your mind and reinvest, you may file an amended return within the replacement period. In the amended return, you elect to defer the gain and claim a refund or credit for the overpayment of tax in the year of conversion.

### Special Statute of Limitations

If you elect to rollover gain, the IRS has an extended period to assess tax. The period of assessment runs for three years from the date you notify it that you have replaced the property, or the date you notify it that you won't replace the property.[22]

### Depreciation Recapture on Conversion of Investment Property

Usually, if you defer the entire gain from an involuntary conversion, the depreciation recapture provisions are overridden.[23] See Appendix B for a discussion of depreciation recapture. In this case, the recapture potential attaches to the replacement property. When you have a taxable disposition of the replacement property, gain is ordinary income to the extent of the recapture potential of both the converted property and the replacement property.

**Example:** Bailor's investment house is destroyed in a storm and she receives insurance proceeds of $90,000. Her basis for the house is $30,000, so her gain is $60,000. The house is subject to $8,000 depreciation recapture. She reinvests

-279-

$100,000 in another rental house within six months. Since no gain is taxed, no recapture is taxed. The $8,000 recapture potential attaches to the new house.

**Example:** Assume the facts of the above example except that she only reinvests $85,000 in the new rental house. $5,000 of the $60,000 gain is taxed ($90,000 proceeds less $85,000 reinvestment). All this gain is ordinary income because it is less than the recapture potential of $8,000.

Even when you reinvest the entire proceeds, recapture might be triggered. This occurs when the replacement property is not depreciable, and therefore cannot be subject to recapture. This is always the case when you reinvest in the stock of a corporation that owns the replacement property. It also occurs when you replace condemned rental real estate with land (that is "like-kind").

**Example:** Assume in the above example that the reinvestment is a purchase of 100% of the stock of a corporation owning the new investment house. Since the stock is not depreciable, the recapture potential of the old house is taxed. Thus, $8,000 of ordinary income is generated.

### Involuntary Conversion of a Principal Residence

If a principal residence is converted by destruction, the rules for the involuntary conversion rollover discussed in this chapter apply. If the residence is converted by condemnation or threat of condemnation, you may irrevocably elect to treat the transaction as a sale and use the home-sale rollover discussed in Chapter 5.[24]

If you use the involuntary conversion rollover to defer gain from condemnation of a principal residence, the reinvestment amount is reduced by the amount excluded under the over-55 exclusion.[25] See Chapter 5 for an illustration of the similar rule for interaction between the over-55 exclusion and the home-sale rollover.

### TAX PLANNING IDEAS FOR INVOLUNTARY CONVERSIONS

Because you have little control over involuntary conversions, it may seem that there is little room for tax planning. In this respect, it is somewhat like trying to prepare an estate plan for somebody who already died. There are, however, several important tax planning opportunities you should consider.

### To Defer or Not to Defer

You must decide whether to elect to defer the gain. Just because deferral is available doesn't necessarily mean that it is desirable. If you have losses from other business or investment activities, gain from an involuntary conversion may be used to offset them. This determination is especially important for capital losses, where deductibility is otherwise limited to $3,000 (see Appendix B).

### Timing of a Condemnation

Although it is not possible (at least not advisable) to control the timing of destruction of property, you may have some leeway for timing its condemnation. If the condemnation takes place near the end of the year, the replacement period is only a little more than two years (three years for condemned real estate). However, if you can delay the condemnation until the beginning of the following year, you have almost three years for replacement (four years for condemned real estate). Often, you can negotiate with the condemning authority for delay of the final condemnation order.

### Preserving the Basis of
### Replacement Property

As an alternative to paying tax on the conversion, you can preserve the cost basis of investment replacement property by acquiring control (more than 80%) of a corporation that owns the replacement property. You may create a new corporation for the specific purpose of acquiring the replacement property, but the corporation must already own the property when you acquire control.[26] Although the basis of the corporation's stock is reduced by the untaxed gain, the basis of the replacement property for the corporation is its cost. If the property produces tax losses, this technique is only advantageous if the corporation has income from other sources to absorb them.

There are risks when you use a corporation to acquire the replacement property. First, if the converted property is subject to depreciation recapture, acquisition of replacement corporate stock triggers immediate taxation of the recapture (see discussion above). Second, you must be careful that the corporation is not a personal holding company subjecting its taxable income to a stiff penalty tax.

### Severance Damages

Severance damages are not condemnation proceeds. Severance damages reduce your amount realized, your gain, and the amount required for you to reinvest to defer the gain.

If you intend to keep the remaining property, you should have as much of the award as possible stipulated as severance damages. This is usually desirable for partial takings for street widening, sidewalks, etc., where you continue to use the remaining property. Since you don't replace the property taken, any gain from its condemnation is taxed. But, if the award is stipulated as severance damages, the basis of the remaining property is reduced, and the gain is postponed until you dispose of the remaining property.

> **Example:** The city condemns a 60 foot strip of Dane's property to install a sidewalk. Of the property's total basis of $90,000, $6,000 is applicable to the strip taken. The condemnation award is $13,000. Since Dane won't reinvest the proceeds, his taxable gain is $7,000 ($13,000 less $6,000). However, if $7,000 of the gain is stipulated as severance damages, the condemnation proceeds are only $6,000 ($13,000 less $7,000), and there is no taxable gain. The basis of the remaining property is reduced to $83,000 ($90,000 less severance damages of $7,000).

### Improving Property You Already Own

If you own several investment properties, the involuntary conversion rollover is available if the proceeds from the conversion of one property are reinvested in the improvement of another if it is similar or related in service or use (or like-kind for a condemnation of real estate).[27] Thus, if you own two investment houses, the rollover applies if you use the proceeds from the conversion of one to improve the other. This makes it unnecessary for you to find another separate property for reinvestment, and makes it possible to upgrade property you already own.

# INVOLUNTARY CONVERSIONS

## FOOTNOTES

1. Generally, see Internal Revenue Code (IRC) §1033.

2. Rev. Rul. 59-102, 1959-1 CB 200; See IRC §165(c)(3) for casualty loss deduction definition.

3. Rev. Rul. 80-175, 1980-2 CB 230 (contains good discussion of law).

4. Rev. Rul. 74-532, 1974-2 CB 270.

5. Rev. Rul. 59-361, 1959-2 CB 183; *Harry G. Masser*, 30 TC 741.

6. Rev. Rul. 74-8, 1974-1 CB 200.

7. *Piedmont-Mt. Airy Guano Co.*, 8 BTA 72.

8. *Davis Co.*, 6 BTA 281.

9. Reg. §1.1033(a)-2(c)(11).

10. Reg. §1.1033(a)-2(c)(7).

11. IRC §1033(b); Reg. §1.1033(b)-1(b).

12. IRC §1033(a)(2)(B).

13. IRC §1033(a)(2)(B), IRC §1033(g)(4).

14. Reg. §1.1033(a)-2(c)(4).

15. IRC §1033(a)(2)(B)(ii); Reg. §1.1033(a)-2(c)(3).

16. IRC §1033(a)(2)(A).

17. *Liant Records, Inc. v. Comm'r.*, 303 F2d 326, (CA 2, 1962).

18. IRC §1033(g); Reg. §1.1033(g)-1.

19. Rev. Rul. 68-37, 1968-1 CB 359; Rev. Rul 271, 1953-2 CB 36.

20. Rev. Rul 59-173, 1959-1 CB 201; Rev. Rul. 64-183, 1964-1 CB 297.

21. Reg. §1.1033(a)-2(c)(2).

22. IRC §1033(a)(2)(C).

23. IRC §1245(b)(4) [personal property] and IRC §1250(d)(4) [real estate].

24. IRC §1.1034(i); Reg. §1.1033(a)-3; Reg. §1.1034-1(h).

25. Reg. §1.121-5(g).

26. *John Richard Corp.*, 46 TC 41 (1966); Rev. Rul. 77-422, 1977-2 CB 307.

27. *Davis, et. al. v. U.S.*, 589 F2d 446, (CA 9, 1979).

# Appendix

# A

# THE INDIVIDUAL TAX CALCULATION

This book is designed for individual taxpayers who own a home or residential investment property. The preceding chapters discuss many items of income, deductions, losses, loss limitations, etc. These items, however, operate within a framework enabling you to come up with the bottom line answer: your taxable income and the amount of tax you owe Uncle Sam.

This appendix describes the mechanics for calculating your individual income tax. Calculation of the income tax's counterpart, the Alternative Minimum Tax, is discussed in Chapter 9.

## THE INDIVIDUAL INCOME TAX FORMULA

The tax formula for individual taxpayers is more complex than those for other taxable entities. This is because the financial affairs of individuals are more complex. For example, corporations are usually engaged in one or more identifiable businesses, so that it is easy to segregate items of income and related expenses. On the other hand, an individual's income may come from many sources: compensation for services, passive investments, operation of businesses, etc. Further, individuals incur personal living expenses and must cope with a variety of personal and family responsibilities.

The individual tax formula is designed to segregate business from personal activities, and to take into account support responsibilities for other individuals. This is done by dividing the calculation into several steps. The first step calculates the net income from busines activities to arrive at a subtotal called *adjusted gross income*. The next step permits a limited range of non-business deductions for personal expenses and expenses incurred for investments and in connection with employment. Finally, family and other support responsibilities are recognized by permitting exemptions for you, your spouse, and those people dependent on you. The individual tax formula is summarized in Figure A-1.

---

### Figure A-1

### INDIVIDUAL INCOME TAX FORMULA

Gross income

**Deduct:** Deductions from gross income

**Equals:** Adjusted gross income (AGI)

**Deduct:** The greater of:

Standard deduction

or

Total itemized deductions

**Deduct:** Personal and dependency exemptions

**Equals:** Taxable income

**Multiply by:** Tax rates according to filing status

**Equals:** Income tax liability

**Deduct:** Tax credits

**Equals:** Income tax payable or refund

---

You determine the amount you owe by applying tables determined by your filing status. You then reduce this amount by tax credits. Tax credits are designed either to prevent double taxation or to provide specific economic incentives.

## Gross Income

Gross income is all income from whatever source derived, except income that is specifically excluded. See Chapter 2 for a discussion of exclusions and their economic impact.

## Deductions From Gross Income

This is where you deduct all your ordinary, necessary and reasonable expenses for a business activity you operate as a proprietor.[1] If your business is operated as a corporation or a partnership, these expenses are deducted on the appropriate tax returns for those entities. The terms *ordinary*, *necessary*, and *reasonable* are narrowly defined by the tax law.

This category of deductions also includes the following items:

o Alimony payments as defined by the tax law (doesn't include child support payments),[2]

o Contributions to Individual Retirement Accounts (IRAs) and self-employed "Keogh" retirement plans,

o Deductions related to rental property as limited by the passive loss rules discussed in Chapter 7,

o Deductions related to royalty income, such and income from copyrights and mineral rights.

o Deductions of expenses you incur as an employee and are reimbursed by your employer.

## Adjusted Gross Income (AGI)

This intermediate step in the tax calculation is roughly equivalent to the financial accounting concept of net business income. AGI is important because it serves as the benchmark for calculating percentage limitations for certain itemized deductions. These may either be "floor" limitations or "ceiling" limitations. The deductions for medical expenses, personal casualty losses, and employee and miscellaneous expenses are subject to a "floor." This means that you are permitted to deduct only the amount exceeding a specified percentage of AGI. The charitable contribution deduction is subject to an AGI ceiling -- a percentage of AGI that caps the amount you may deduct.

### Itemized Deductions

At this point in the calculation you have the choice of reducing your AGI by the standard deduction (see below), or by *itemizing* certain specified expenses if the total of the itemized deductions is more than the standard deduction. Itemized deductions include a limited number of personal expenses, expenses relating to investment activities, and unreimbursed expenses you incur during your employment.

o **Medical Expenses.** Qualifying medical expenses for yourself, your spouse, and your dependents are deductible to the extent that they exceed 7.5% of AGI,[3]

o **Charitable Contributions.** Contributions of money and property to qualifying charitable organizations are deductible subject to a general ceiling of 50% of AGI. Other ceilings of 30% of AGI and 20% of AGI apply depending upon the nature of the property you contribute and the nature of the charity.[4]

o **Personal Casualty Losses.** Casualty losses to property you own for personal use are deductible to the extent the losses exceed 10% of AGI. See Chapter 4.

o **State and Local Income and Real Estate Taxes.** Income taxes imposed by state and local governments are deductible without limitation. See Chapter 4 for a discussion of the deduction for real estate taxes. State and local sales taxes are not deductible.

o **Employee and Miscellaneous Investment Expenses.** These expenses are deductible for the amount in excess of 2% of AGI.[5] Employee expenses include those for transportation (not commuting), travel, and all expenses of outside salesmen. Also included are the following unreimbursed expenses incurred by employees: entertainment, professional dues and subscriptions, education, job hunting, home office (see Chapter 4), uniforms, and union dues. Miscellaneous investment expenses include safe-deposit box rental, hobby expenses (see Chapter 7), and fees paid for tax assistance, investment counseling, and IRA custodians. Reimbursed expenses of employees are deducted before arriving at AGI.

o **Mortgage Interest for a Principal Residence and a Second Home.** See Chapter 4.

o **Moving Expenses.** See Chapter 4.

For tax years 1991 through 1995, if your AGI is above an *applicable amount* you lose a portion of your itemized deductions. The applicable amounts for 1992 and 1993 are $105,250 and $108,450, respectively. The applicable amounts for married persons filing separately are $52,625 and $54,225, respectively.[6] The reduction applies for all itemized deductions except medical expenses, casualty and theft losses, and investment interest. The reduction is equal to the lesser of: (1) 3% of the threshold amount, or (2) 80% of your itemized deductions other than those specified above. See the example at Figure 9-2 in Chapter 9.

### Standard Deduction

Instead of itemizing deductions, you may elect to use the standard deduction.[7] You do this when the amount of your itemized deductions is less than the specified standard deduction. The amount of the standard deduction depends upon your filing status as follows:

|  | *1992* | *1993* |
| --- | --- | --- |
| Unmarried | $3,600 | $3,700 |
| Head of Household | $5,250 | $5,450 |
| Married Filing Jointly | $6,000 | $6,200 |
| Married Filing Separately | $3,000 | $3,100 |

An additional standard deduction is available for taxpayers and spouses who are over 65 years of age or are blind. For an unmarried taxpayer the additional standard deduction for 1992 and 1993 is $900. For a married taxpayer, the additional standard deduction for 1992 and 1993 is $700.

If an individual may be claimed as a dependent on another taxpayer's return, his standard deduction for 1992 and 1993 is limited to the greater of $600, or the amount of his earned income.[8] See Chapter 2 for a discussion of splitting income with other taxpayers.

The basic standard deduction, the additional standard deduction and the special standard deduction for a taxpayer who can be claimed as a dependent by another, are indexed for inflation each year.

### Personal and Dependency Exemptions

The tax law recognizes that a certain amount of income should be free of tax to support yourself, your spouse, and those people dependent on you. This is accomplished by permitting you to reduce AGI by personal and dependency exemptions.[9]

Personal exemptions are for yourself and your spouse if you file a joint return. Dependency exemptions are for certain people whom you support. The amount of each personal and dependency exemption is $2,300 for 1992, and $2,350 for 1993. The exemption amount is adjusted each year for inflation.

To qualify as a dependent, an individual must satisfy each of five different tests:

o **Support.** You must provide more than one-half of the support of the individual. Support includes food, clothing, shelter, medical and dental care, education, etc.

o **Relationship.** The individual must either be related to you or be a member of your household. The law specifies what relatives (and in-laws) qualify under this test.

o **Gross Income.** The individual's gross income must be less than the exemption amount (i.e., less than $2,300 for 1992, and $2,350 for 1993).

o **Joint Return.** The individual cannot file a joint return with his or her spouse unless the return is filed solely to obtain a refund of tax withheld.

o **Citizenship.** The individual must be a citizen or resident of the United States, Canada, or Mexico for some part of the taxable year.

If a person qualifies as a dependent on someone else's return, he is not entitled to a personal exemption for himself.[10] For example, if a child qualifies as a dependent for his parents, he may not deduct a personal exemption for himself on his return.

The law phases out the tax benefit that high income taxpayers get from personal and dependency exemptions. The phase-out begins at certain thresholds of adjusted gross income (adjusted annually for inflation) that depend on your filing status, as follows:[11]

|  | *1992* | *1993* |
|---|---|---|
| Unmarried | $105,250 | $108,450 |
| Head of household | $131,550 | $135,600 |
| Married -joint | $157,900 | $162,700 |
| Married - separate | $ 78,950 | $ 81,350 |

When AGI exceeds these thresholds, you lose 2% of the exemptions amount for every $2,500 (or fraction) of AGI exceeding the threshold amounts ($1,250 for marrieds filing separately). See the example at Figure 9-2 in Chapter 9. Note that this example is calculated using 1992 rates and limitation amounts.

## FILING STATUS

Your figure out your tax liability by applying rates in tables applicable to your filing status. See Tables A-1 and A-2 for the rates for 1992 and 1993, respectively. Your filing status depends upon whether you are married, and the state of your spouse's health (i.e., whether he or she is dead or alive). There are five filing statuses for individuals to determine which of four separate rate tables to use:

o **Unmarried.** Taxpayers who have never been married or who are separated from their spouse under a final divorce decree or decree of separate maintenance.[12]

o **Married Filing Jointly.** Married persons may elect this status. The rate schedule is the lowest for individual taxpayers.[13]

o **Married Filing Separately.** This is the filing status for married persons who do not elect to file jointly. It is the highest individual rate schedule, and is advantageous in only a few situations. The primary impact of this filing status is to complicate the law by making it necessary to cut many limitations, deductions, etc., in half for taxpayers who use it (i.e., the $25,000 special deduction for rental passive losses is $12,500 for married persons filing separately - see Chapter 7).[14]

o **Head of Household.** You use this status if you are unmarried and support a dependent in your home. The rates are two-thirds of the anount between those for unmarried taxpayers and taxpayers who are married filing jointly. To qualify as a head of household, you must be unmarried and pay more than half the cost of maintaining a household that is the principal home of a dependent relative (as specified in the law). There are exceptions for abandoned spouses, parents, and non-dependent children.[15]

o **Surviving Spouse.** If your spouse is deceased, you are a surviving spouse for the two years *following* the death of your spouse if you maintain a household for a dependent son or daughter.[16] For this two-year period, you may use the rate schedule for married persons filing jointly. You may not, however, deduct an exemption for your deceased spouse during this period.

### Table A-1
### INDIVIDUAL INCOME TAX RATES - 1992

| Tax Rate | Married Joint | Single | Head of Household |
|---|---|---|---|
| 15% | First 35,800 | First 21,450 | First 28,750 |
| 28% | 35,801-86,500 | 21,451-51,900 | 28,751-74,150 |
| 31% | Over 86,500 | Over 51,900 | Over 74,150 |

### Table A-2
### INDIVIDUAL INCOME TAX RATES - 1993

| Tax Rate | Married Joint | Single | Head of Household |
|---|---|---|---|
| 15% | First 36,900 | First 22,100 | First 29,600 |
| 28% | 36,901-89,150 | 22,101-53,500 | 29,601-76,400 |
| 31% | Over 89,150 | Over 53,500 | Over 76,400 |

# THE INDIVIDUAL TAX CALCULATION

## FOOTNOTES

1. Internal Revenue Code (IRC) §62.

2. IRC §215.

3. IRC §213.

4. IRC §170.

5. IRC §67.

6. IRC §68.

7. IRC §63(c).

8. IRC §63(c)(5).

9. IRC §§151 and 152.

10. IRC §151(d)(2).

11. IRC §151(d)(3).

12. IRC §1.

13. IRC §1(a).

14. IRC §1(d).

15. IRC §2(b).

16. IRC §2(a).

# B

# CAPITAL ASSET AND
# RELATED TRANSACTIONS

The Tax Reform Act of 1986 (1986 TRA), by eliminating most of the tax advantages for long-term capital gains, greatly reduced the importance of capital gain and loss tax planning. Such gains are taxed as ordinary income, but are subject to a maximum tax rate of 28%. This is only three percentage points lower than the maximum individual tax rate of 31% (see Appendix A).

The tax mechanics for capital asset transactions are still important, however, since Congress retained them intact to facilitate reinstatement of preferential treatment. We must still go through the mechanics to determine the net result of capital asset transactions. For example, if the result is a loss, we must continue to deal with the limitation on capital loss deductions.

Since real estate transactions usually produce gains, you may think that it is a waste of time to examine the capital gain and loss rules. Remember, however, that you might have other capital asset transactions, such as sales of securities, that produce losses. Here, the calculations are important. Further, if you have capital losses, the analysis is important to determine whether tax deferral is desirable for gains.

Thus, although the capital asset rules are less important than they were, they continue to be relevant in many situations. This appendix discusses the tax treatment of capital asset transactions, the related subject of business asset tax treatment, and the distinction between dealers and investors. The discussions apply only for individual taxpayers. Corporate capital asset transactions are treated differently.

## TAX CONSEQUENCES OF CAPITAL GAINS AND LOSSES

Capital gains or losses result from sales or exchanges of capital assets. The definition of capital assets is the key to capital gain and loss analysis.

The tax law defines capital assets in negative terms: all assets are capital assets except those specifically excluded.[1] The excluded assets are:

o Inventory and stock in trade;

o Property held primarily for sale to customers in the ordinary course of business. Such real estate is called *dealer* property, and is discussed below;

o Accounts and notes receivable resulting from the sale of inventory or dealer property;

o Real estate and depreciable property (including depreciable personal property) used in a trade or business. Although these are not capital assets, gains and losses from their sale get preferential treatment, as described below;

o Other assets not important for real estate investment such as certain copyrights, memoranda, discounted government bonds, and government publications.

In addition to statutory non-capital assets, the courts have created two other categories of non-capital assets.

**Assets That Are an Integral Part of a Business.** In the famous *Corn Products*[2] case, the Supreme Court held that even though an asset may not fall into one of the specific statutory categories, it is not a capital asset if it is an integral part of the taxpayer's business. In that case, corn futures purchased to hedge the price of the taxpayer's inventory (corn) were held not to be capital assets.

**Anticipations of Ordinary Income.** If you sell a right to receive future ordinary income, the proceeds from the sale are ordinary income.[3] For instance, if you sell your right to receive dividends or interest, the sale proceeds are ordinary income. Similarly, if a tenant forfeits a security deposit because he breaks a lease, the deposit is treated as a settlement for the future rent, and is ordinary income.

Aside from these exceptions, most non-business assets are capital assets. These include your investment real estate and securities, personal automobiles and residences, household goods, and personal effects such as clothing or jewelry.

### Holding Period

Capital gains and losses are classified as long-term or short-term depending upon how long you owned the asset. An asset owned for one year or less is short-term.[4] An asset owned for more than one year is long-term. An asset becomes long-term on the day following the date of acquisition, one year later. If you acquire the asset on the last day of the month, it becomes long-term on the first day of the thirteenth following month.

> **Example:** Mehler buys investment real estate on January 4, 19X1. It becomes a long-term asset on January 5, 19X2. If the property is bought on January 31, 19X1, it becomes long-term on February 1, 19X2.

The date of purchase or sale of real estate is generally the date of closing, not the date of contract of sale.

In tax-deferred exchanges (see Chapter 11), home-sale rollovers (see Chapter 5), and involuntary conversion rollovers (see Chapter 12), the holding period of the property given up or sold is *tacked* or added to the holding period of the property received or the reinvestment property.[5]

### The Netting Process

The first step in determining capital gain or loss tax consequences is to offset capital losses against capital gains. You first offset long-term losses against long-term gains. Then you offset short-term losses against short-term gains. If these offsets result in a net gain and a net loss (one long-term and one short-term), you offset the net gain and net loss against each other.[6]

**Example:** Moore has four capital asset transactions during the year that produce the following gains and losses: long-term gain of $8,000; long-term loss of $2,000; short-term gain of $1,000; short-term loss of $1,500. A net long-term gain of $6,000 results from offsetting the long-term items. The offset of the short-term items results in a net short-term loss of $500. These are further offset to produce a net long-term gain of $5,500.

This process can result in six possible combinations, three involving gains, and three involving losses. There can be a net short-term gain; a net long-term gain; and two gains, one short-term and one long-term. All these gains are taxed as ordinary income, with the long-term gains subject to a maximum tax rate of 28%.

Similarly, there can be a net short-term loss; a net long-term loss; and two losses, one short-term and one long-term. You deduct up to $3,000 of losses from gross income to arrive at adjusted gross income (see Appendix A for discussion of the individual tax formula).[7]

If your capital losses exceed $3,000, you carry the excess forward to offset capital gains generated in future years.[8] The losses retain their short- or long-term character in the carryforward years. If the losses are not fully used (by offsetting gains and deducting $3,000) in the subsequent year, you continue to carry them forward in similar manner indefinitely. If you have both a net short-term loss and a net long-term loss, you use the short-term loss first to take the $3,000 deduction.

**Example:** In 19X1 Magnotti has a short-term loss of $18,000 and no capital gains. He deducts $3,000 of the loss in 19X1, and he carries forward the remaining $15,000 to 19X2. The carryforward enters the 19X2 netting process as a short-term loss to be offset first against 19X2 short-term gains, and then against 19X2 long-term gains. If there are no capital asset transactions in 19X2, he deducts another $3,000, leaving a balance of $12,000 to carry forward to enter the 19X3 netting process as a short-term loss. This continues until the carryforward loss is exhausted.

**Example:** Assume that in 19X1, Magnotti's netting process produces a short-term loss of $2,000, and a long-term loss of $10,000. He deducts $3,000 in 19X1. This fully exhausts the $2,000 short-term loss, and uses $1,000 of the long-term loss. He carries the remaining $9,000 long-term loss forward to enter the 19X2 netting process as a long-term loss to be offset first against long-term gains, and then against short-term gains.

There is one exception to the rule that you can carry capital losses forward indefinitely. If you die when you have an unused capital loss carryforward, the carryforward is buried with you, and cannot be used by your estate or beneficiaries.

## REAL AND DEPRECIABLE PROPERTY USED IN A BUSINESS

Real or depreciable properties used in your business are not capital assets. However, if you have owned them for more than one year, under Section 1231 of the Internal Revenue Code you get preferential tax treatment when you dispose of them. These assets are called Section 1231 assets to distinguish them from capital assets. Examples are business automobiles, land and buildings used in your business, office furniture and equipment, etc.

If you have several sales of Section 1231 assets during the year, you must offset any losses against gains. If the result of the offset is a gain, it is treated as a long-term capital gain and you offset it against losses from sales of capital assets in the capital gain and loss netting process. If the result is a loss, you deduct it in full. The loss is not subject to the $3,000 deduction limitation for capital losses.

Example: McFeeter has two sales of business property during the year: a building at a loss of $5,000, and a machine at a gain of $1,500. She owned both assets for more than one year. The gain and loss are offset, producing a net Section 1231 loss of $3,500. The loss is fully deductible from ordinary income.

Example: Assume the facts of the above example, except that the loss is $1,500 and the gain is $5,000. The offset produces a net Section 1231 gain of $3,500. This gain is included with all other long-term capital gains in the normal capital gain and loss netting process.

In one situation, a net Section 1231 gain is *not* treated as a long-term capital gain. This happens if you have deducted Section 1231 losses in prior years. Gains are taxed as ordinary income to the extent of the losses deducted during the five preceding years.[9]

**Example:** In 19X1, DeJong has a Section 1231 transaction resulting in a loss of $2,000 that he deducts in full from ordinary income. In 19X2, he has a Section 1231 transaction producing a gain of $5,000. $2,000 of the gain is taxed as ordinary income because of the 19X1 deduction. The remainder ($3,000) is treated as a long-term capital gain.

## DEALER VS. INVESTOR

Capital assets do not include property held primarily for sale to customers in the ordinary course of a business (dealer property). Gain from its sale is ordinary income, and loss is fully deductible from ordinary income. Sometimes it is difficult to determine whether you hold a particular property as a dealer (ordinary asset) or as an investor (capital asset). The guidelines are unclear, and the status turns on the special facts and circumstances of each case.

Before the 1986 TRA, your strategy was to establish investor status to get favorable long-term capital gain treatment. However, now your strategy is probably reversed. Since long-term capital gains are now taxed as ordinary income, dealer vs. investor status is irrelevant for gains. For losses, however, the distinction remains important. Losses from investment properties are capital losses, subject to the $3,000 deduction limit. However, you may deduct dealer property losses without limitation. It would seem, therefore, that the goal now is to establish dealer status so that you are guaranteed ordinary loss treatment.

There is a downside risk to this strategy. There is a strong possibility that the long-term capital gain preference will be reinstated. If you establish dealer status, you are stuck with ordinary income treatment if you sell the property for a gain. It is important to be aware of the problem, and be careful to establish circumstances supporting whichever status your strategy dictates.

Other important tax implications turn on dealer classification. For instance, dealer property does not qualify for installment reporting (see Chapter 10) or tax-deferred exchanges (see Chapter 11). However, dealer property is not subject to the passive loss limitation (see Chapter 7).

Dealer vs. investor status is determined by the circumstances surrounding your ownership of the property. It is irrelevant whether you are a licensed real estate professional. Substantial real estate activity may make you a dealer even though you don't have a real estate license. Conversely, you are not automatically classified as a dealer because you have a real estate license.

Dealer property is that held *primarily* for sale rather than that held *primarily* for investment. Primarily means *principally,* or *of first importance.*[10] Thus, you can have both dealer and investor intent for the same property at the same time. The more important intent prevails. Obviously you should avoid sending out signals of more than one intent. Many factors have been discussed by the courts to distinguish dealers from investors.[11] No one factor is conclusive. Generally, a judge's "gut" reaction controls the outcome. Some of the factors most often cited are:

o **Ordinary or General Business of the Owner.** If you are involved in some aspect of the real estate business, it is more difficult to establish investor status.

o **Extent of Advertising and Promotion for Sale.** Dealers usually engage in active selling activities, whereas investors usually hold property for relatively long periods for appreciation in value or investment income. The more you engage in selling activities, the more you look like a dealer, particularly if you haven't owned the property very long.

o **Listing for Sale With a Real Estate Broker.** For a non-licensee, this indicates an intent to sell.

o **Frequency, Number, and Continuity of Sales.** Many sales of similar properties within a relatively short time period indicate dealer status. There are no "magic" numbers. Such questions as "How many sales are too many?", and "How long must I own the property before selling it?", have no clear numerical answers. Each case is examined according to its own facts and circumstances.

o **Extent and Nature of Sales.** The amount of your income resulting from real estate activities is compared to your income from non-real estate activities. Size of profit on particular sales -- small individual profits on many sales indicate dealer activity; larger profits on fewer sales --indicate investment intent.

o **Purpose for Acquiring Property.** It is important to document the intent you desire from the outset. You can do this with statements in legal documents, correspondence, files, etc.

o **Purpose for Owning Property After You Acquire It.** Any changes of intent must be supported or refuted by convincing evidence.

o **Extent of Improvements.** Extensive improvements indicate dealer intent, particularly when you subdivide land.

o **Purpose for Ownership at the Time of Sale.** The cumulative result of all of the above factors.

Two types of activities are suspect, and may classify you as a dealer even though you are not otherwise engaged in real estate activities:

o **Trading Activities.** Frequent purchases and sales, particularly if the properties are similar, e.g., all single family homes or all commercial.

o **Subdividing Activities.** Dividing large tracts of land into smaller *retail* parcels for resale. This is essentially a manufacturing operation which is dealer activity. There is a relief provision for certain small subdividers, but its requirements are so restrictive that it is not often useful.[12]

In general, the more passive you are about a particular property, and the more you appear reluctant to sell, the less likely that you will be classified as a dealer.

### Tax Planning for Dealer or Investor Status

You can take certain steps to establish yourself as a dealer or an investor. Sometimes these actions are self-serving, and as such, they are not conclusive. However, it is best to take the steps anyway. At the very least, forcing yourself to make the right "noises" makes it less likely that you will make the wrong "noises."

**Accounting Records.** Investment properties should be carefully segregated in your accounting records. This is particularly important if you are otherwise engaged in the real estate business. Sometimes you should segregate investment properties into separate legal entities such as trusts or partnerships. Note, however, that using corporations for investment property ownership can be dangerous.

**Files and Correspondence.** It is important to establish your intent when you acquire the property. Once dealer (or investor) intent attaches, it is difficult to prove that you have changed your intent. Correspondence between you and real estate professionals, attorneys, etc., before acquisition should document why you want the property. If you want to establish investment intent, you should emphasize your desire for income and appreciation, and indicate that you intend to own the property for a long time.

**Sales and Promotion Activities.** Active selling and promotion activities are inconsistent with investor status. Your *reluctance to sell* is important. You should keep sales activities to a minimum.

**Acquisition and Selling Expenses.** An investor's expenses for acquiring property add to its basis (see Chapter 3). Expenses for selling property reduce the amount realized from the sale. Such expenses of a dealer are deductible as business expenses. Thus, you should handle these expenses in the manner consistent with the status you desire.

## DEPRECIATION RECAPTURE

The purpose for the depreciation recapture rules is to convert long-term capital gain into ordinary income. The idea is that because you reduced ordinary income when you took depreciation deductions, some of your gain should be ordinary income when you dispose of your investment.

### Depreciation Recapture for Real Estate

For real estate, there is recapture only if you use accelerated cost recovery deductions. Thus, for property placed into service after 1986, recapture is irrelevant because only straight-line recovery is allowed (see Chapter 8).

The rules remain important for gains from dispositions of real estate placed into service before 1987. Although the traditional function of the rules is now largely irrelevant, the old recapture rules might accelerate taxation of gain for the following types of dispositions of pre-1987 property:

o Installment sales (see Chapter 10);

o Like-kind exchanges (see Chapter 11); and

o Involuntary conversions (see Chapter 12).

Also, you must divide gains into their capital gain and recaptured ordinary income elements to determine how much capital gain is available to absorb capital losses. Only the portion classified as capital gain enters into the capital gain netting process (see discussion above).

This section discusses the recapture rules for real estate placed into service after 1980.[13] Other rules apply for property placed into service before 1981. If you did not use accelerated recovery for pre-1987 real estate, but elected an alterative straight-line recovery period, there is no recapture when you sell the property.

The operation of the pre-1987 recapture rules depends upon whether the real estate is residential or nonresidential. Real estate is residential if at least 80% of the gross receipts is from the rental of dwelling units. All other real estate is nonresidential (see Chapter 8).

For residential real estate, gain from disposition is treated as ordinary income to the extent of the excess of the accelerated cost recovery you deducted over what you would have deducted using the same straight-line recovery period. The remaining gain is long-term capital gain.

**Example:** On October 1, 19X1, McGinley purchased a rental duplex for $120,000. $100,000 of the purchase price is allocated to the building. He uses accelerated cost recovery with the 19-year recovery period (see Table 8-1, Chapter 8). He sells the property on December 31, 19X4 for $200,000. He has deducted $26,500 of cost recovery. Straight-line recovery using the 19-year recovery period would have been $17,000. The excess of accelerated recovery taken over straight-line is $9,500 ($26,500 less $17,000). McGinley's gain is calculated as follows:

| Amount realized | | $200,000 |
|---|---|---|
| Less: Adjusted basis | | |
| Cost | $120,000 | |
| ACRS deducted | 26,500 | 93,500 |
| Gain | | $106,500 |

$9,500 of the gain is ordinary income. The remaining $97,000 ($106,500 less $9,500) is long-term capital gain.

The rule for nonresidential real estate is different. Gains from sales of nonresidential property are ordinary income to the extent of all accelerated cost recovery deducted.

**Example:** Assume in the above example that the property is a warehouse. The ordinary income from the sale is $26,500, the total amount of ACRS deducted. The remaining $80,000 ($106,500 less $26,500) is long-term capital gain.

**Personal Property**

For personal property, the recapture rules are more severe.[14] Recapture applies regardless of the method of depreciation, ACRS or MACRS used. Thus, ordinary income is generated even if you use an alternative straight-line election under depreciation, ACRS or MACRS (see Chapter 8). The rule is very simple: gains from dispositions of business or investment personal property are ordinary income to the extent of all depreciation, ACRS or MACRS deducted.

# FOOTNOTES

1. Internal Revenue Code (IRC) §1221.
2. *Corn Products Refining Co. v. U.S.*, 350 US 46; (1955).
3. *Hort v. Comm'r*, 313 US 28; (1941).
4. IRC §1223.
5. IRC §1223.
6. IRC §1223.
7. IRC §1211.
8. IRC §1212.
9. IRC §1231(c).
10. *Malat v. Riddell*, 383 US 569; (1966).
11. *U.S. v. Winthrop*, 417 F.2d 905; (CA 5, 1969).
12. IRC §1237.
13. IRC §1250.
14. IRC §1245.

# INDEX

## A